IMAGES
of America

10th Mountain Division at Camp Hale

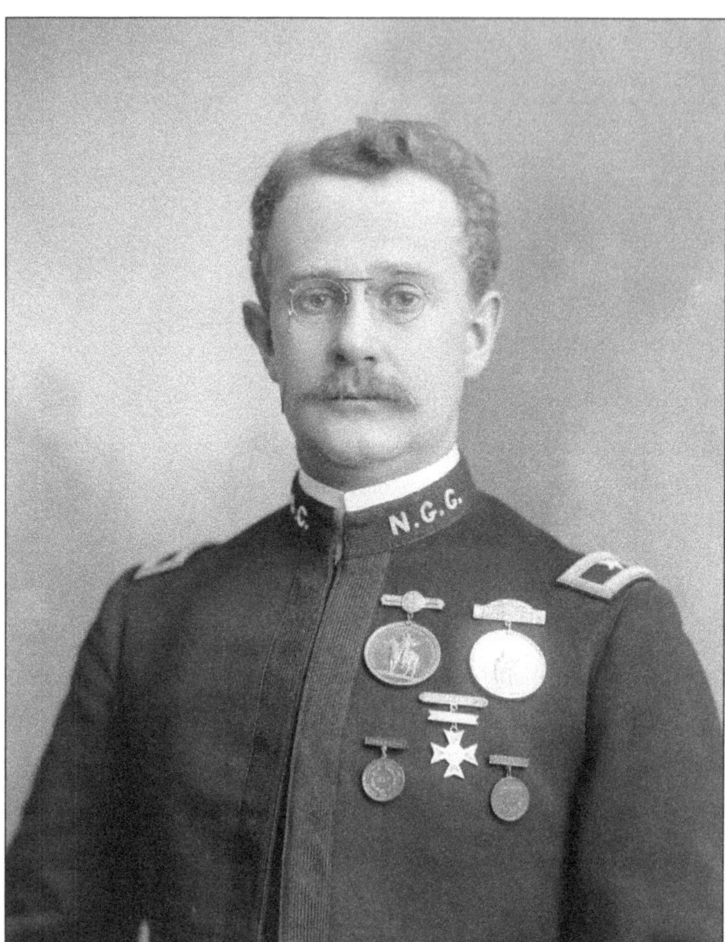

Camp Hale was named to honor one of Colorado's most distinguished soldiers: Brig. Gen. Irving Hale (1861–1930). He was a Denver native, an 1884 graduate of the US Military Academy at West Point, the commander of the Colorado Regiment that captured Manila during the Spanish-American War in 1898, and one of the founders of the Veterans of Foreign Wars organization. (Courtesy of the 10th Mountain Division Resource Center at the Denver Public Library.)

On the Cover: Soldiers of the 10th Light Division (later redesignated the 10th Mountain Division) march in formation through the snowy streets of Camp Hale, Colorado, in March 1943. (Courtesy of the 10th Mountain Division Resource Center at the Denver Public Library.)

IMAGES
of America

10TH MOUNTAIN DIVISION AT CAMP HALE

Flint Whitlock and Eric Miller

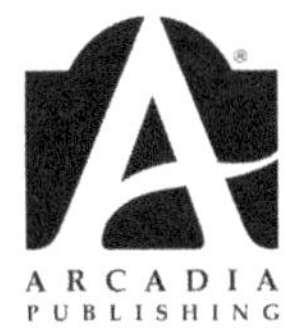

ISBN 978-1-4671-0917-8

Published by Arcadia Publishing
Charleston, South Carolina

Library of Congress Control Number: 2022944003

For all general information, please contact Arcadia Publishing:
Telephone 843-853-2070
Fax 843-853-0044
E-mail sales@arcadiapublishing.com
For customer service and orders:
Toll-Free 1-888-313-2665

Visit us on the Internet at www.arcadiapublishing.com

Dedicated to the courageous men of the 10th Mountain Division who served their country so gallantly during World War II—and afterward—and to Private First Class John D. Magrath, Medal of Honor recipient.

Contents

Acknowledgments

The authors wish to thank a number of individuals and organizations without whose kind assistance this book would not have been possible. These include Keli Schmid, special collections librarian of the 10th Mountain Division Resource Center at the Denver Public Library; Chris Juergens, Anschutz associate curator of Military History, along with Viviana Guajardo and Jori Johnson, at History Colorado; Jen Mason and Dana Mathios of the Colorado Snowsports Museum and Hall of Fame in Vail; Megan Cerise and Anna Scott at the Aspen Historical Society; Jennifer Maruffo, local history coordinator at the Lake County (Leadville) Public Library; Ann Schroeder at the US Ski and Snowboard Hall of Fame in Ishpeming, Michigan; Rouene Brown, widow of William "Sarge" Brown, a 10th Mountain Division veteran and a founder of Vail; and David J. Little, historian for the 10th Mountain Division Foundation, whose knowledge of all things 10th is encyclopedic.

Others deserving of thanks are Nancy Kramer, president of the 10th Mountain Division Foundation; Sandy Kent; Ann Schroeder; Ella Warren Burnett; and our superb editor at Arcadia Publishing, Caitrin Cunningham.

Credits in the captions are as follows: DPL stands for the 10th Mountain Division Resource Center at the Denver Public Library, HC stands for History Colorado, CSSM stands for the Colorado Ski & Snowboard Museum & Ski Hall of Fame, AHS stands for the Aspen Historical Society, LCPL stands for Lake County (Colorado) Public Library, LCCC stands for Lake County Civic Center, and USS&SHOF stands for US Ski & Snowboard Hall of Fame.

Introduction

The story of Camp Hale, Colorado, begins with the creation of the unit most associated with it—the US Army's 10th Mountain Division.

Three New England ski enthusiasts were responsible for the 10th's creation: Charles Minot "Minnie" Dole, a New York insurance executive; Roger Langley, president of the US Ski Association; and Roland Palmedo, an investment banker. In 1936, they combined to create the National Ski Patrol System, with Dole as its president.

In the 1930s, the United States and the rest of the world were just beginning to climb up from the depths of the Great Depression. But dark developments were taking place in Germany. In January 1933, extreme nationalist Adolf Hitler, through some shrewd political maneuvering, was appointed chancellor, and the nation fell under the control of the Nazi party. That same year, the Nazis established concentration camps, in which they began incarcerating their political opponents.

War clouds had already begun building elsewhere on the horizon. In September 1931, Japan had invaded Manchuria, and in 1937, it would invade China. Future plans called for the invasion and conquest of Pacific Rim nations where vital raw materials such as oil and rubber could be secured for the use of Japan's war machine.

In 1935, the German parliament, essentially under Nazi control, passed a series of draconian laws—known as the Nuremberg Laws—that stripped German Jews of their civil rights and left them vulnerable to future depredations.

The year 1936 was also a fateful year. Nazi Germany staged two successful Olympic Games: the Winter Games in the Garmisch-Partenkirchen region of Bavaria, and the Summer Games in Berlin. Both were highly successful and presented a face to the world that Germany, defeated in World War I, had remarkably transformed itself into a modern, civilized nation. But to many observers, it was all a façade, a smokescreen, a clever public-relations ploy to disguise the nation's darker side and its plans for the future.

Behind the peaceful mask of the Olympics, Germany was preparing for war. Angered by the Treaty of Versailles that ended World War I—and humiliated and bankrupted Germany in the process—Hitler was determined to exact revenge on the victorious Allies.

Once the 1936 Olympics were over, and in violation of the Treaty of Versailles, Hitler reverted to his scheme to rebuild Germany's armed forces. In addition to creating new ships and planes, he also ignored the treaty's stipulation of an army restricted to 100,000 men. Many of the men in his new army were skilled skiers and mountaineers—and many had taken part in the 1936 Winter Olympics—for Hitler knew that any upcoming war might very well include combat in cold and mountainous regions. In 1940, Germany had organized three mountain divisions, known as *Gebirgsjägers*.

Hitler began his ambitious plan to gain control of much of Europe; no sooner had the Summer Games ended in August 1936 than Hitler allied his army and air force—along with that of Fascist Italy under Benito Mussolini—with Spanish colonel Francisco Franco in his efforts to defeat the ruling government during the Spanish Civil War. Many historians have called this a "dress rehearsal" for World War II.

That same year, Hitler also sent troops into the Rhineland to reclaim what the Treaty of Versailles had stripped from Germany in 1919. When no nation (or even the League of Nations) did anything other than issue weak protests, Hitler was emboldened to go for more. In March 1938, Germany annexed Hitler's home country of Austria and then demanded that the German-speaking border areas of Czechoslovakia, known as the Sudetenland, be given to Germany.

At Munich in September 1938, Hitler bluffed the British and French prime ministers into allowing Germany to have the Sudetenland (without the Czechs' consent), promising them that he had no further plans for German expansion.

Another conflict soon erupted—this time on the border between Finland and the Soviet Union on November 30, 1939, when Josef Stalin's Red Army invaded its smaller neighbor. This was known as the "Winter War," or Russo-Finnish War. However, so skilled were the Finns at moving large numbers of ski-equipped troops swiftly and silently through the snowy Finnish forests that the Soviets were soundly defeated, losing nearly 168,000 dead and missing, with some 5,500 more taken prisoner. (The poor performance of the Red Army was one reason why Hitler decided to attack the Soviet Union in the summer of 1941, thus breaking a non-aggression pact that he and Stalin had signed.)

Watching all these worrying developments, of course, were Minnie Dole, Roger Langley, and Roland Palmedo. What if the United States were caught up in the conflict? What if the United States became involved, fighting in cold and mountainous regions of Europe? Would the US Army be ready? After all, the Army preferred to train in the warm, flat, Southern states and was ill-prepared for anything else. A few units had received cold-weather training (notably the 1st, 3rd, 5th, 6th, 41st, and 44th Infantry Divisions), but there was no concerted effort to develop one or more divisions specifically prepared for that type of combat environment.

To rectify the situation, Dole, Langley, and Palmedo established the National Volunteer Winter Defense Committee and took it upon themselves to try and convince Gen. George C. Marshall, the Army's chief of staff, of the need to form and train units that could fight and survive in Europe's harsh alpine regions.

In his voluminous correspondence with General Marshall, Dole used the Russo-Finnish War as a perfect example of why the US Army needed winter- and mountain-trained troops. At first, Marshall was unmoved; if America became embroiled in the conflict, he said, the Army would need regular infantry and armor and artillery troops—not a specialized mountain division or two.

Undeterred, Dole kept up his campaign. Finally, perhaps worn down by Dole's unrelenting barrage of letters, Marshall relented, and in October 1941 authorized the trio's self-proclaimed National Volunteer Winter Warfare Defense Board to recruit men for what would eventually become the 10th Mountain Division—the first and only time a civilian agency was given such authority.

The indefatigable Dole, along with his compatriots, began their recruiting campaign, contacting every ski area, ski patrol chapter, and college and high school ski team in the country. Ads, articles, and notices were placed in every ski publication, and a filmmaker, John Jay, created a recruiting film that he showed to packed theaters across the nation. Dole and company also involved the American Alpine Club, which informed its members about the creation of a fledgling mountain-warfare unit. Applications for the all-volunteer unit poured in. For many young men of draft age, skiing for the Army seemed like the perfect way to serve their country in the event war broke out.

Early volunteers needed to submit three letters of recommendation from athletic coaches, school faculty, church officials, civic leaders, or anyone else of stature who could attest to the applicant's outstanding character and abilities. Many of those early applicants were young Americans who had grown up on skis, while others were foreign-born skiers and mountaineers who had arrived in the United States before their countries were threatened or invaded by Nazi Germany. Once the pool of early volunteers had been exhausted, the ranks were filled by draftees—many of whom had never seen snow or a mountain and who hated cold weather.

Initially, the US War Department established the 1st Battalion of the 87th Mountain Infantry Regiment, with its headquarters at Camp Lewis, Washington, and its training area on the slopes of 14,408-foot Mount Rainier. The Army requisitioned the 100-room Paradise Lodge (which opened in 1917) on the mountain's southern slopes and turned it into barracks for the battalion.

While the troops began training there under Lt. Col. Onslow Rolfe, the Army went on a nationwide search for a permanent home for what would become a 14,000-man division. The sites considered were Camp Lewis; Camp Snelling, Minnesota; Camp Ord, California; Camp Ethan Allen, Vermont; West Yellowstone, Montana; and most improbably, the Great Sand Dunes National Monument in Colorado.

The *Colorado Encyclopedia* reads, "With the groundwork set, in November 1941, the government created the Mountain Winter Warfare Board to design and test winter equipment and transportation." A month later, the United States found itself at war.

The site that seemed to meet all of the Army's criteria was a high mountain valley, 9,250 feet above sea level, in the Colorado Rocky Mountains known as both Eagle Park and the Pando Valley, 100 miles west of Denver and some 15 miles north of the old mining town of Leadville.

The location seemed perfect. It had a highway and a railroad line and a source of water (the Eagle River) running through it. The snowfall averaged 250 inches a year. It was remote enough to conduct training without disturbing any nearby urban areas and large enough to create a full-size cantonment area, artillery range, and two ski-training areas. In total, the new camp would encompass nearly 250,000 acres—one of the largest in the United States.

There were plenty of 12,000-foot-high mountains surrounding Eagle Park/Pando Valley where troops could learn how to ski the military way, and plenty of cliffs and craggy rock outcroppings where soldiers could acquire the skills of mountain climbing. There were a few towns (Leadville, Red Cliff, and Minturn) close by where the soldiers could socialize during their off-duty hours.

While the first group of soldiers was being recruited and trained at Mount Rainier, Camp Hale was being built—and what an incredible feat of wartime engineering and construction it proved to be.

Moving with unusual swiftness even for wartime, in March 1942, the Army decided that Eagle Park/Pando Valley was where the new, as-yet-unnamed camp would be built. A tremendous number of Herculean tasks needed to be accomplished within a very short time: An engineering company and a construction company would need to be contracted to do the work; detailed engineering plans would need to be drawn up; thousands of workers would need to be hired and housed somewhere nearby; and a huge amount of lumber, concrete, pipe, electrical conduit, and other building materials would need to be fast-tracked and delivered to the site. Basically, an entire city was built from scratch in just a few months.

On April 6, 1942, Leadville's leading weekly newspaper, the *Carbonate Chronicle*, reported that the Army had selected Pando as the site for an as-yet-unnamed training camp for mountain troops: "Climatic conditions are superb . . . for winter comes early to this area, and leaves late. Indications are that the army will train thousands of soldiers at Pando, giving them the skill and seasoning necessary for wartime service in the coldest fighting zones."

Incredibly, the contract to build the camp was signed on April 7, 1942—and work began three days later.

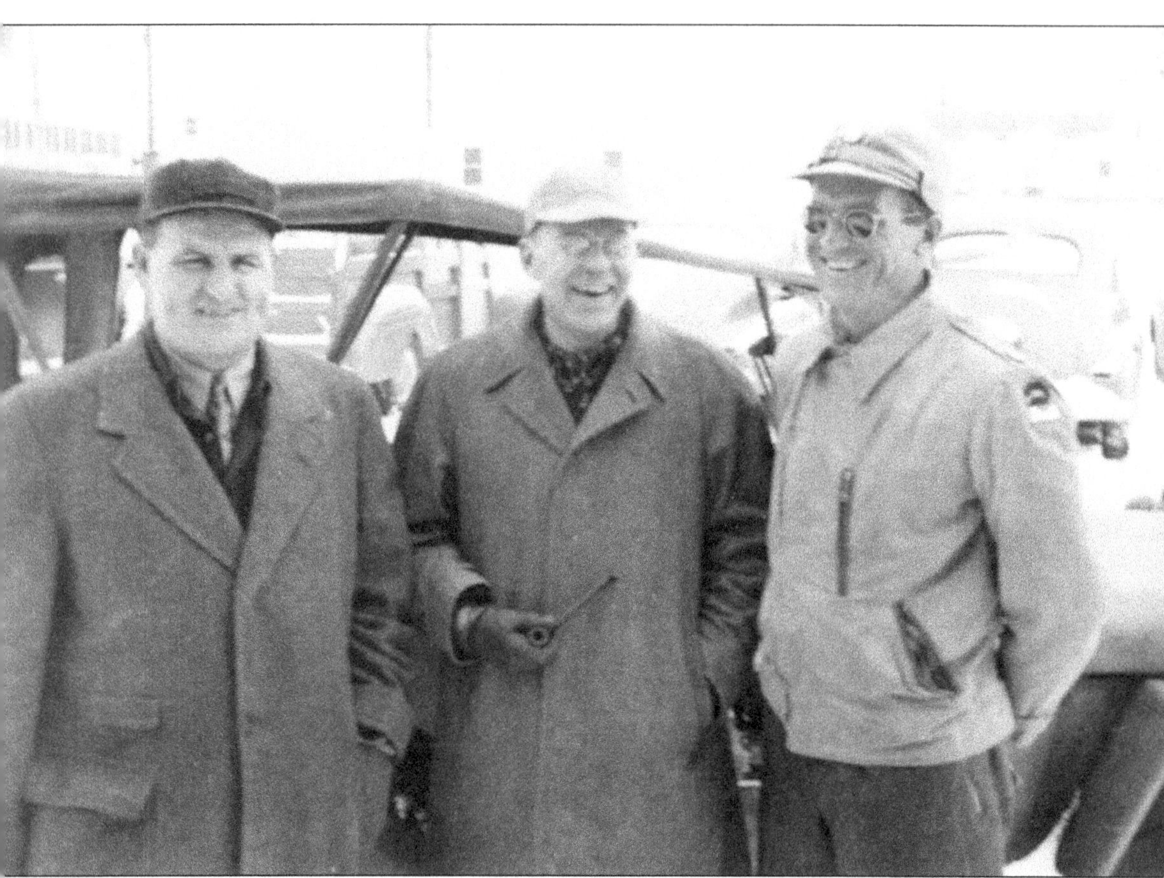

From left to right, Roger Langley, Charles Minot "Minnie" Dole, and Roland Palmedo were the three civilians behind the creation of what would become the 10th Mountain Division. Here they are standing beside a jeep at Camp Hale in 1943. (Courtesy of DPL.)

One

Birth of a Dream

Once the Army decided to form a unit of mountain soldiers and build a training camp in the Colorado Rockies, there was not a minute to lose. While the 1st Battalion of the 87th Mountain Infantry Regiment was receiving recruits and being equipped at Camp Lewis, Washington, and trained on the southern slopes of Mount Rainier, construction of the still unnamed camp in Colorado had already begun.

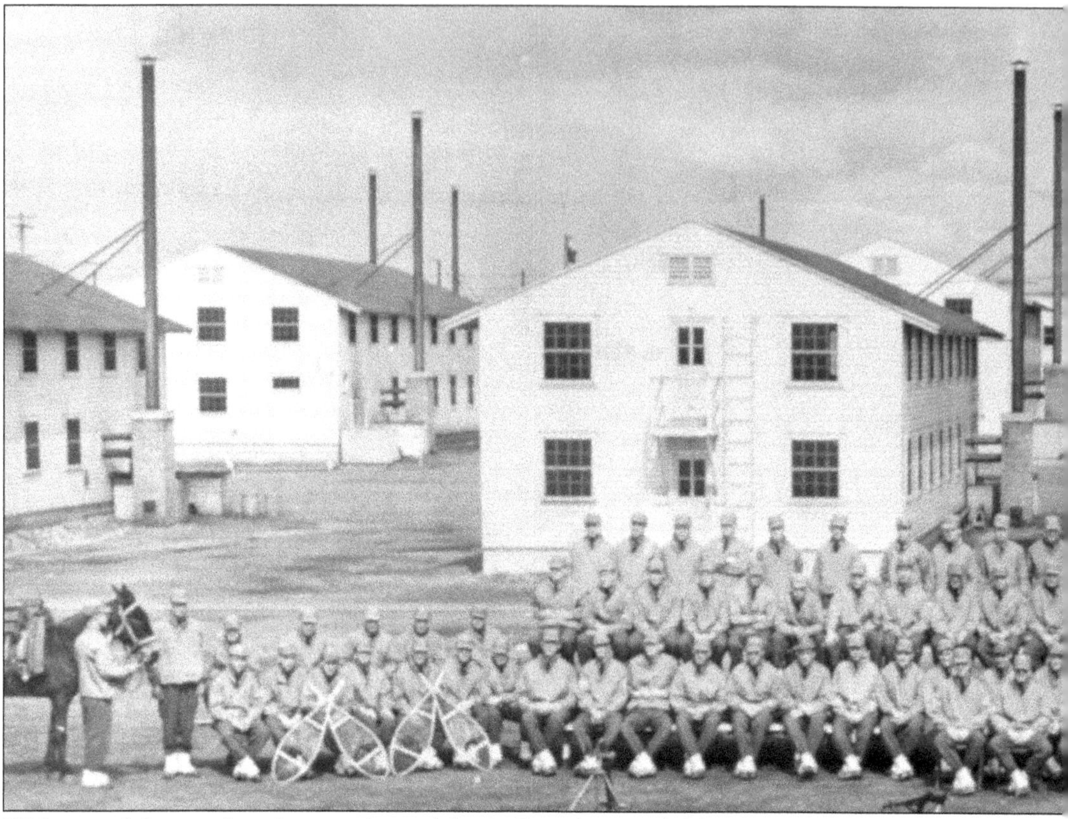

With two of their pack mules, members of the 1st Battalion, 87th Mountain Infantry Regiment, pose for a group photograph in the cantonment (barracks) area of Camp Lewis, Washington, in

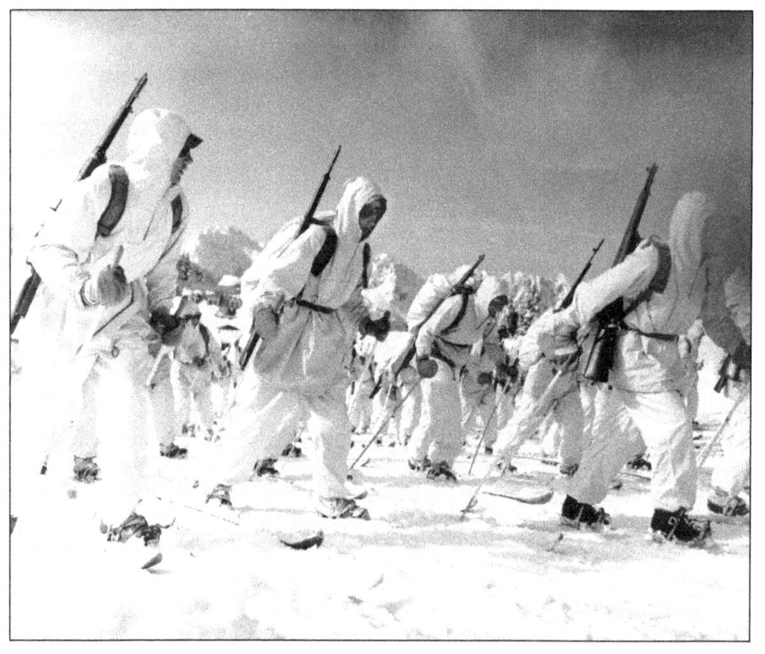

Outfitted in white snow-camouflage uniforms, men of the 1st Battalion, 87th Mountain Infantry Regiment, glide across the snow while on a training maneuver at Mount Rainier. Many of the finest skiers in the United States and Europe were already a part of the unit by this time. (Courtesy of DPL.)

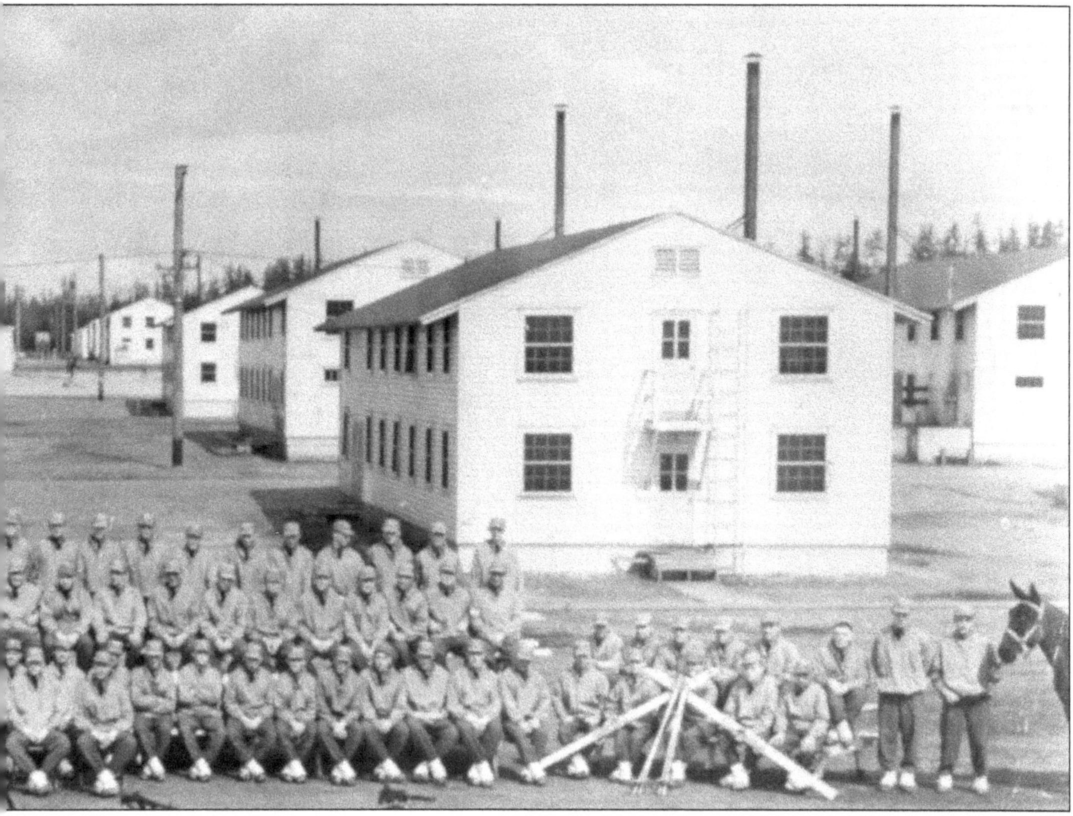

the summer of 1942. The unit would move to Camp Hale in the fall. (Courtesy of DPL.)

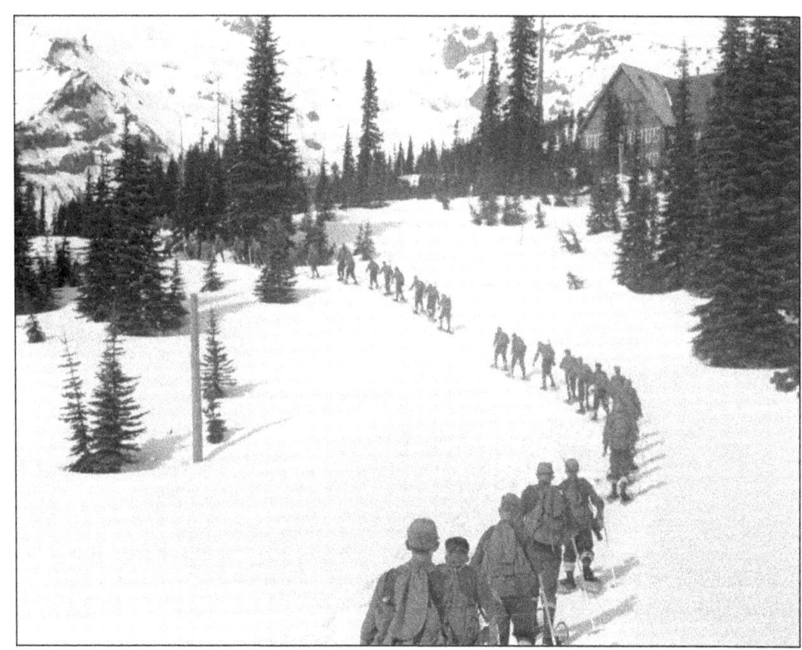

Trudging uphill toward Paradise Inn (behind the trees at right), a line of 87th men learn how to use snowshoes. (Courtesy of DPL.)

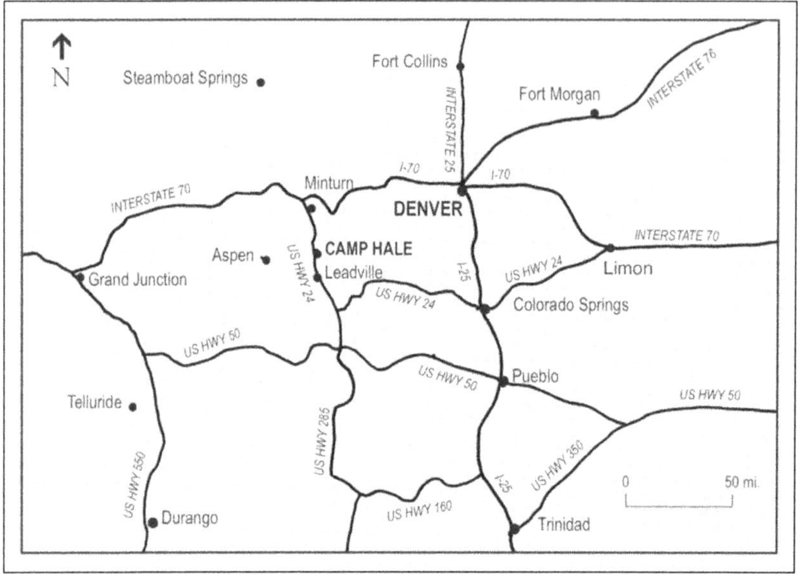

This map shows the location of Camp Hale relative to other Colorado towns and major roads, including the interstate highways that did not exist until the 1960s and 1970s. (Map by Flint Whitlock.)

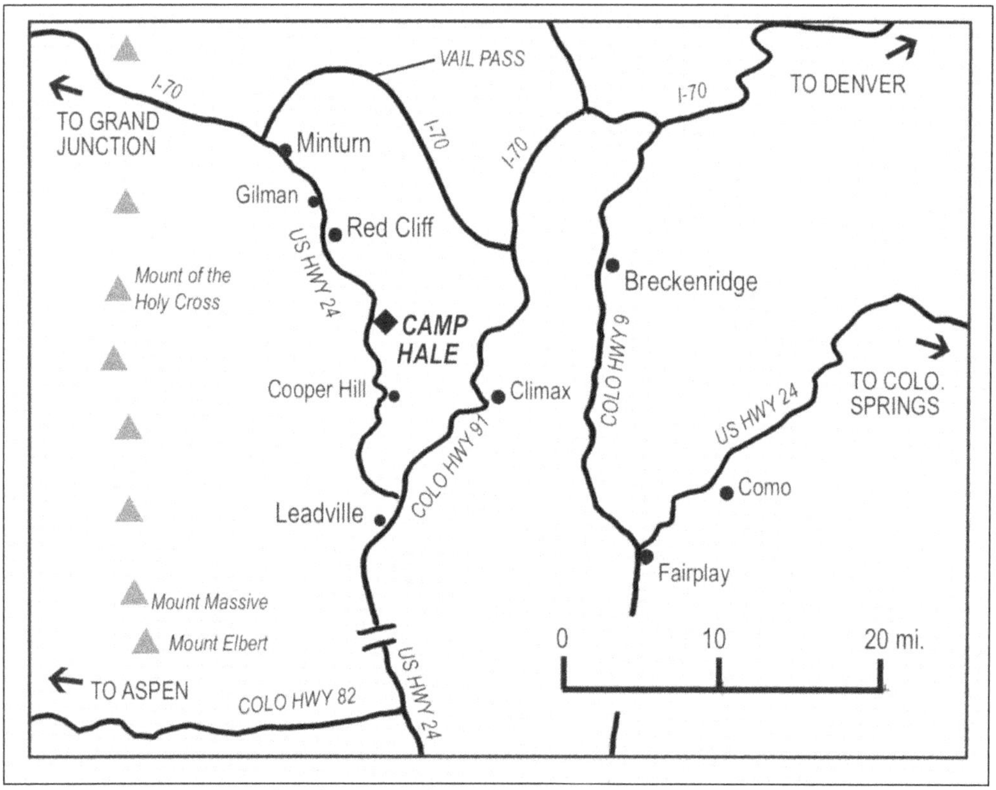

Camp Hale was in central Colorado, halfway between the railroad town of Minturn and the former gold-and-silver mining town of Leadville. Denver was 100 miles to the east. (Map by Flint Whitlock.)

Two

The Camp before the Camp

At the end of March 1942, Army Ground Forces (AGF) authorized the building of the camp at Pando. After a quick bid process, AGF selected the Kansas City engineering firm of Black & Veatch, and Platt Rogers Inc., a Colorado-based industrial-building company, which then hired 10,000 men who became the workers known as Pando Constructors. The initial budget was $5 million, which would balloon to $30 million by the time the project was completed.

The site was nearly a mile wide by three miles long, and seemed to possess everything the Army wanted. There was enough acreage for a thousand structures, plus even more for an artillery range. A water supply, in the form of the Eagle River, weaved its crooked way through the swampy valley floor. There were plenty of places to climb and plenty of snow and cold weather. US Highway 24 ran through it, as did the tracks for the Denver & Rio Grande Western Railroad. Three small towns (Minturn, Red Cliff, and Leadville) were close enough to provide places for off-duty relaxation, and Denver was about 100 miles away. A more ideal place to train a mountain division is hard to imagine.

(In addition to Camp Hale, the US government was also building or enlarging scores of other Army posts, air bases, and naval facilities across the country at the same time.)

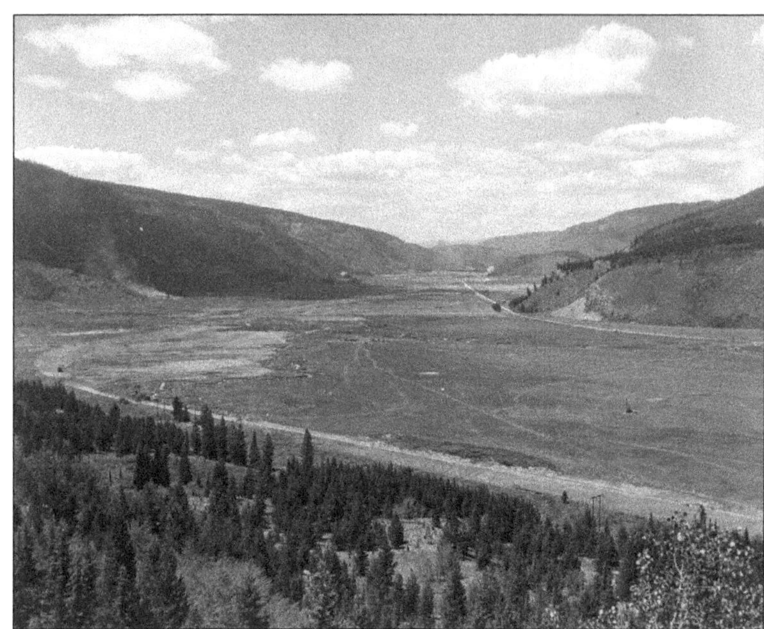

In April 1942, the Pando Valley was empty, but a flurry of construction was about to begin. With the war on, and America's military draft gobbling up almost every able-bodied man, finding 10,000 construction workers to build Camp Hale was an incredible feat in itself. (Courtesy of DPL.)

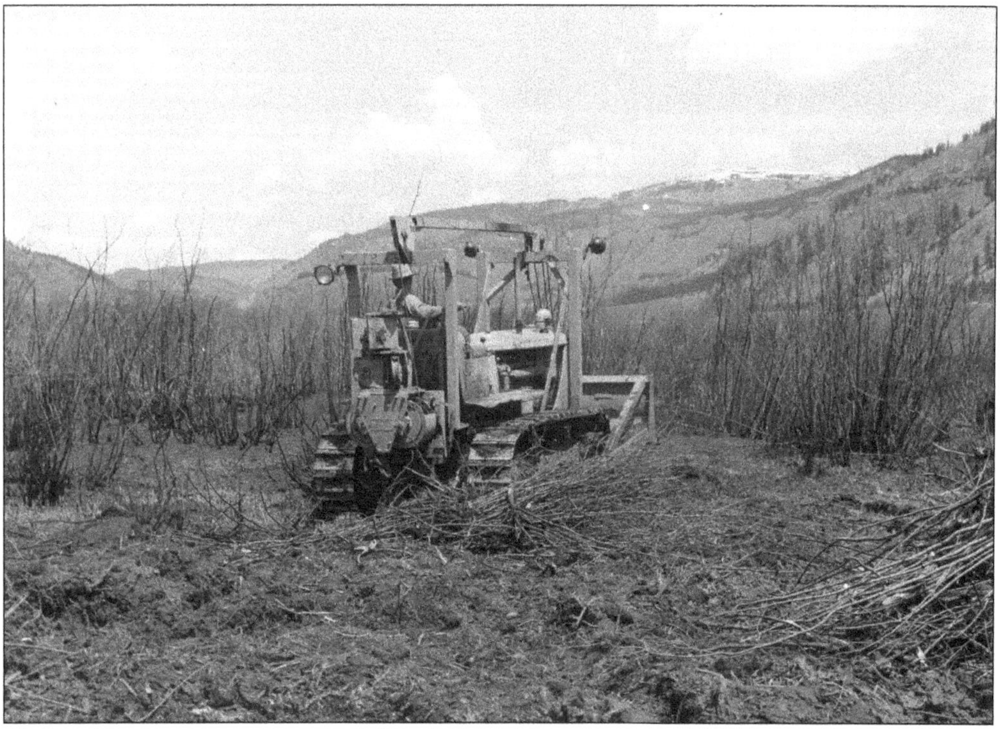

The land for the cantonment area and artillery range was purchased from property owners, mostly ranchers. Here, a bulldozer is clearing foliage from the valley floor. Much of the work, however, had to be done by hand. (Courtesy of DPL.)

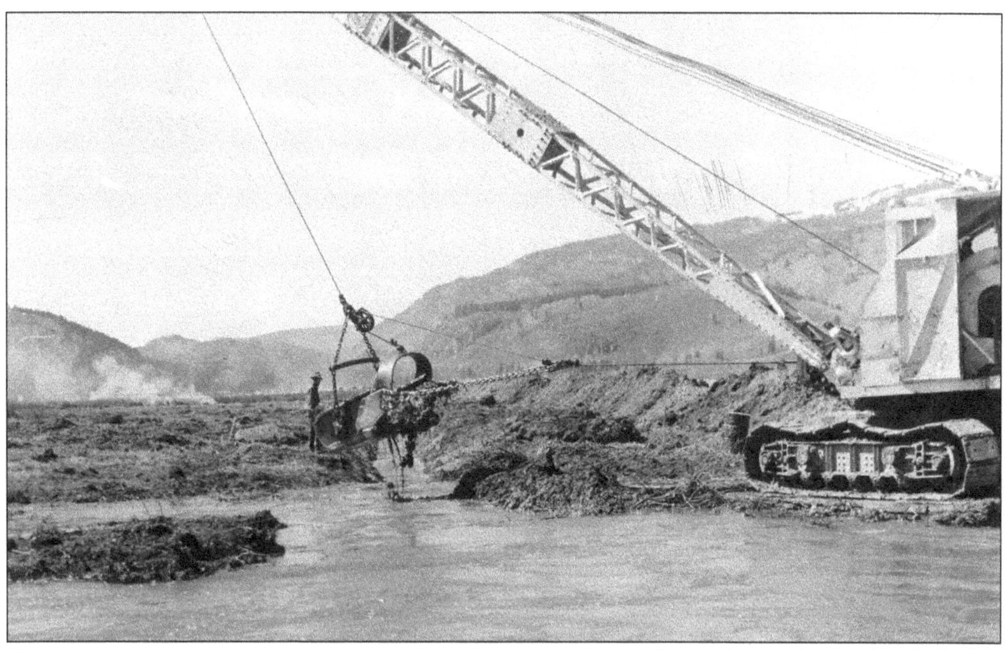

Heavy equipment was necessary to widen, deepen, and straighten the Eagle River, which ran through the site. (Courtesy of DPL.)

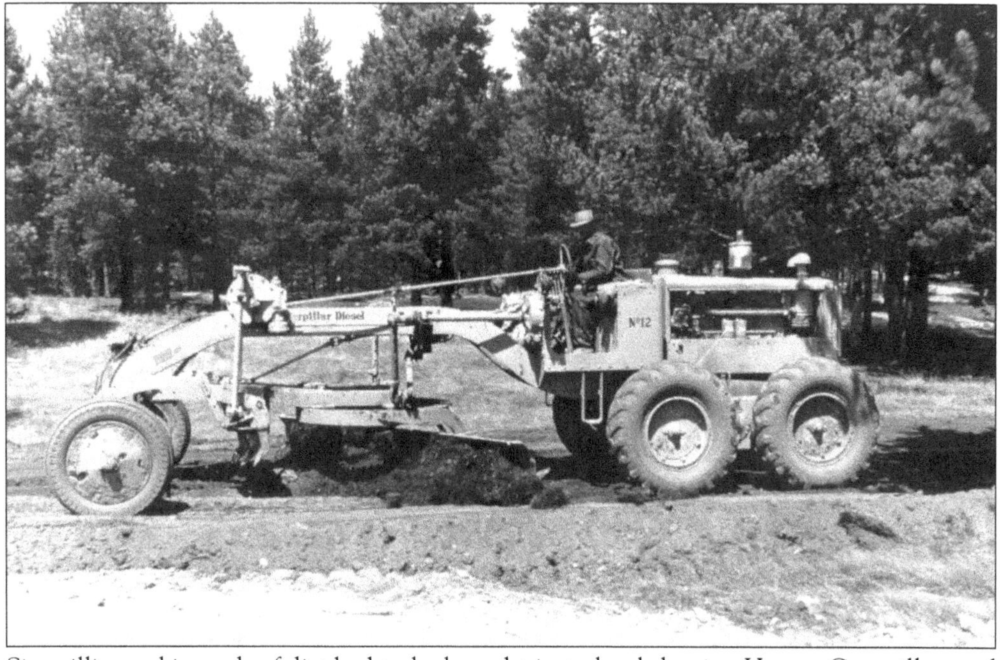

Six million cubic yards of dirt had to be brought in to level the site. Here, a Caterpillar road grader smooths the ground in preparation for construction of the buildings. (Courtesy of DPL.)

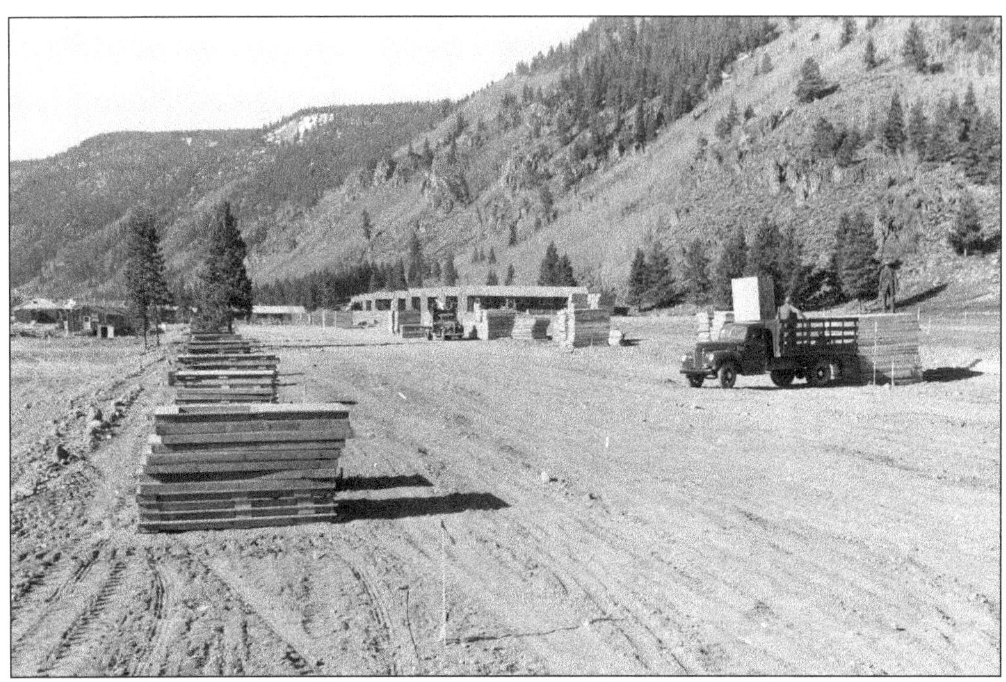

Once the Pando Valley was cleared of vegetation and the ground leveled, and before they could start to build the military camp, Pando Constructors first had to build their own temporary housing area near the Pando railroad depot. (Courtesy of DPL.)

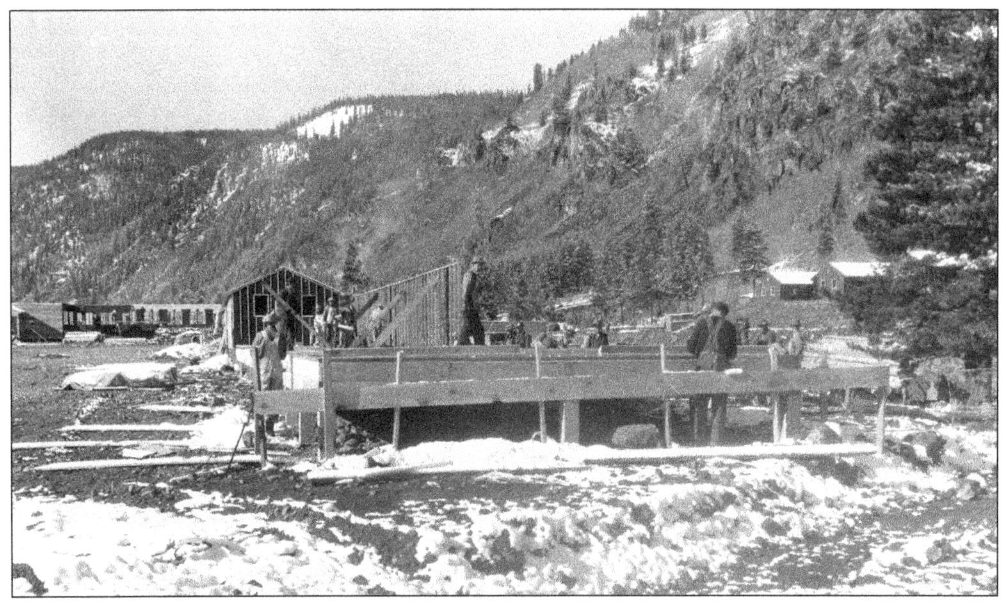

Workers nail together one of the 88 barracks at the Pando Constructors' camp. In addition to the workers' camp that was designed to hold 8,000 men, another 2,800 lived off-site in trailers and homes that had been boarded up for years in Leadville, Minturn, and Red Cliff. (Courtesy of DPL.)

Men employed by Pando Constructors become railroad workers as they lay ties for the Denver & Rio Grande Western spur tracks, which will run into the warehouse area. (Courtesy of DPL.)

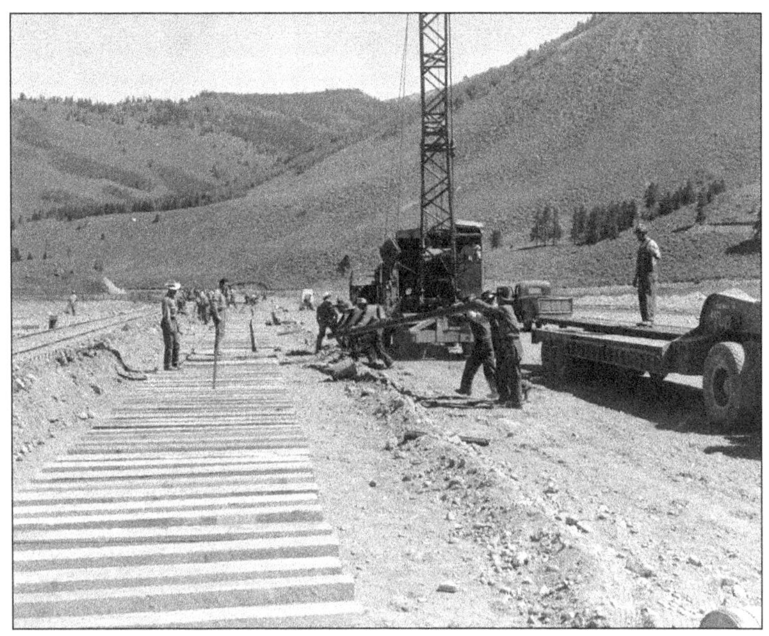

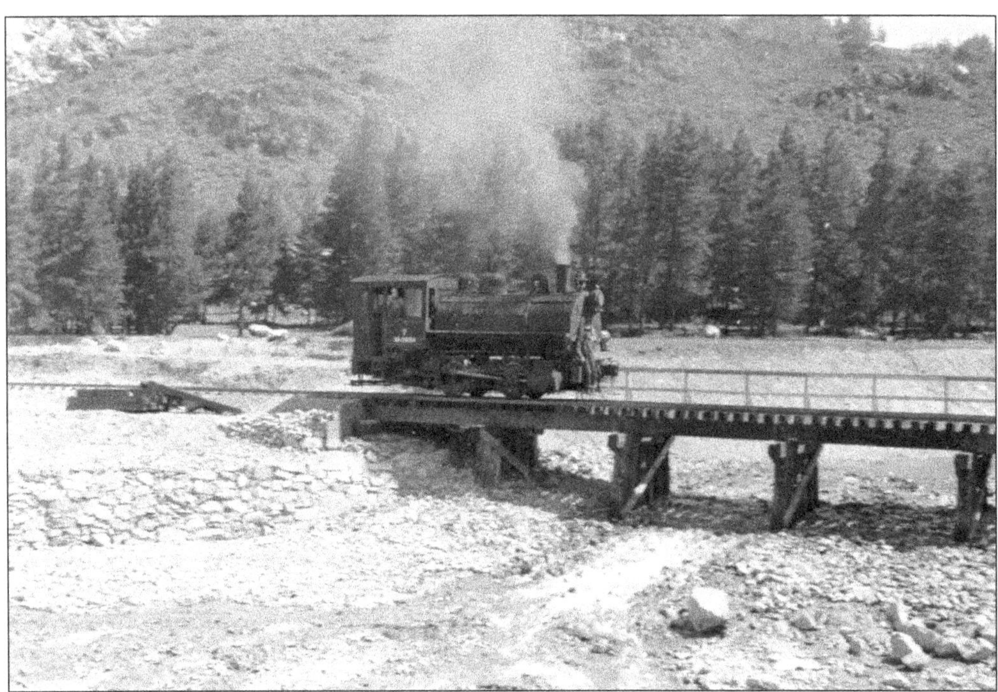

A small switching engine crosses a temporary bridge over the Eagle River. Dozens of freight cars carrying building materials arrived at the valley daily and had to be shunted to the proper job-site location. (Courtesy of DPL.)

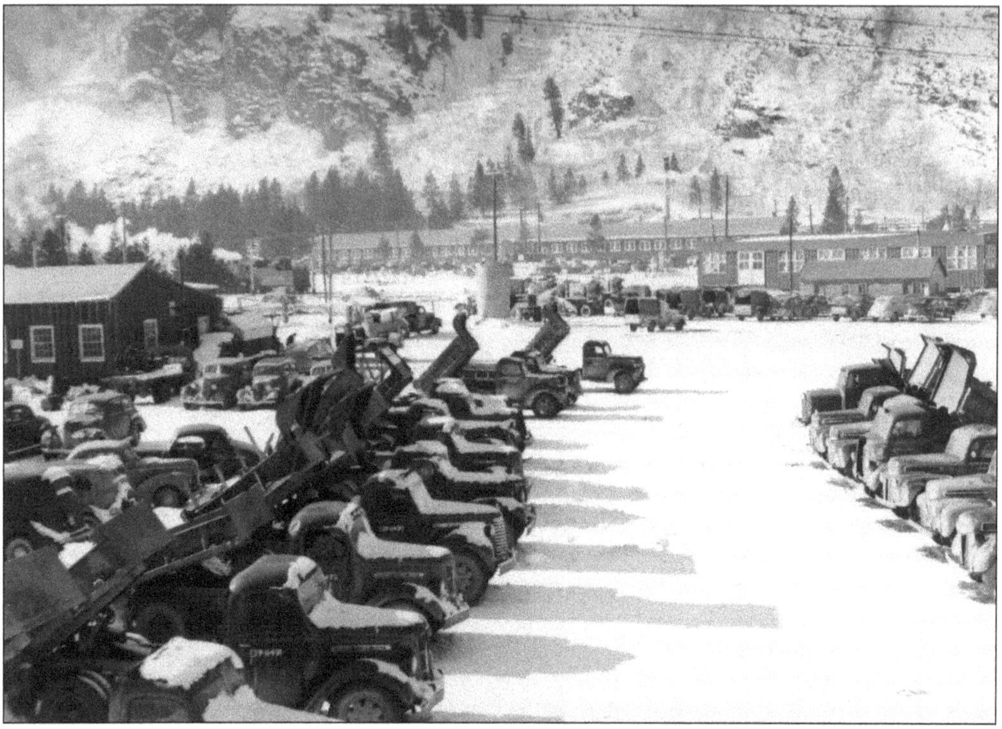

Dump trucks, workers' cars, and other vehicles fill the Pando Constructors' motor pool. For those thousands of workers who did not live in the camp's temporary barracks, getting to work from towns such as Leadville, Red Cliff, and Minturn on winding, two-lane US Highway 24 was a crowded and sometimes dangerous commute, especially during the winter of 1942–1943. (Courtesy of DPL.)

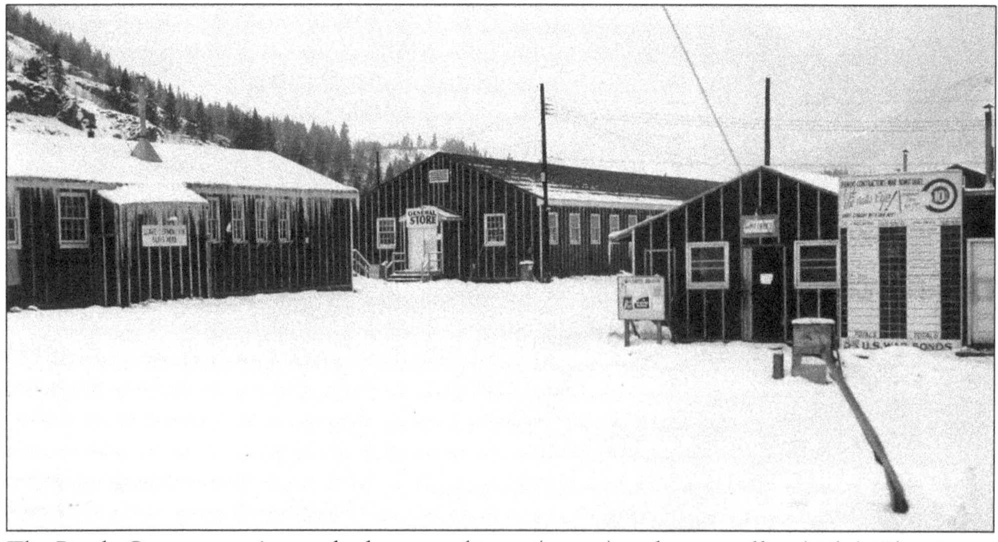

The Pando Constructors' camp had a general store (center) and a post office (right). The sign at right tracked the workers' purchases of war bonds. (Courtesy of DPL.)

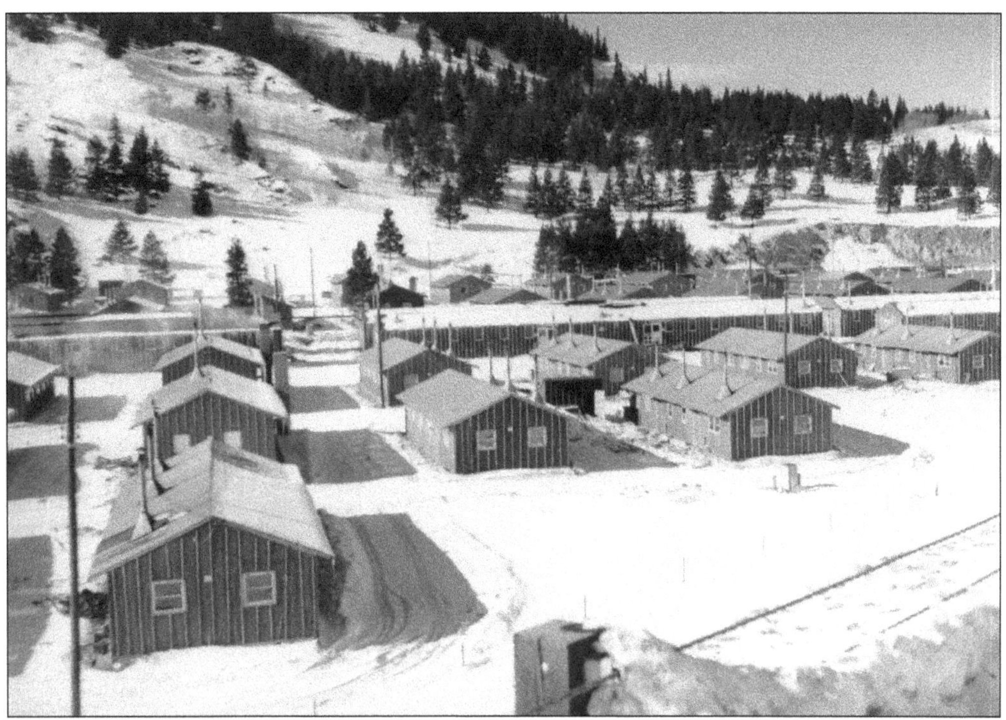

Snow blankets the temporary tar paper barracks at the Pando Constructors' camp. The workers tried never to let weather conditions slow their progress. (Courtesy of DPL.)

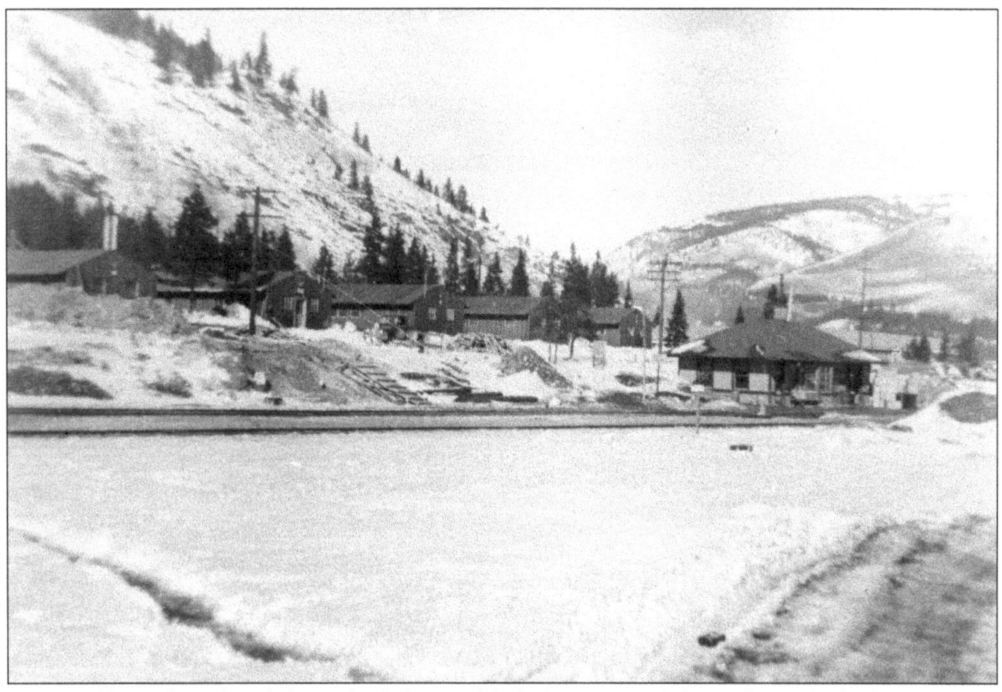

The small Pando railroad depot (right) is visible below some of the 88 barracks built for and by the Camp Hale construction workers. Virtually no trace of the depot or workers' camp remains today. (Courtesy of DPL.)

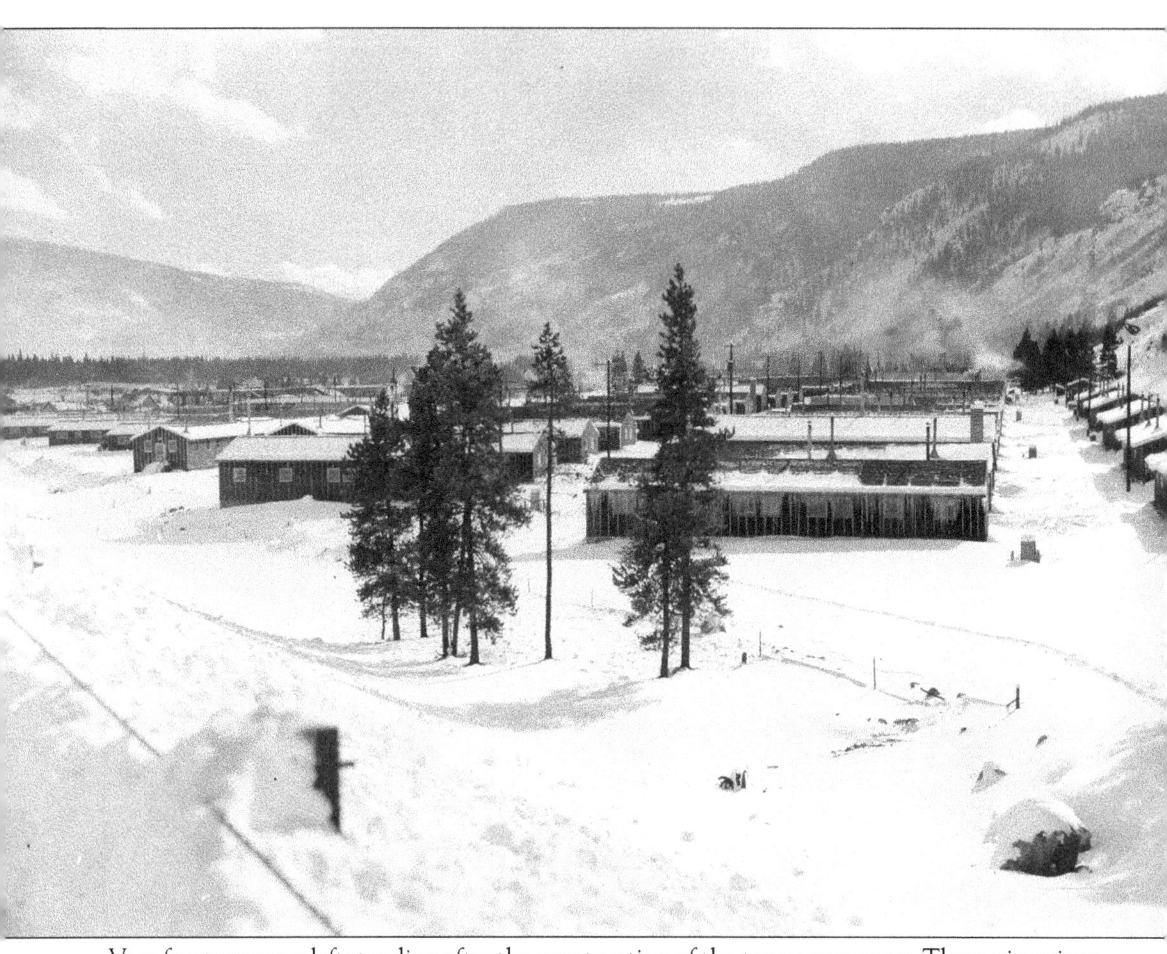

Very few trees were left standing after the construction of the temporary camp. These nine pines at the northern end of the construction workers' camp were an exception. (Courtesy of DPL.)

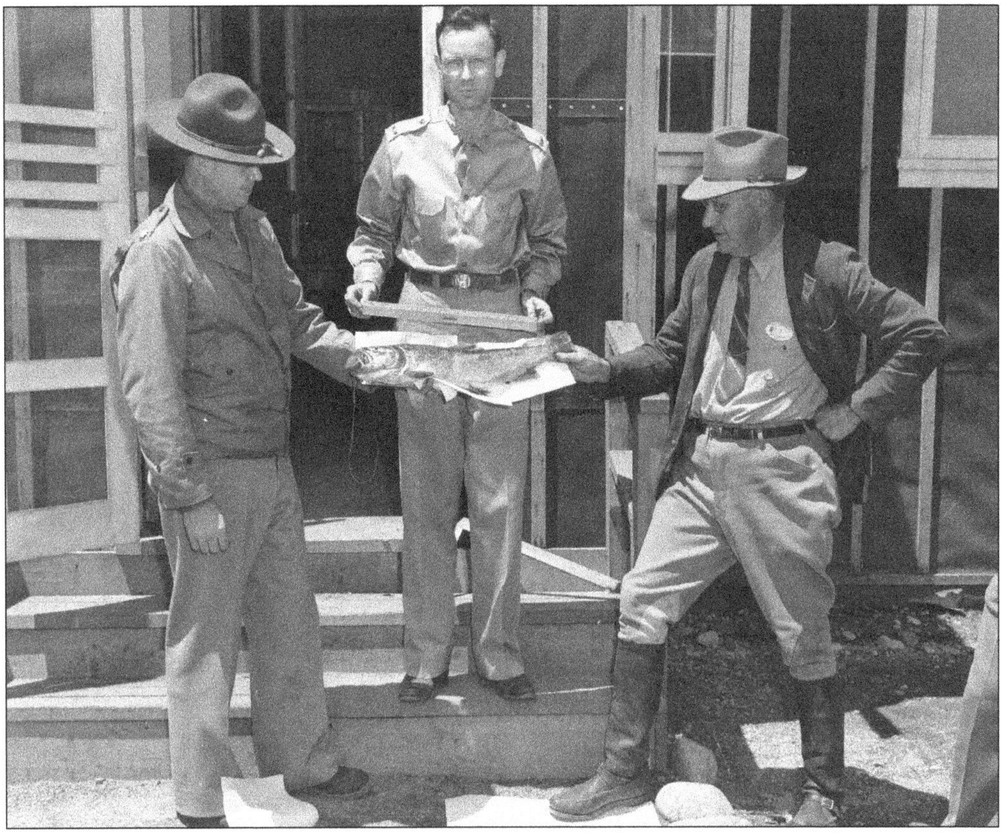

Two Army officers and a Pando Constructors foreman (right) measure a trout that one of them has caught in the Eagle River. While working six days a week, the Pando Constructors workmen had very little free time to engage in recreational activities. (Courtesy of DPL.)

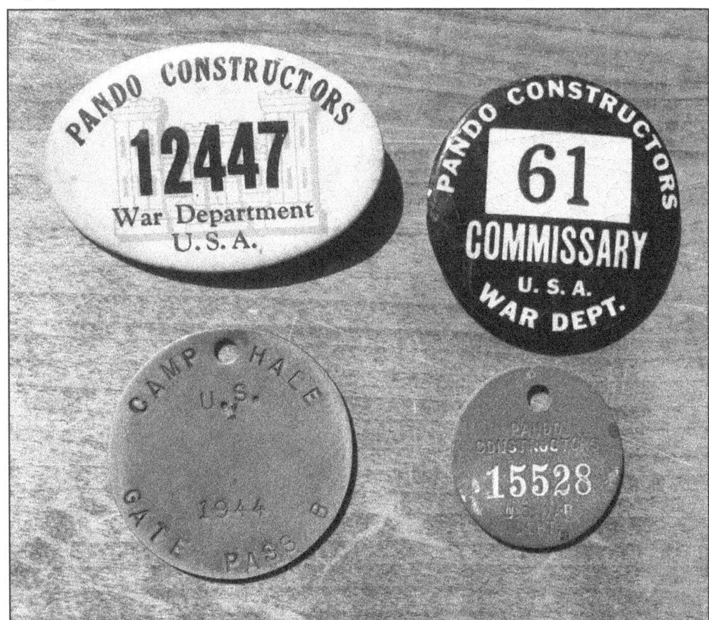

Pando Constructors employees needed a variety of badges to gain access to the work site and other facilities. (Courtesy of David J. Little.)

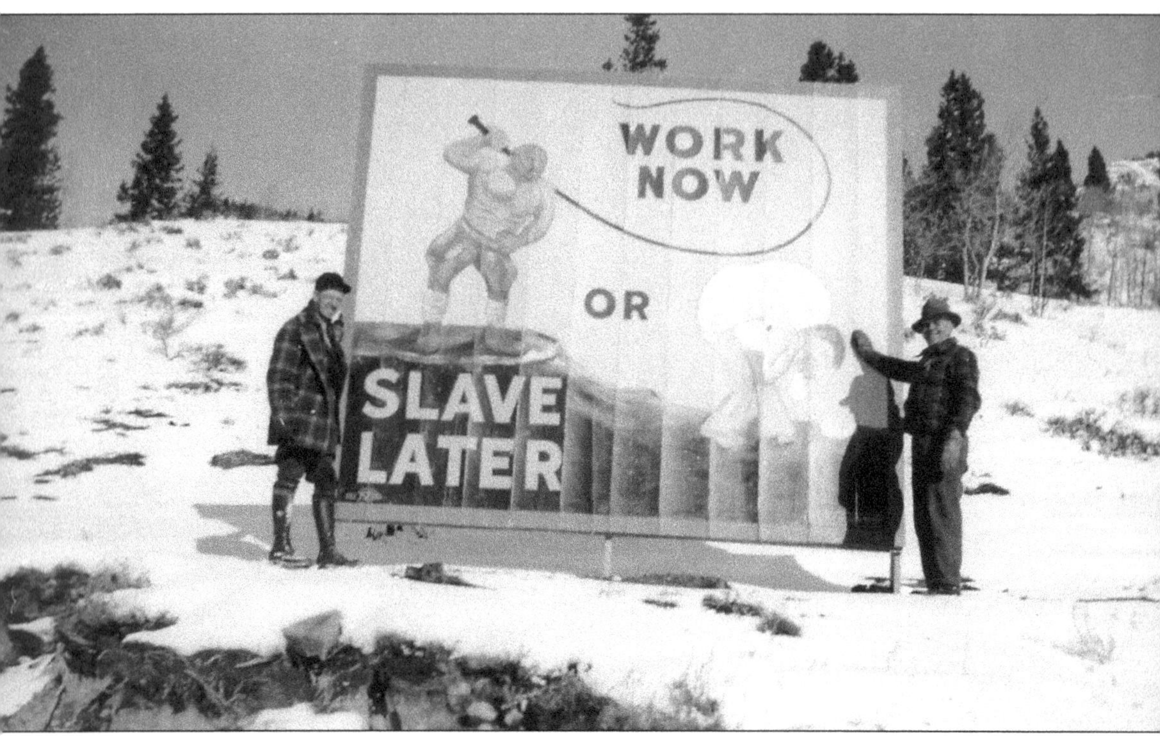

A billboard at the construction workers' camp graphically warned what might happen if the Allies lost the war, and encouraged everyone to make a maximum effort. The year 1942 was a dark one for Americans and their allies, who were on the defensive against the Axis forces on practically every battlefront. There was no assurance that Nazi Germany, Fascist Italy, or Imperial Japan could be defeated, which made the completion of Camp Hale and other US military facilities that much more important. (Courtesy of DPL.)

Three

Building Camp Hale

By the middle of 1942, the Pando Constructors had finished their temporary camp and had concurrently begun work on the military cantonment area. It was now time to finish what they had started back in April: the main camp.

The original plan called for a camp housing 20,353 officers and enlisted men and 11,288 pack animals. This was reduced a month later to 16,392 humans and 3,925 animals.

Built here in just seven months were 226 barracks, 33 administration buildings, a 676-bed hospital, a veterinary hospital, five churches and chapels, a hundred mess halls, a bakery, three theaters, one field house, indoor pistol ranges, seven post exchanges, two service clubs, one officers' club, horse and mule barns, grain storage, coal storage, numerous warehouses, a stockade, vehicle-maintenance facilities, weapons ranges, six underground ammunition magazines, four water-storage tanks, three fire stations, a school, a post office, medical and dental clinics, a combat village, two ski areas, and more.

On July 4, 1942, a flag-raising ceremony was held at Pando and the Army camp was officially named Camp Hale.

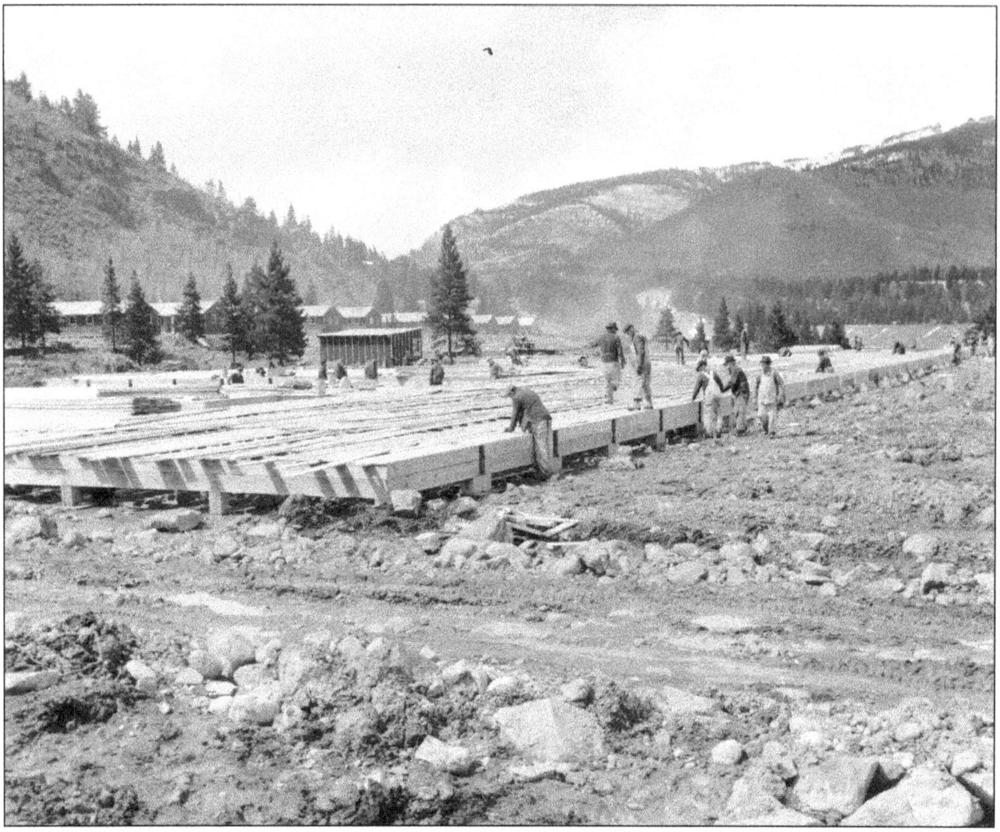

Workers lay out planks for a large building. The temporary camp for the Pando Constructors is visible in the distance behind the trees. (Courtesy of DPL.)

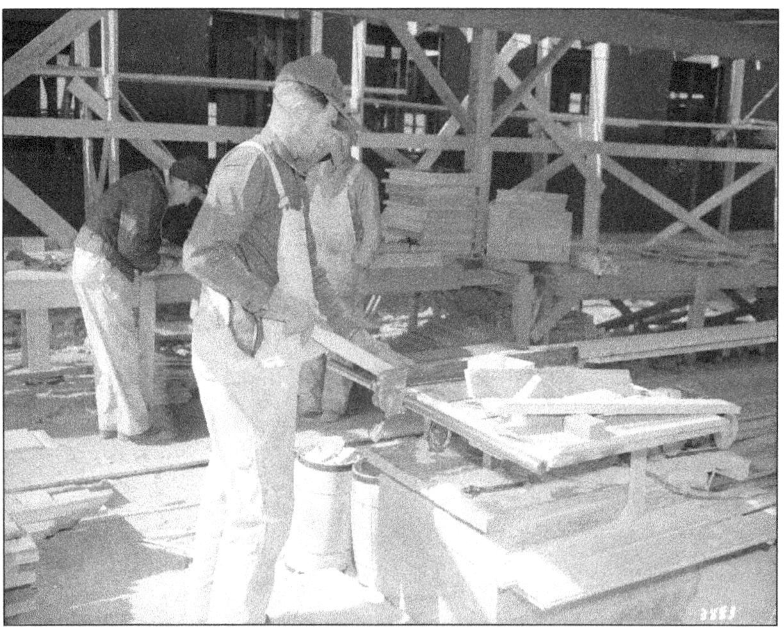

Even getting electricity to the work site was a major accomplishment. Here, a worker uses an electric table saw to trim boards to size. (Courtesy of HC.)

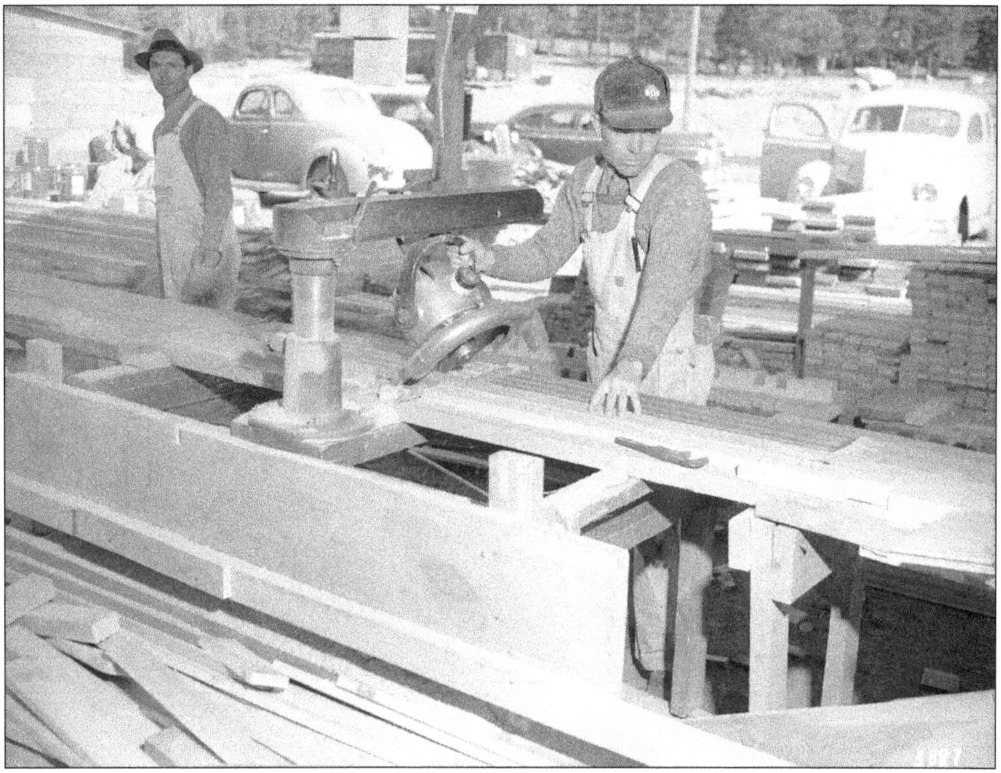

A carpenter cuts a board to length. In order to meet the deadline, work went on six and sometimes seven days a week. (Courtesy of DPL.)

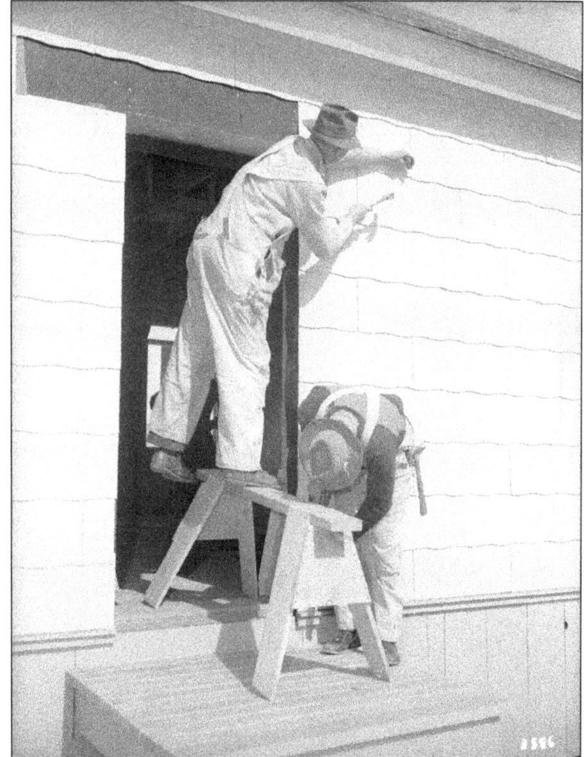

Workmen nail asbestos-cement siding onto one of the barracks buildings. It was a fire- and weather-resistant product, but the cancer-causing properties of asbestos were not then well known. (Courtesy of HC.)

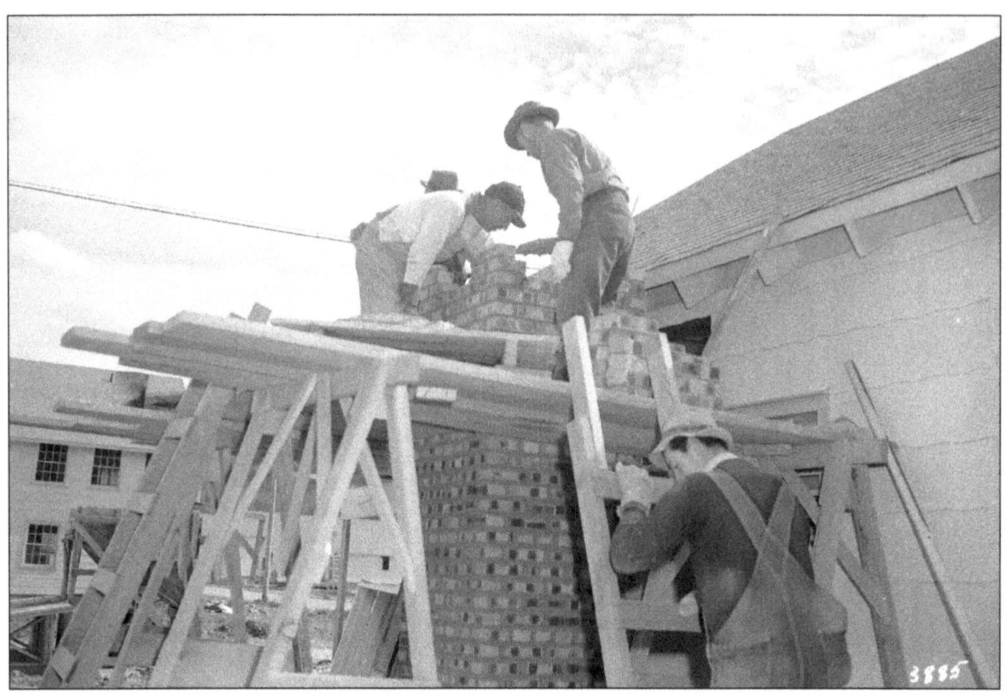

Bricklayers assemble a chimney beside one of the camp buildings. Each building had at least one coal-burning stove, which created serious pollution problems in the Pando Valley. (Courtesy of HC.)

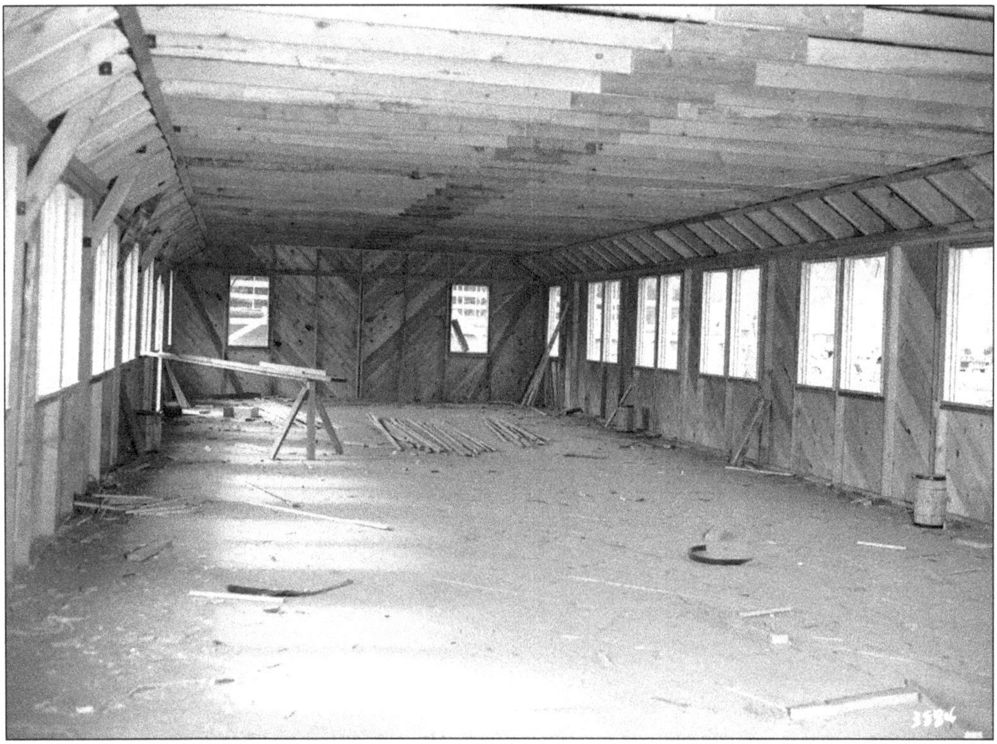

The interior of a building—perhaps an administrative or hospital building—begins to shape up. (Courtesy of HC.)

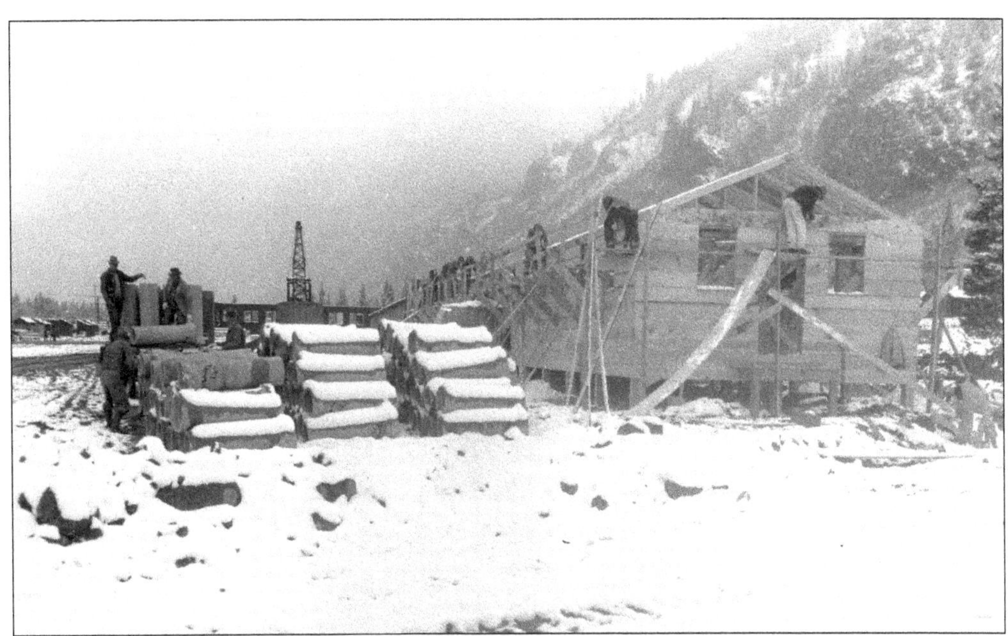

A two-story building in the cantonment area goes up as a stack of snow-dusted sewer pipes wait to go underground. (Courtesy of DPL.)

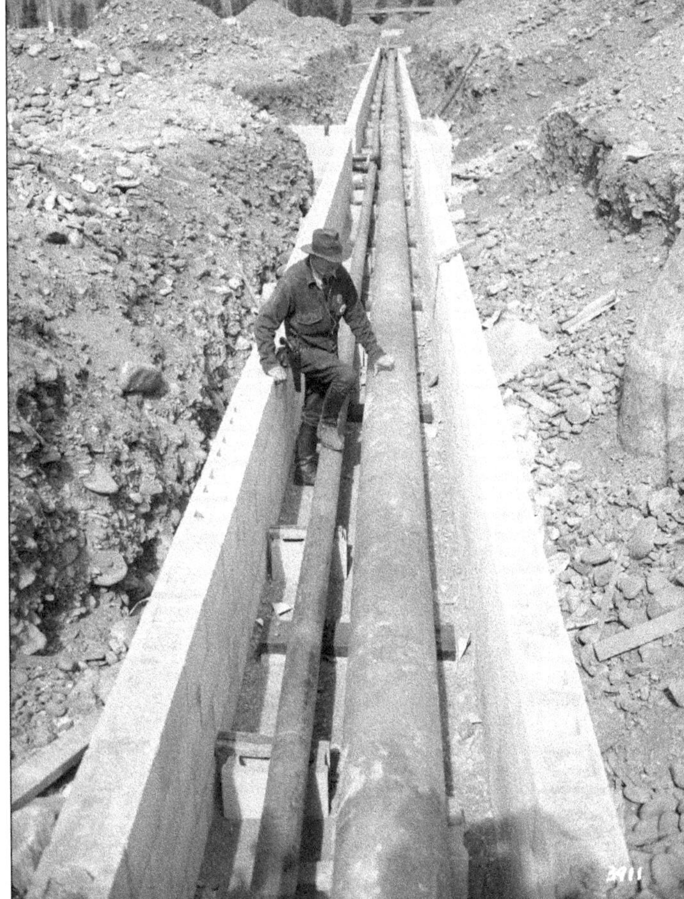

An inspector, with a large pistol on his belt (probably as protection against wild animals that roamed the valley), checks out water and sewer lines. After the first lines were buried, it was discovered that they froze—and had to be re-buried deeper. (Courtesy of HC.)

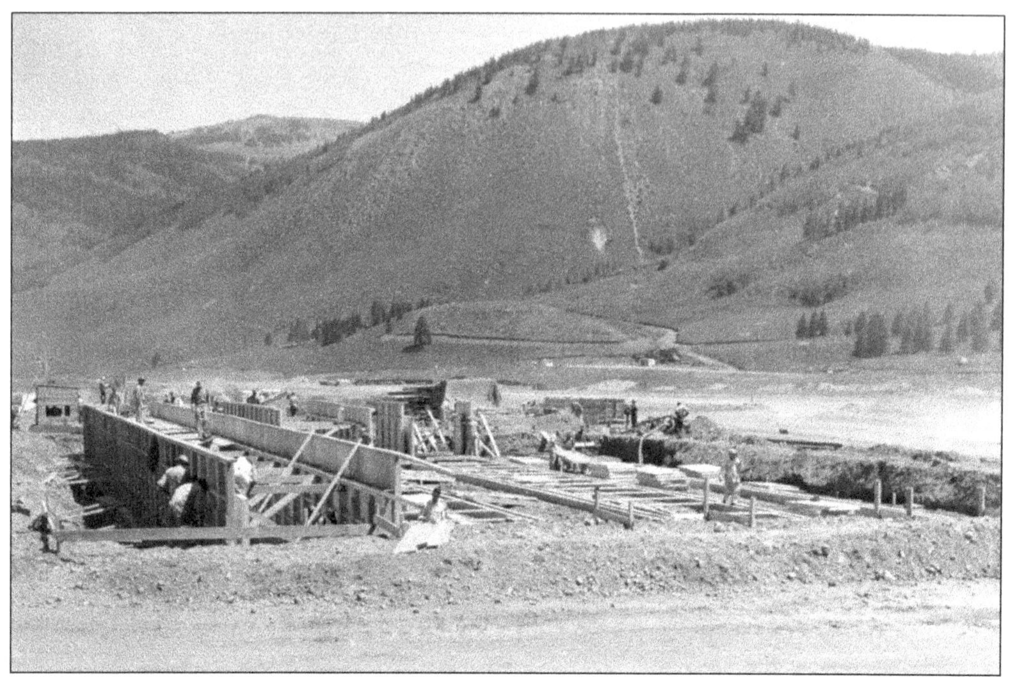

Attention to detail and craftsmanship were important to Pando Constructors. Here, wooden forms are constructed before concrete foundations are poured. The foundations can still be seen at the camp today. (Courtesy of HC.)

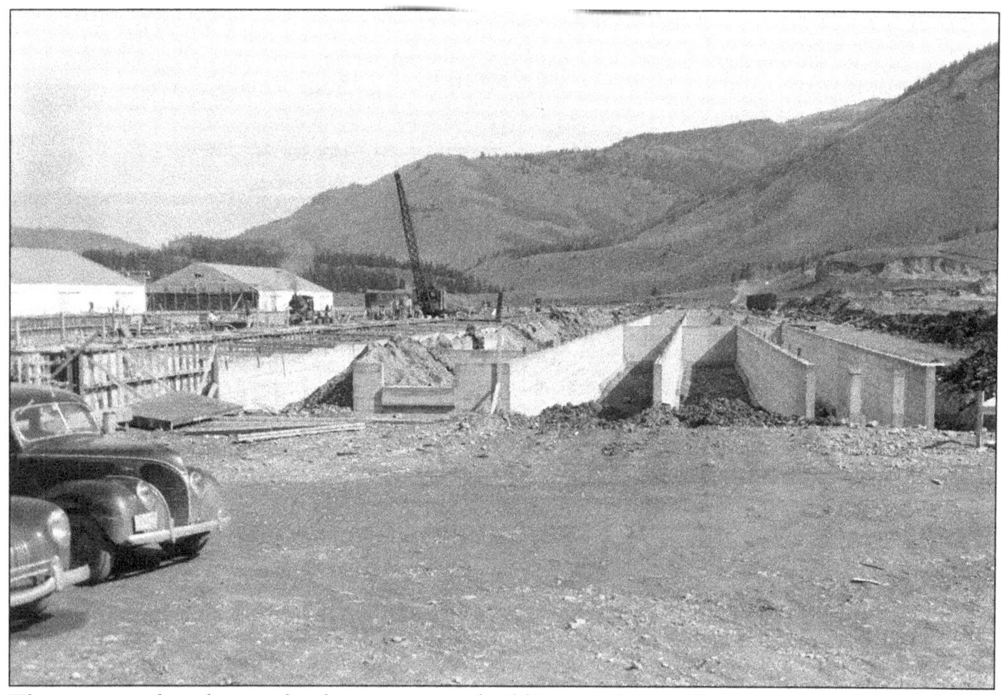

The concrete foundations for three immense buildings in the warehouse area on the north end of the camp have been laid and await the finishing touches—floors, walls, roofs, and more. (Courtesy of HC.)

The stalls in one of the camp's seven mule stables are nearing completion. Even the construction in the barns was meticulous and of the highest craftsmanship. (Courtesy of HC.)

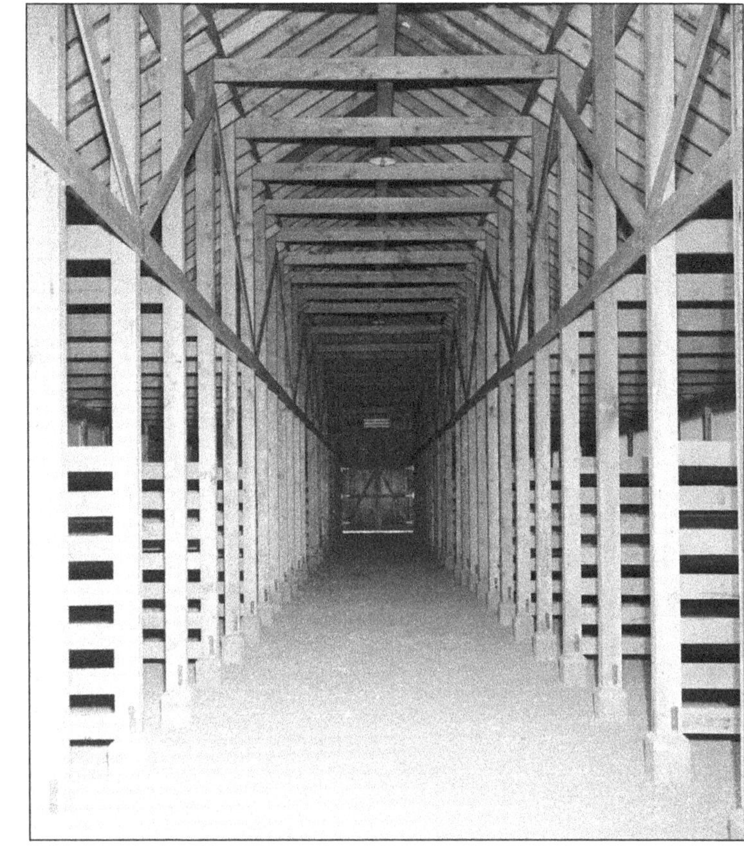

Two men prepare to install a sink while working on the interior of a two-story building. Although the November deadline loomed, there is no indication that any shortcuts were taken by the builders. (Courtesy of HC.)

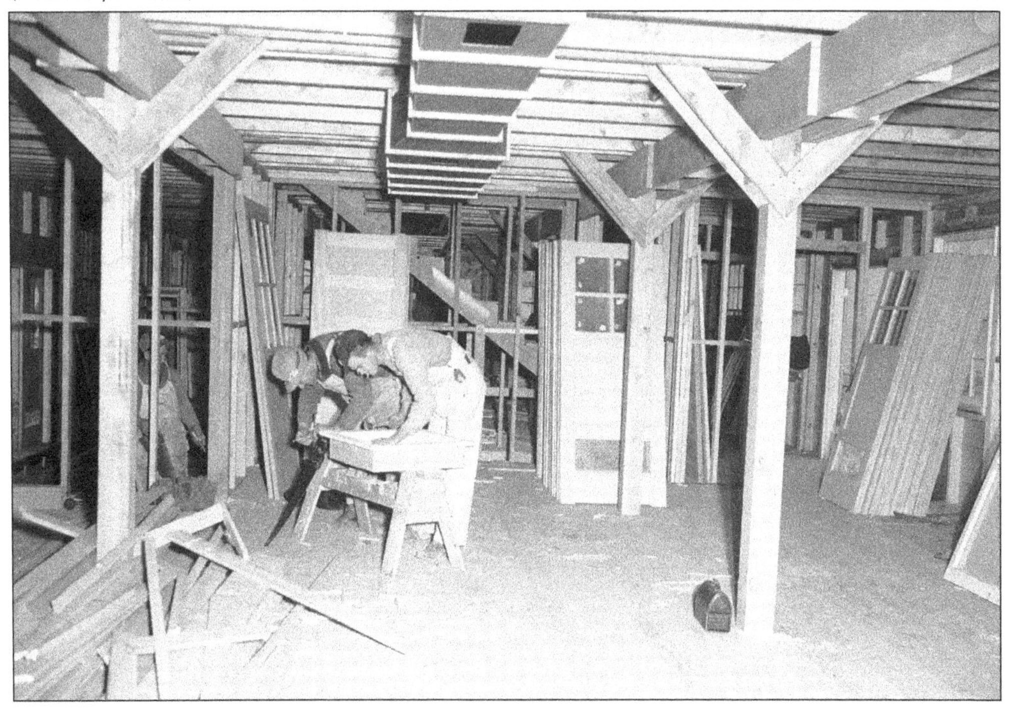

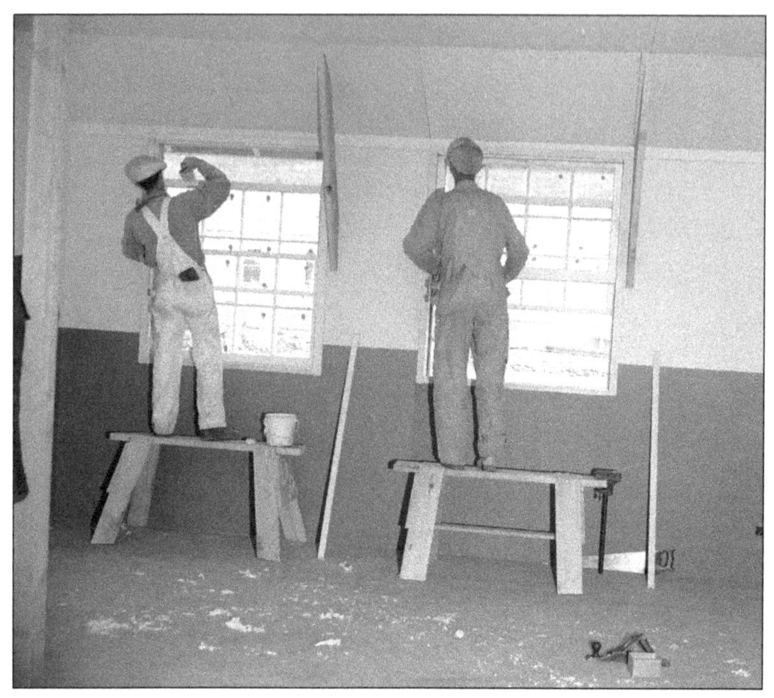

Workers install a pair of windows in one of the buildings. One day in August 1942, a total of 61 carpenters and 4 shinglers set out to build a complete 63-man barracks building in record time. They did—in 7 hours and 45 minutes, breaking the old national record by more than three hours. (Courtesy of HC.)

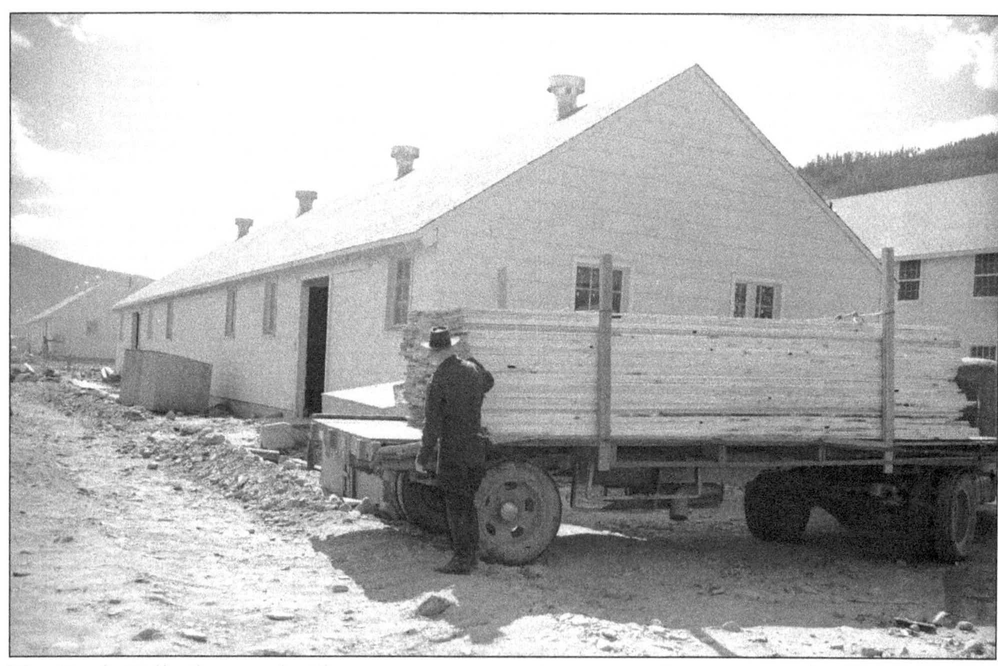

The Pando Valley hummed with non-stop construction activity for seven months. Here, a lumber truck delivers boards to a building in the hospital area. (Courtesy of HC.)

Although the ground is still rough, rows of buildings in the hospital area appear to be nearly complete during the summer of 1942. (Courtesy of DPL.)

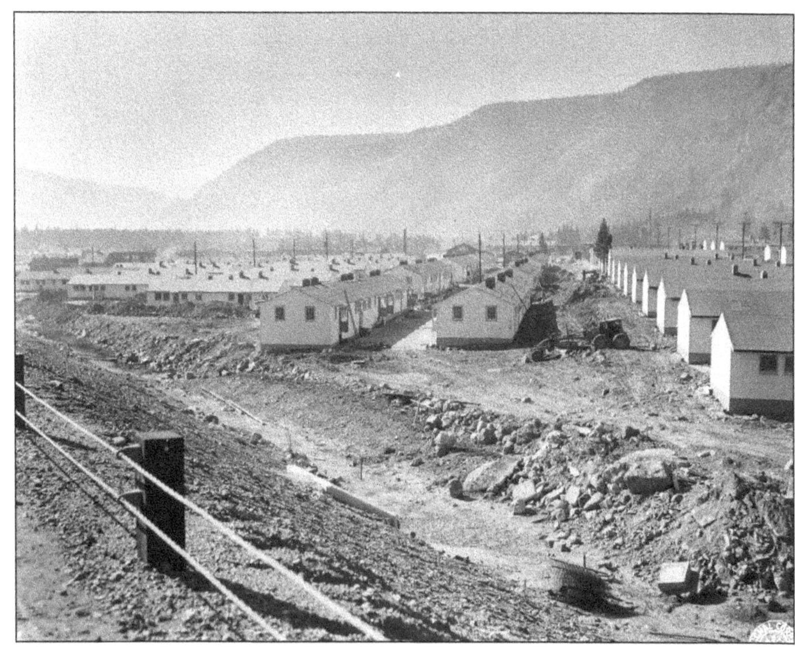

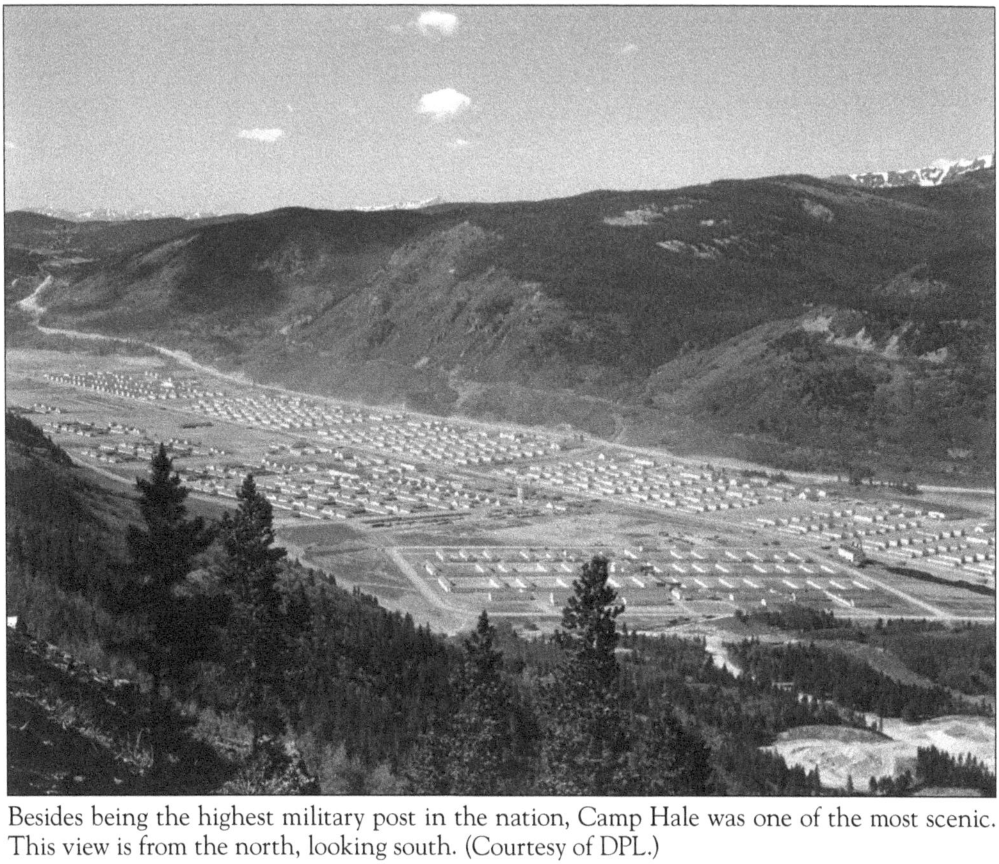

Besides being the highest military post in the nation, Camp Hale was one of the most scenic. This view is from the north, looking south. (Courtesy of DPL.)

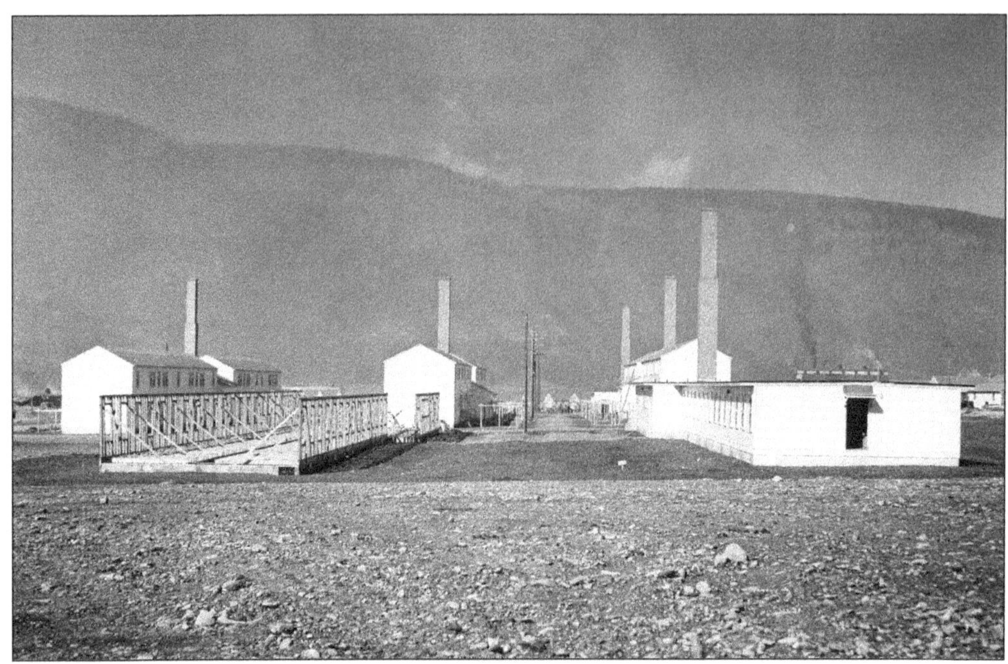

Gleaming white buildings replace the once-overgrown valley floor. The same buildings are shown below in a more complete state. (Courtesy of DPL.)

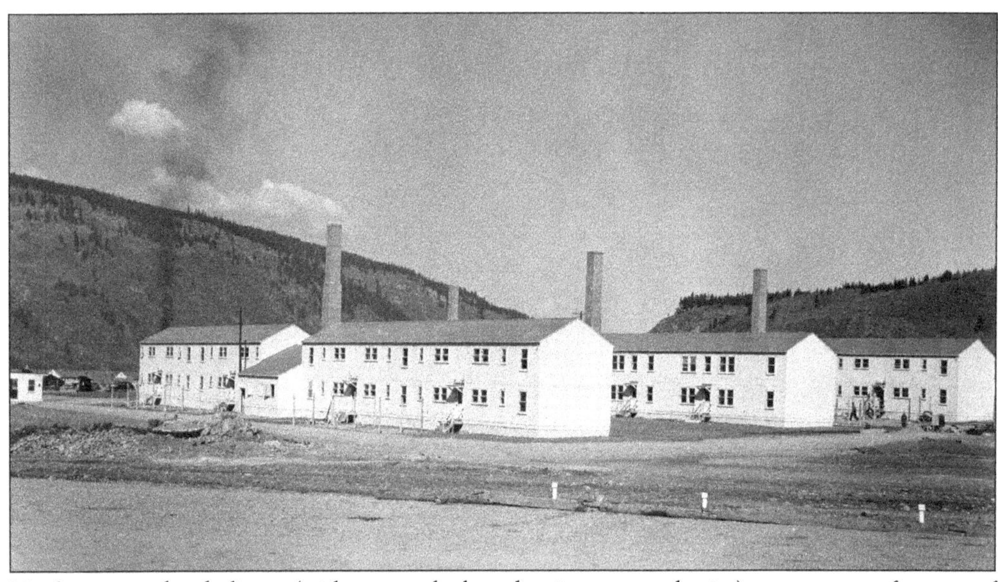

Uniformity and orderliness (without much thought given to aesthetics) are common features of all military posts and bases built during and after World War II; Camp Hale was no exception. By the summer of 1942, the site has begun to take on the look of a real Army camp, but much interior finishing work remains to be done before soldiers can occupy it. (Courtesy of DPL.)

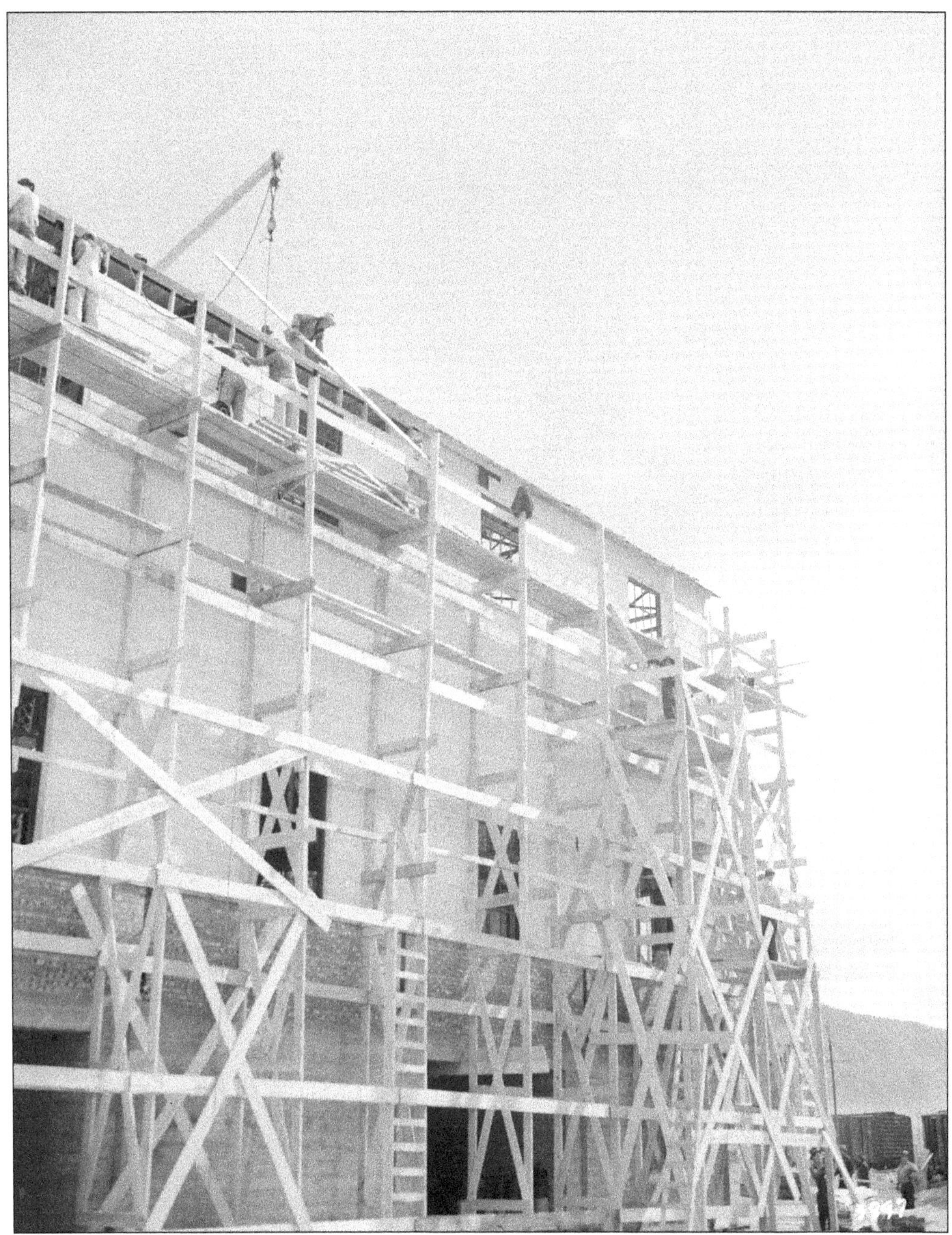

Scaffolding rises on the exterior of a three-story building. Millions of board feet of lumber were used in the construction of the camp. (Courtesy of HC.)

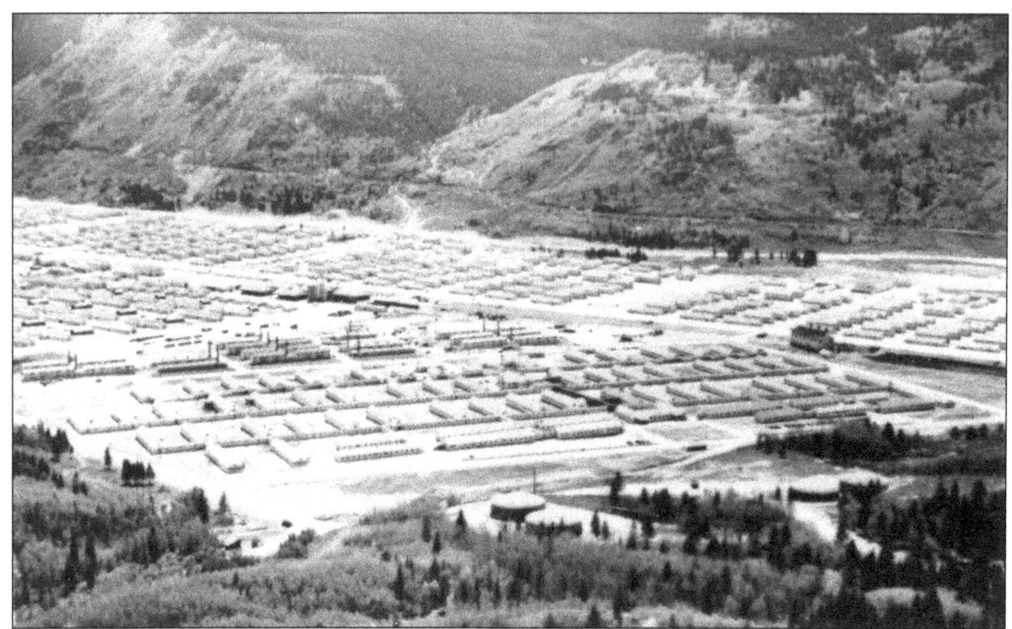

Camp Hale's cantonment area covered 1,457 acres of the Pando Valley floor. Here, the northern end of the camp is dusted with the first traces of snow in the fall of 1942. (Courtesy of DPL.)

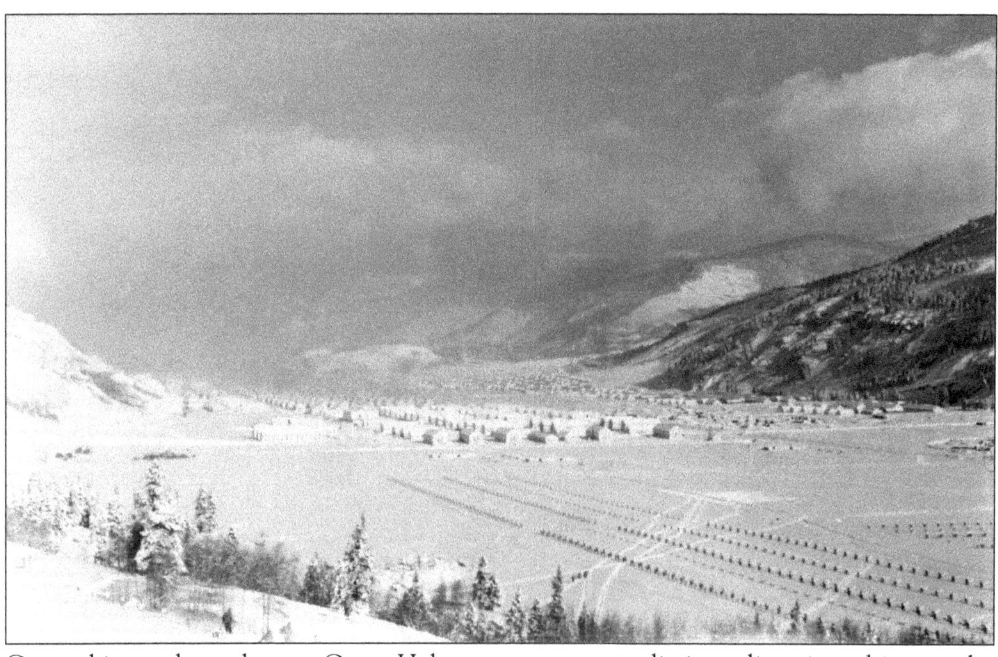

Covered in smoke and snow, Camp Hale presents a contradiction: glistening white powder and black coal smoke in December 1942. The area in the foreground is the bayonet-drill range. (Courtesy of DPL.)

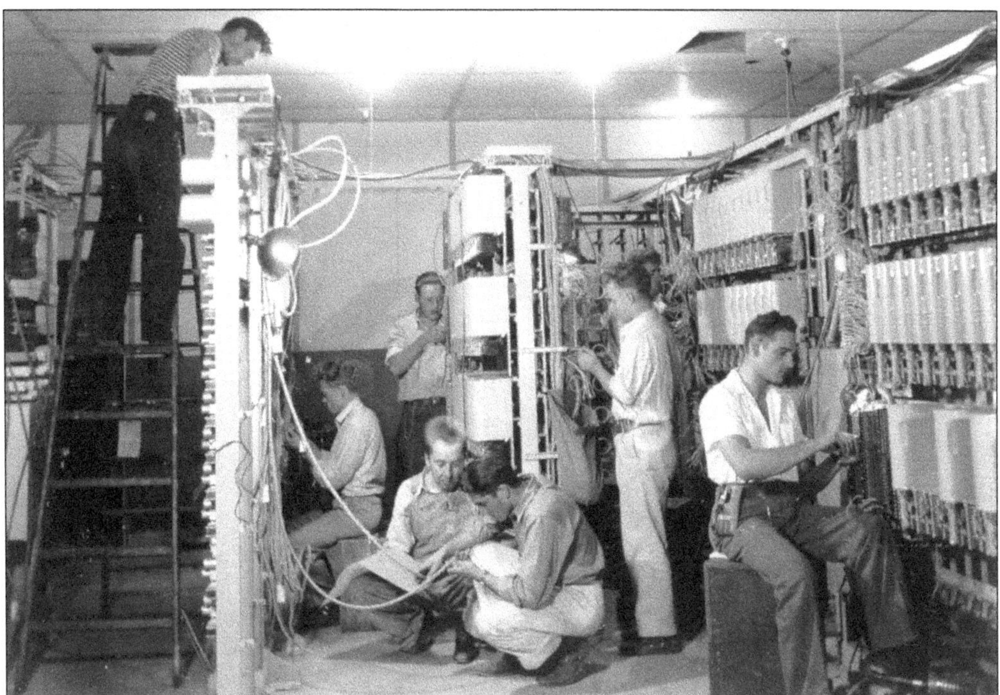

Civilian communications specialists from Mountain States Telephone and Telegraph Company (later Mountain Bell) work to install a state-of-the-art telephone switching system. Hundreds of miles of telephone wire and cable were installed at the camp. (Courtesy of DPL.)

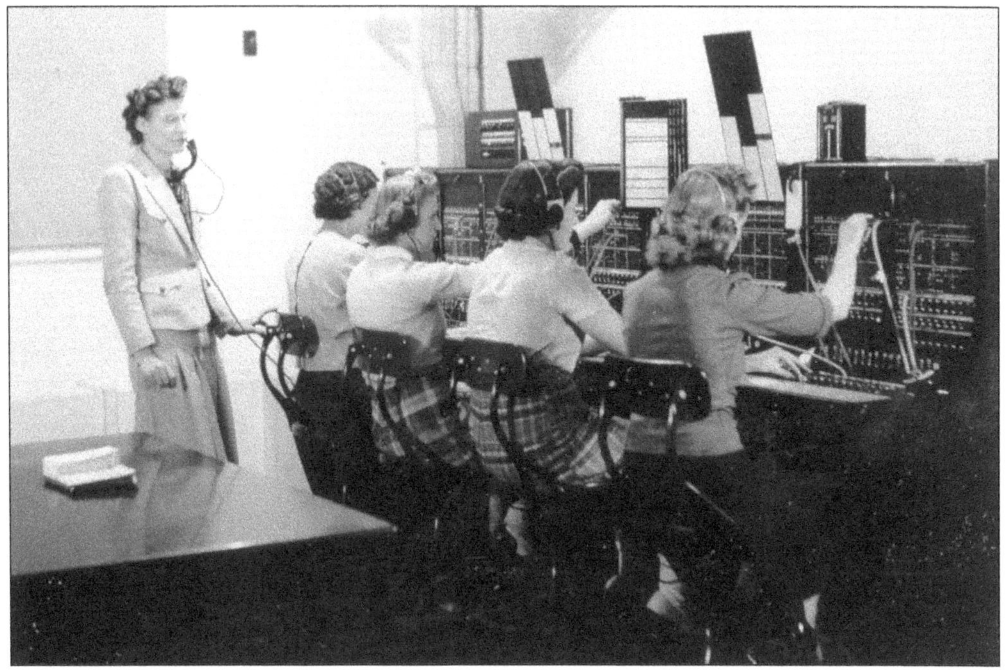

Long before the days of cellular phones, civilian telephone operators were required to place calls. Here, four operators work at a bank of switchboards under the watchful eye of a supervisor. (Courtesy of DPL.)

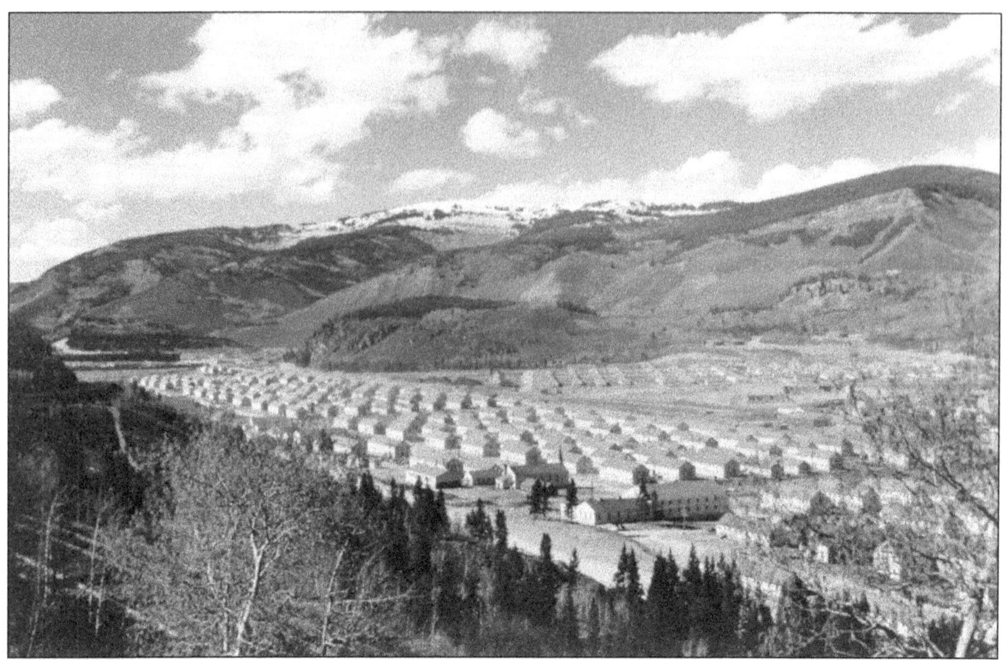

A valley filled with row after row of white-painted buildings was an inspiring sight that demonstrated America's commitment to winning the war. This view is from the southwest, looking north. (Courtesy of DPL.)

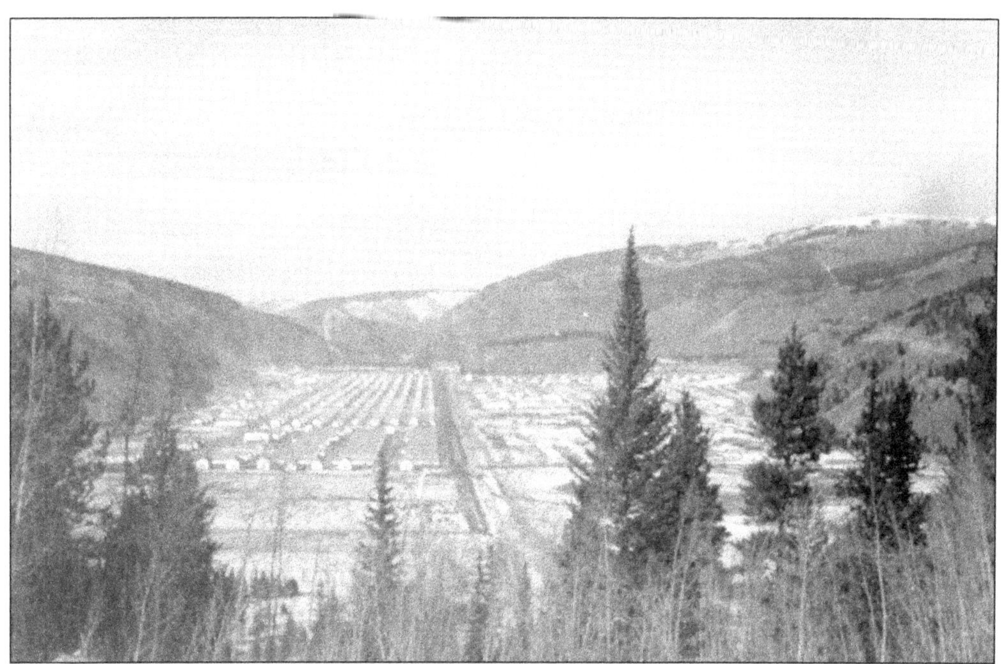

In only seven months, Camp Hale was completed and ready for the thousands of men (and women) who would inhabit it. Camp Hale was truly an astounding feat of wartime engineering and construction; the unsung 10,000–12,000 men who built it deserve much credit for all their hard work. (Compare this image with the one on page 16.) (Courtesy of DPL.)

Four

On to Colorado

While Camp Hale was being finished in the summer and early fall of 1942, and Lt. Col. Onslow Rolfe's 1st Battalion, 87th Infantry Mountain Infantry Regiment, continued to train at Camp Lewis, Washington, a detachment of soldiers from the 1st Battalion was sent to build a small camp at the ghost town of Ashcroft, 12 miles south of Aspen, Colorado. The remainder of the battalion was sent to Hunter Liggett Military Reservation in California to prepare to participate in a large-scale amphibious invasion of Kiska Island in the Aleutian chain that the Japanese had seized. (That invasion, known as Operation Cottage, would involve over 34,000 US and Canadian troops and take place in August 1943, but the Japanese secretly abandoned Kiska shortly before the Allies arrived. Unfortunately, the 87th would suffer 30 deaths due to booby traps and friendly-fire incidents.)

This "test detachment" (25 skier-mountaineers, 25 mule drivers, 10 service personnel, 3 officers, and 24 mules) from the 87th was to perform a variety of training tasks, such as building various types of bridges and cable aerial tramways under the guidance of the US Army Corps of Engineers.

One of the 87th men recalled, "Materials used had to be carried by men or mules. We were supplied with wire rope, u-hooks, dynamite, axes, adzes, shovels, hammers and nails. All other material was 'native,' logs and rocks. A suspension bridge across East Maroon ravine and a Swiss A-frame bridge across the beaver dam in Ashcroft were built. As proof of sound construction, bridges were crossed by men and reluctant mules upon completion of projects."

After the 87th moved on to Camp Hale late in 1942, many of the men, charmed by the beauty of Aspen, returned in the winter in their free time to ski the slopes there.

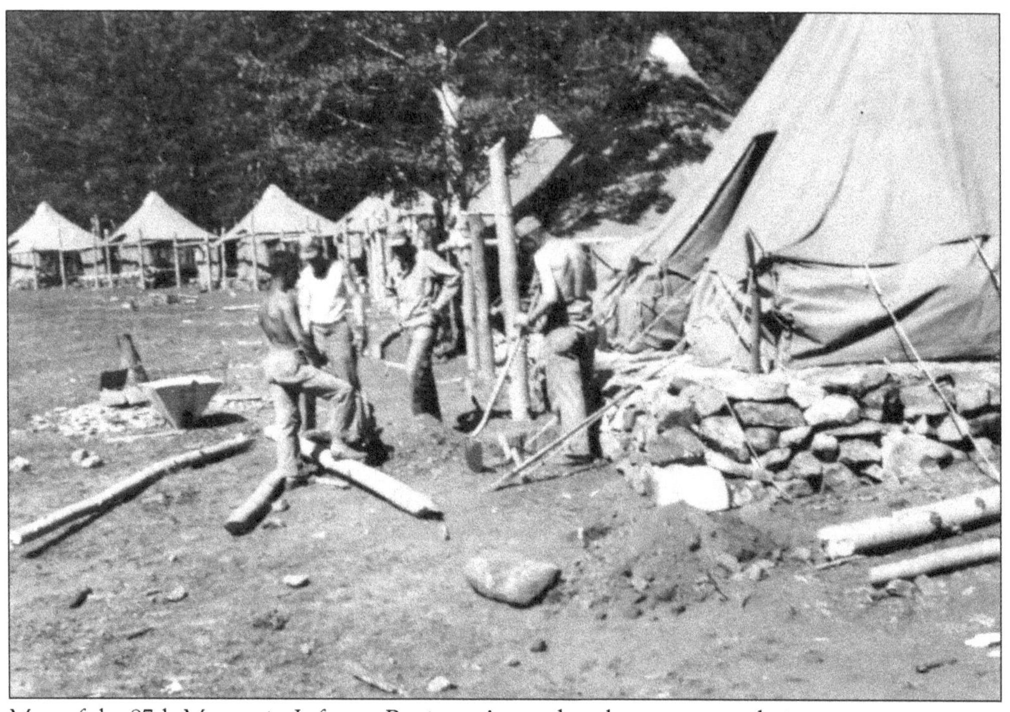

Men of the 87th Mountain Infantry Regiment's test detachment set up their temporary camp at Ashcroft, near Aspen. (Courtesy of AHS.)

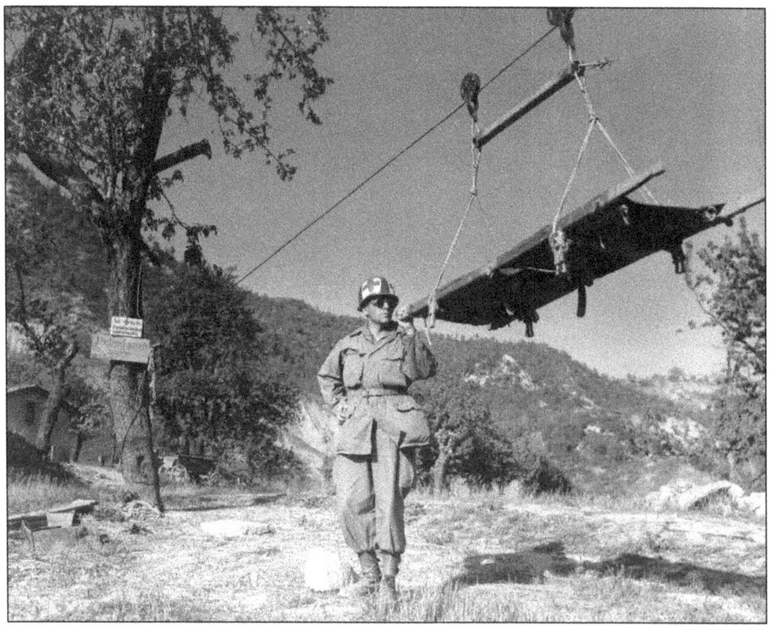

A medic stands next to a litter suspended from a cable. A similar device would be used in Italy to bring wounded soldiers down from Riva Ridge, the scene of the 10th's first major combat action in February 1945. (Courtesy of DPL.)

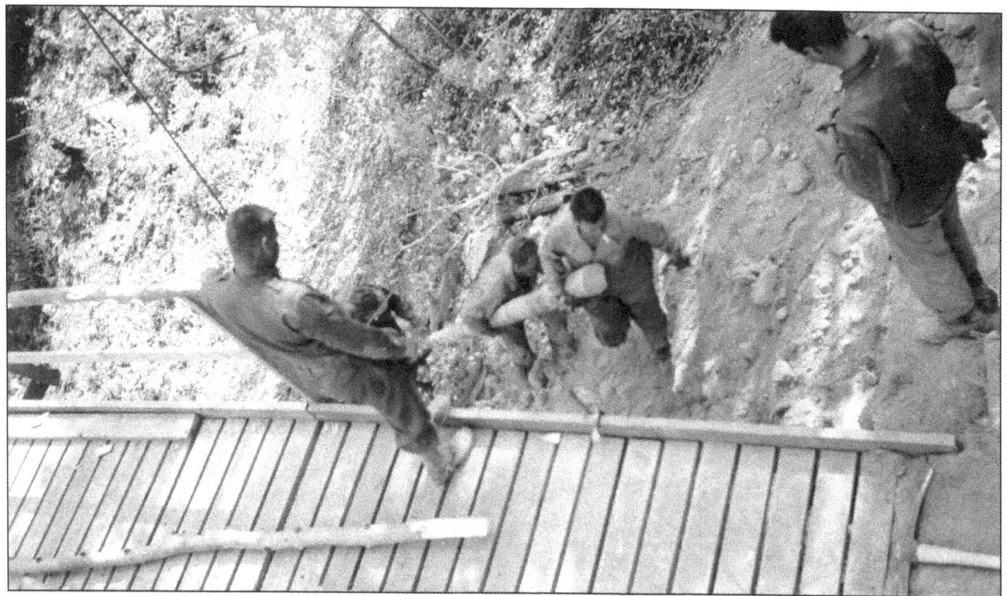

Learning how to be combat engineers, 87th Regiment soldiers carry a log to be used in the construction of a footbridge over Maroon Creek at Ashcroft. (Courtesy of AHS.)

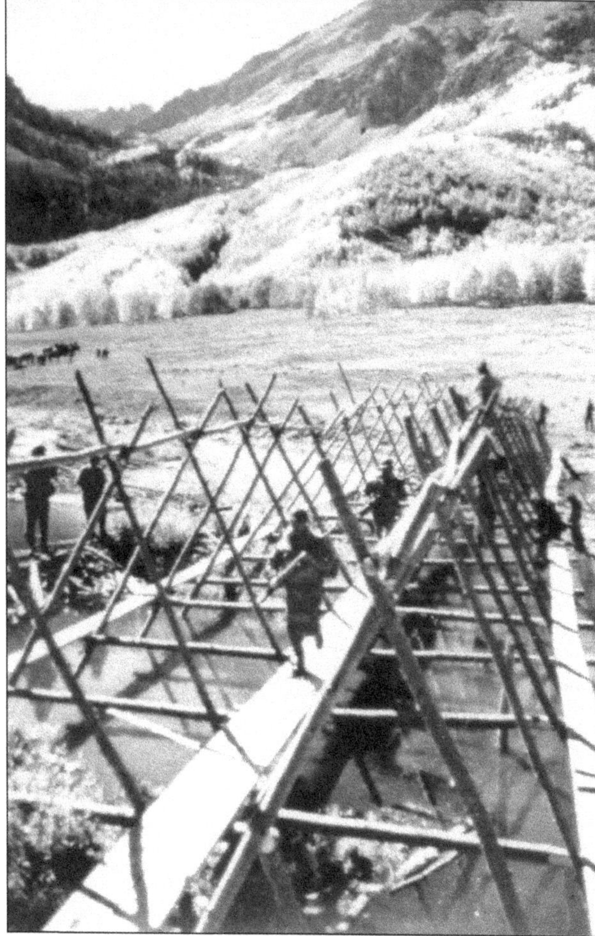

During their stay in the Aspen/Ashcroft area, men of the 87th constructed several bridges, such as this Swiss A-frame. (Courtesy of AHS.)

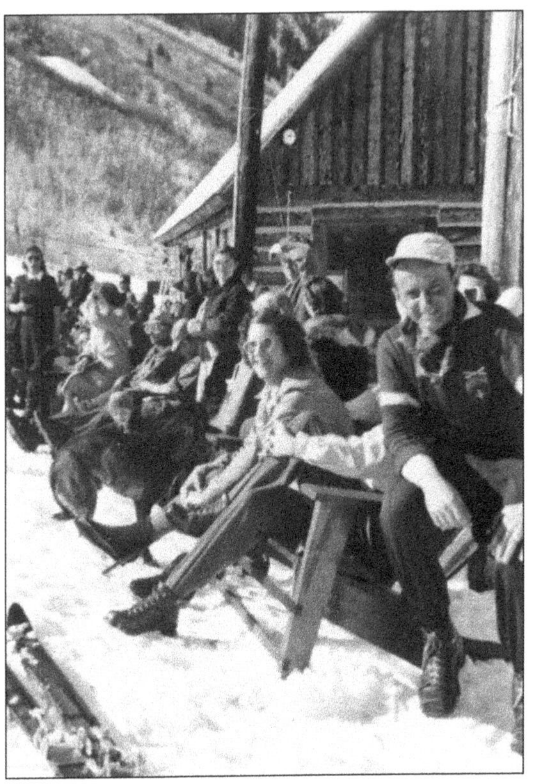

Once Camp Hale opened and a week of ski training was not enough for some hard-core skiers, they headed to Aspen for some freestyle skiing or ski races on the weekends—and some female companionship. (Courtesy of DPL.)

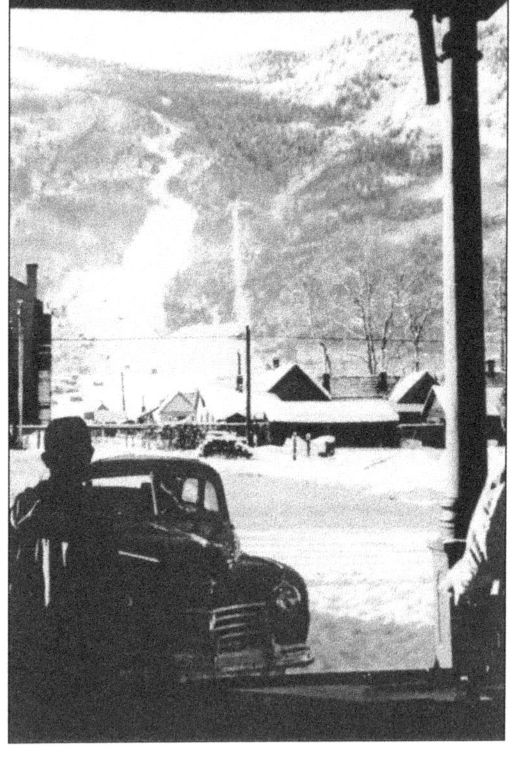

A soldier of the 87th looks across the town of Aspen toward Roch Run and Corkscrew, two ski runs on Aspen Mountain that were carved in the 1930s by Andre Roch, a Swiss mountaineer and Aspen ski pioneer. Both runs are still in use. (Courtesy of Rouene Brown.)

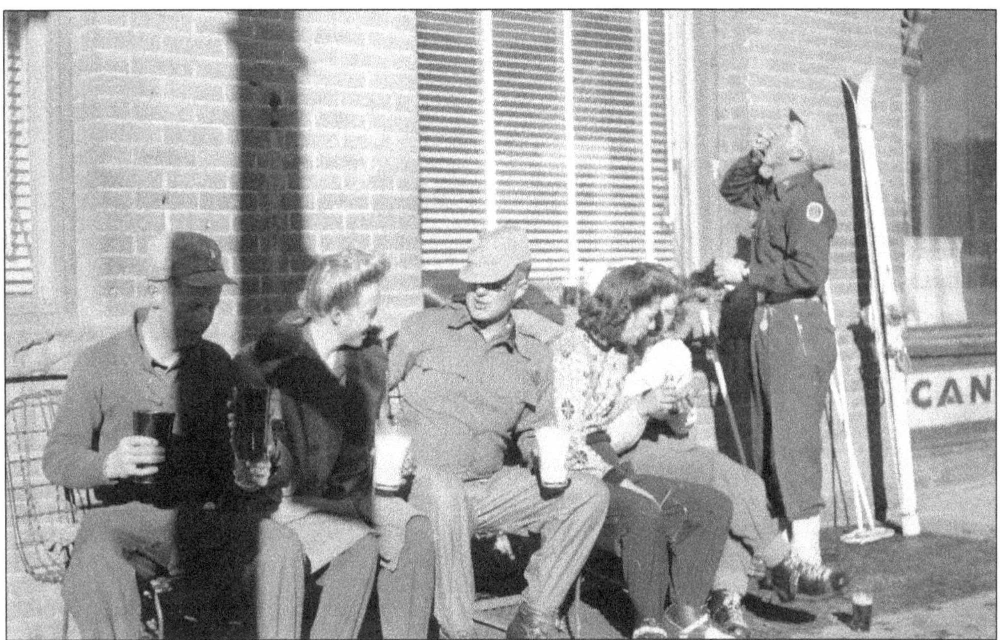

Three soldiers and three women enjoy the sun outside Aspen's Jerome Hotel while drinking a concoction known as "Aspen Crud"—half ice cream, half bourbon. The hotel bar still serves the drink. (Courtesy of DPL.)

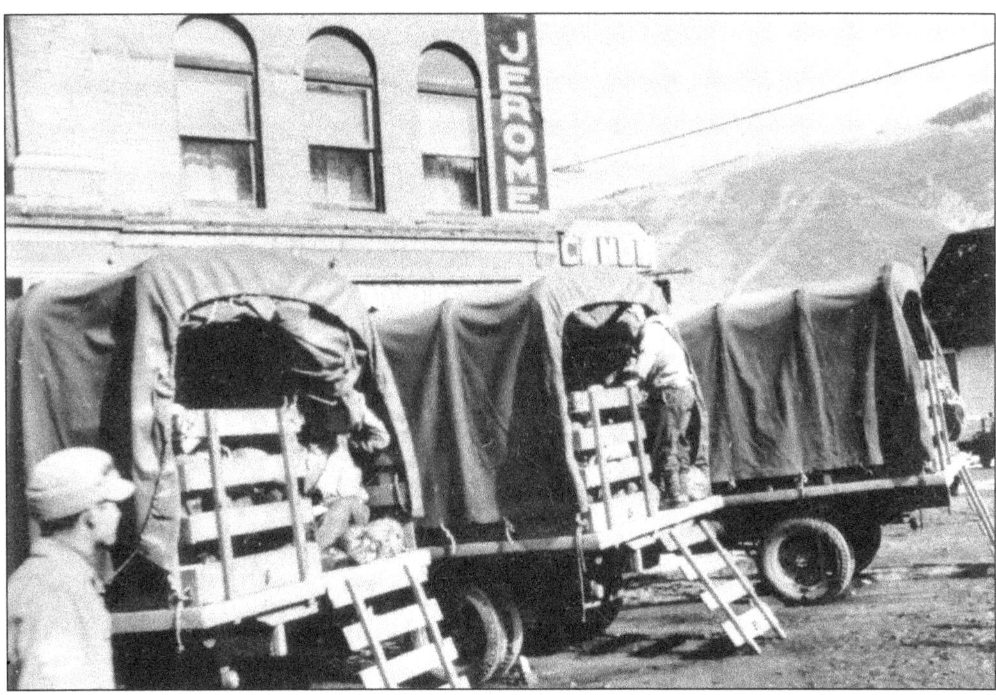

The Jerome Hotel offered rooms for $1.50 per night. Here, with their ski weekend over, 10th troopers climb into Army trucks that will take them back to Camp Hale. (Courtesy of AHS.)

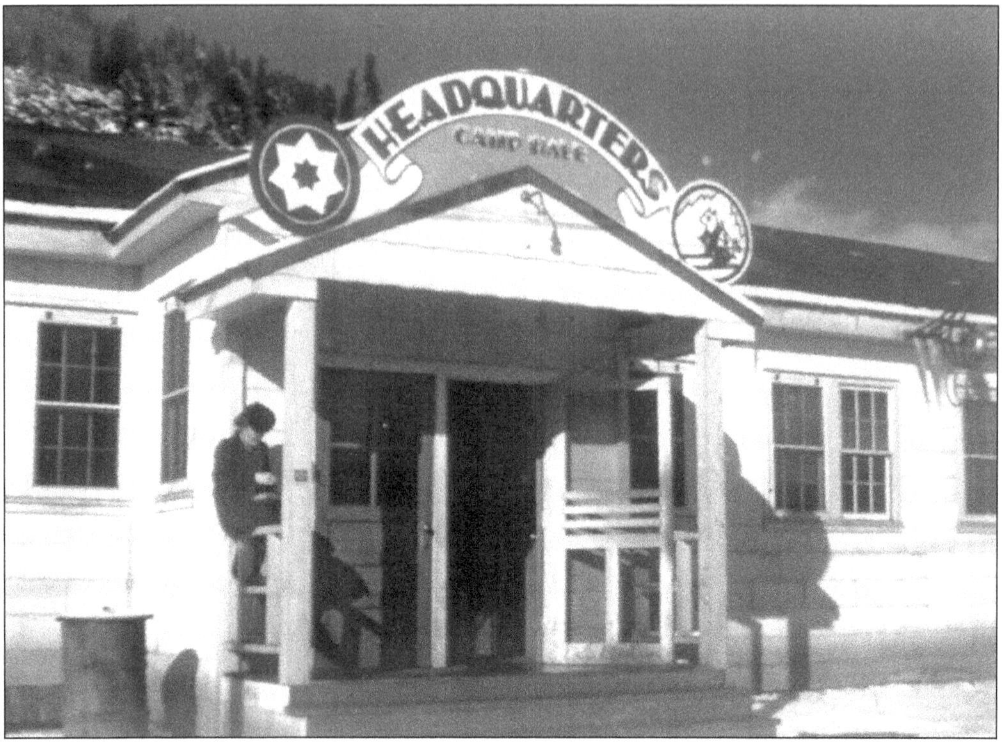

In October 1942, members of the 7th Service Command arrived at Pando to manage the new camp. This photograph shows the camp headquarters. The sign bears the emblem of both the 7th Service Command, the command that all Colorado bases were under, and the whimsical, unofficial emblem of the 10th (the "Pando Commandos")—a cartoon of an armed panda on skis. (Courtesy of DPL.)

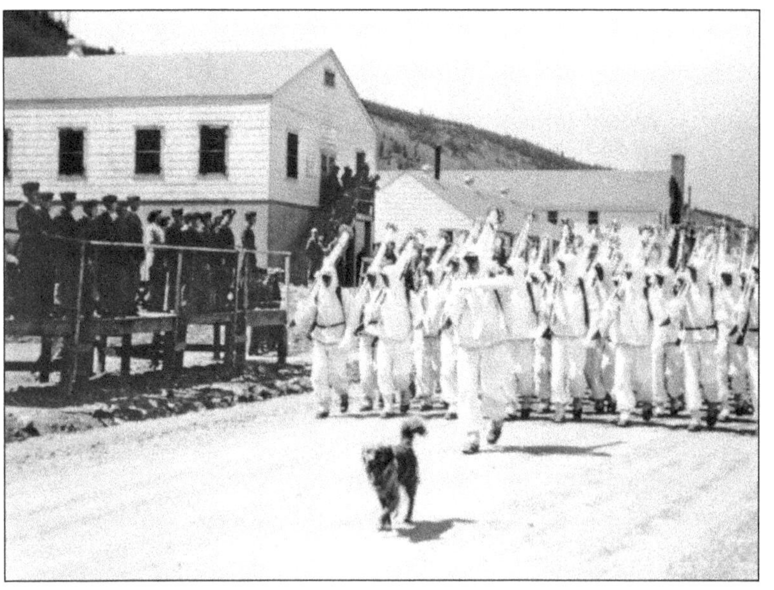

With a stray dog leading them, a platoon of 10th men in whites and carrying skis march past a reviewing stand at Camp Hale. The troops, inspired by their European-born comrades, often sang while they marched. (Courtesy of Rouene Brown.)

Marching is a time-proven method of moving a group of soldiers in an orderly way from one place to another. Here, marching in formation with rifles on their shoulders, are members of the 126th Engineer Battalion on their way to a lecture. Marching was not the troops' favorite activity; they would much rather have been skiing, climbing, or hiking. (Courtesy of DPL.)

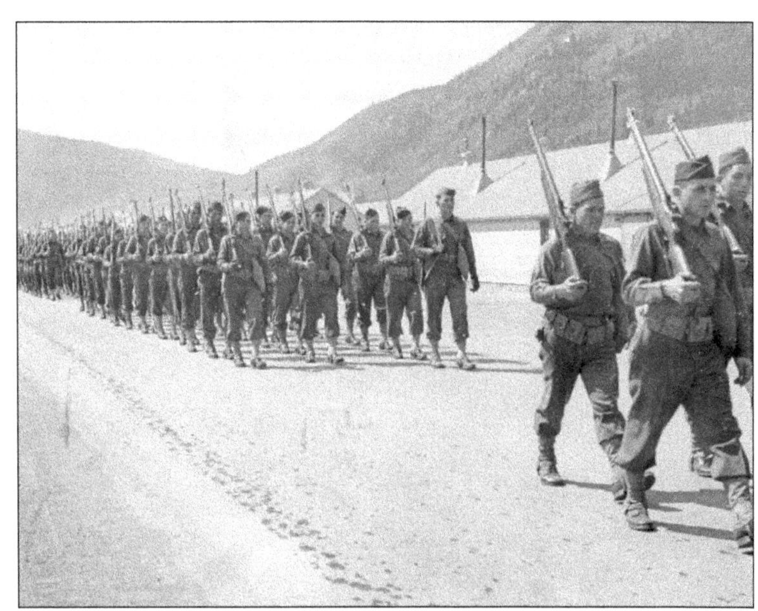

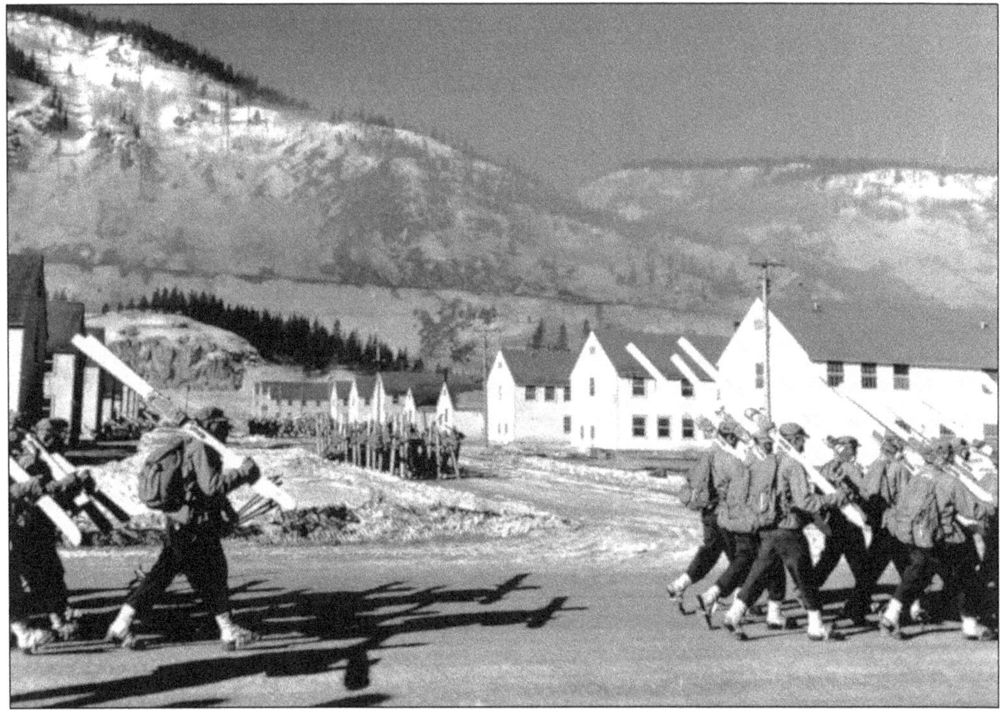

Dressed in ski parkas tucked into their trousers, and carrying skis and rucksacks, men of the 10th Light Division march through the streets of Camp Hale singing their song, "90 Pounds of Rucksack." This photograph was taken during the filming of *Mountain Fighters* (see chapter nine). (Courtesy of DPL.)

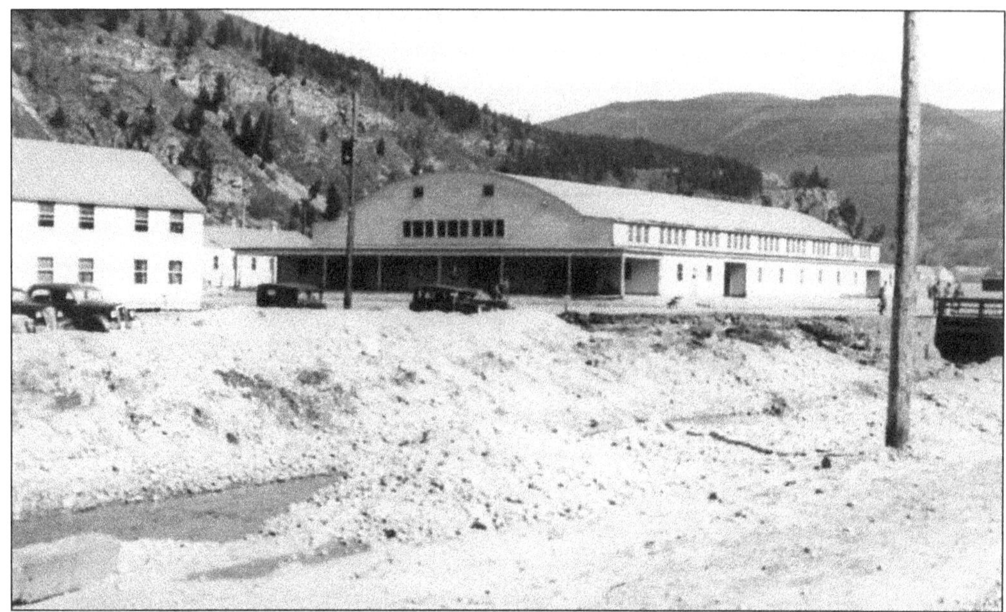

The largest building at Camp Hale—the 18,000-square-foot field house—was the scene of ceremonies, basketball and volleyball games, exhibition boxing matches (world heavyweight champion Joe Louis once staged an exhibition here), concerts, and dances. (Courtesy of DPL.)

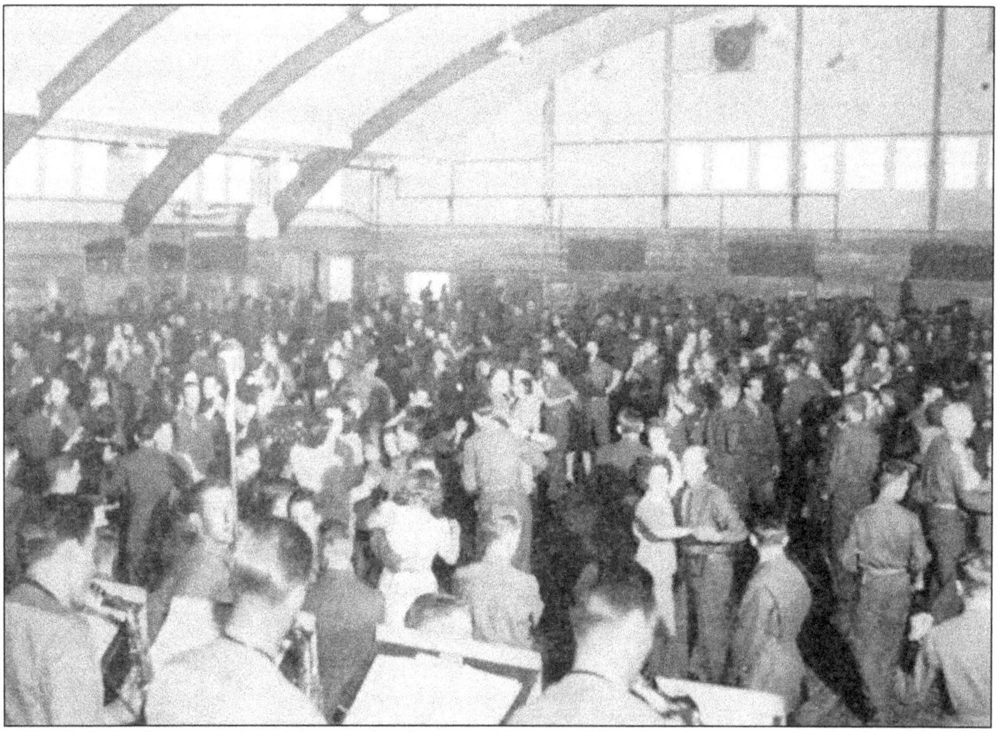

The Richard Himber Essex House Orchestra (foreground) was a big-name band of the period. Here, in August 1943, the band plays while the entire floor of the field house is covered with dancing couples. Young ladies were often brought in from surrounding towns for such occasions. (Courtesy of DPL.)

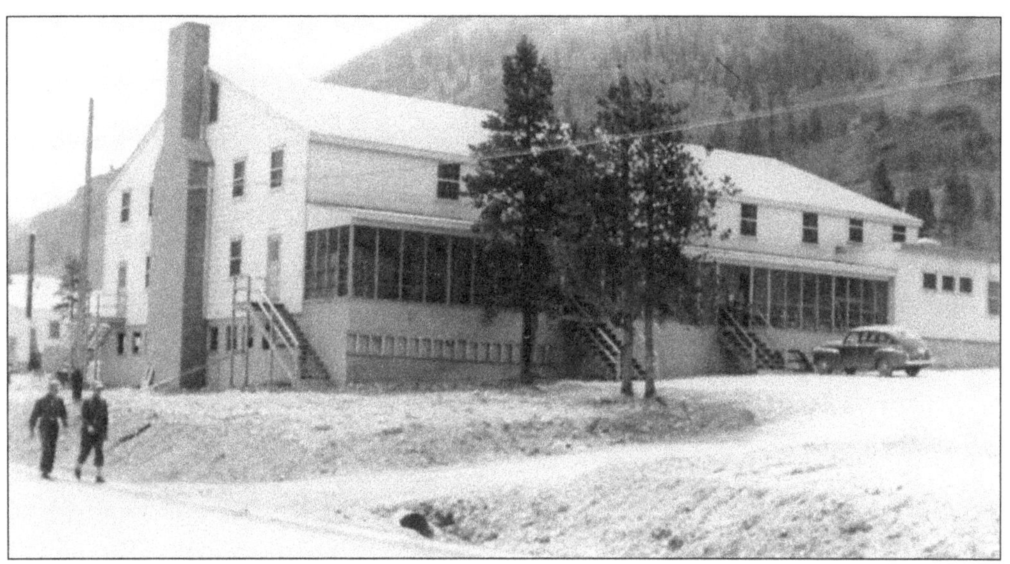

Camp Hale offered many facilities, such as the Service Clubs run by the United Service Organization (USO), for enlisted troops to use during their off-duty hours, and provided a place where soldiers could relax, listen to records, read, write letters home, and hold parties and dances. This large building with a screened-in porch was Service Club No. 1. (Courtesy of DPL.)

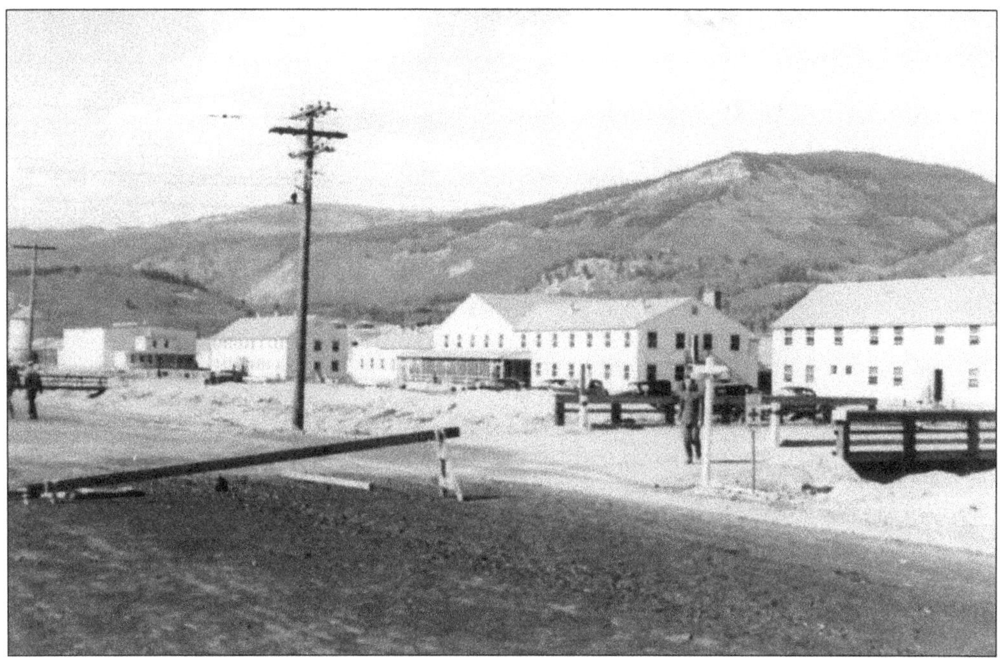

Social mixing of officers and enlisted personnel was frowned upon by the armed forces, so the officers and enlisted men had their own separate recreation facilities. This photograph shows the officers' club at center. (Courtesy of DPL.)

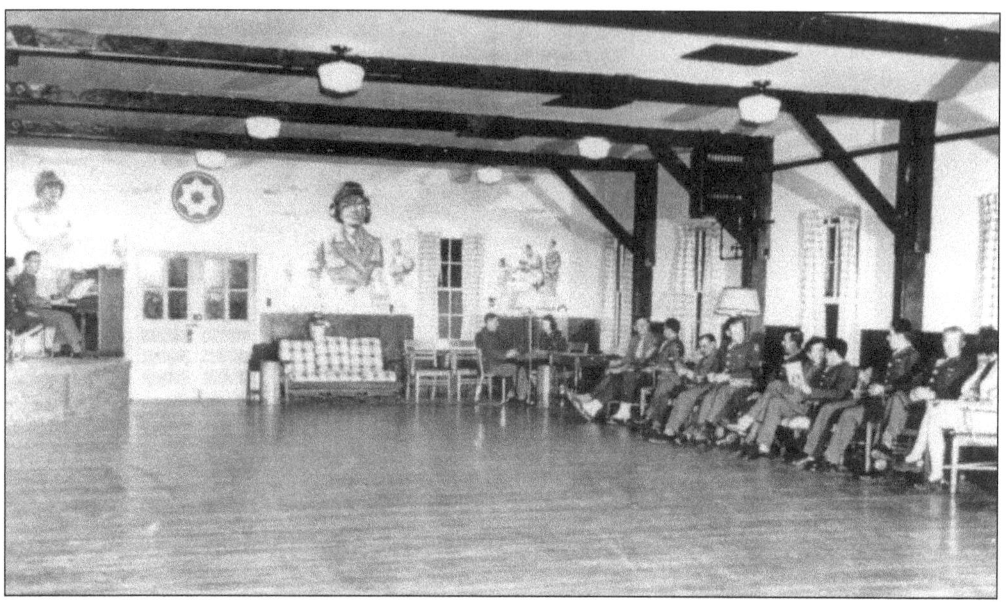

The Service Clubs, run by USO personnel, performed a valuable role by helping soldiers relax and forget about the stresses and strains of training. Here, enlisted men in their Class A uniforms, some with dates, listen to a soldier playing the piano, at left. (Courtesy of DPL.)

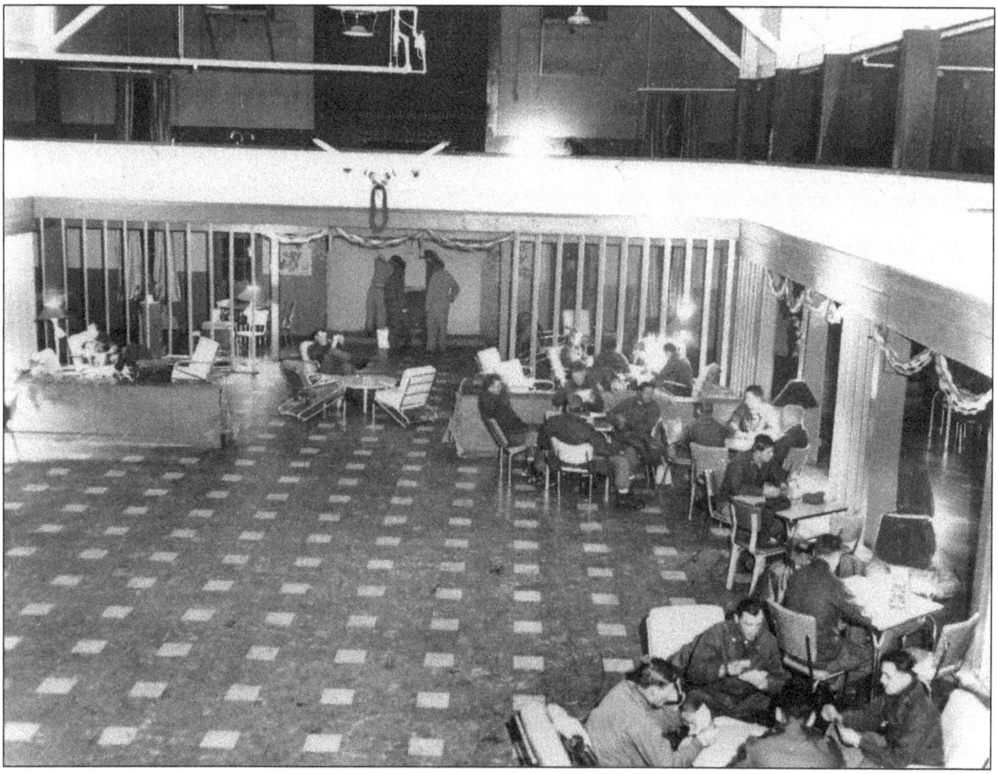

The spacious floor at the Service Club allowed for regular game nights, live musical performances, and public appearances by celebrities who wanted to be photographed "entertaining the boys in uniform." (Courtesy of DPL.)

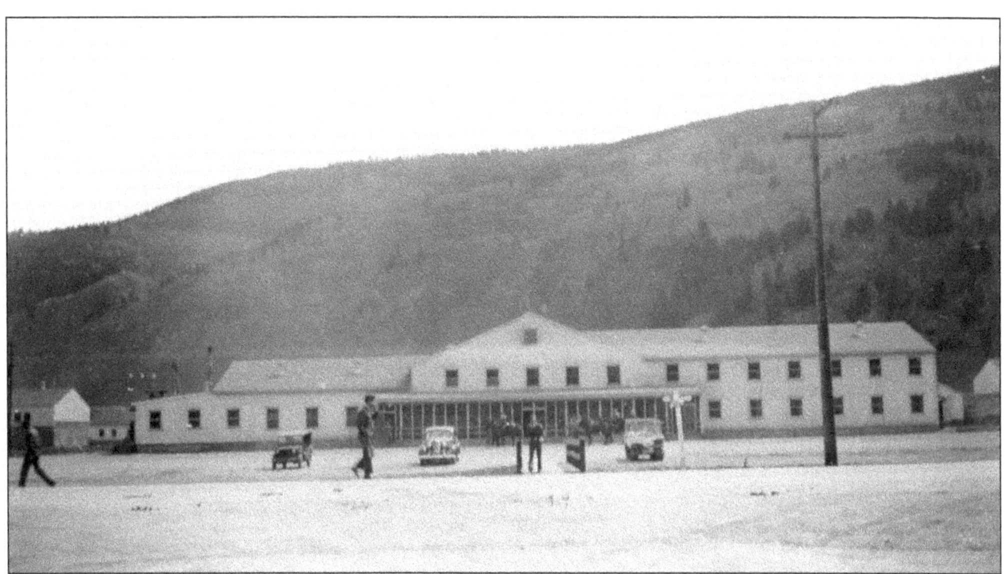

No matter their rank, officers (and civilian guests) could socialize at their own club, shown here. (Courtesy of DPL.)

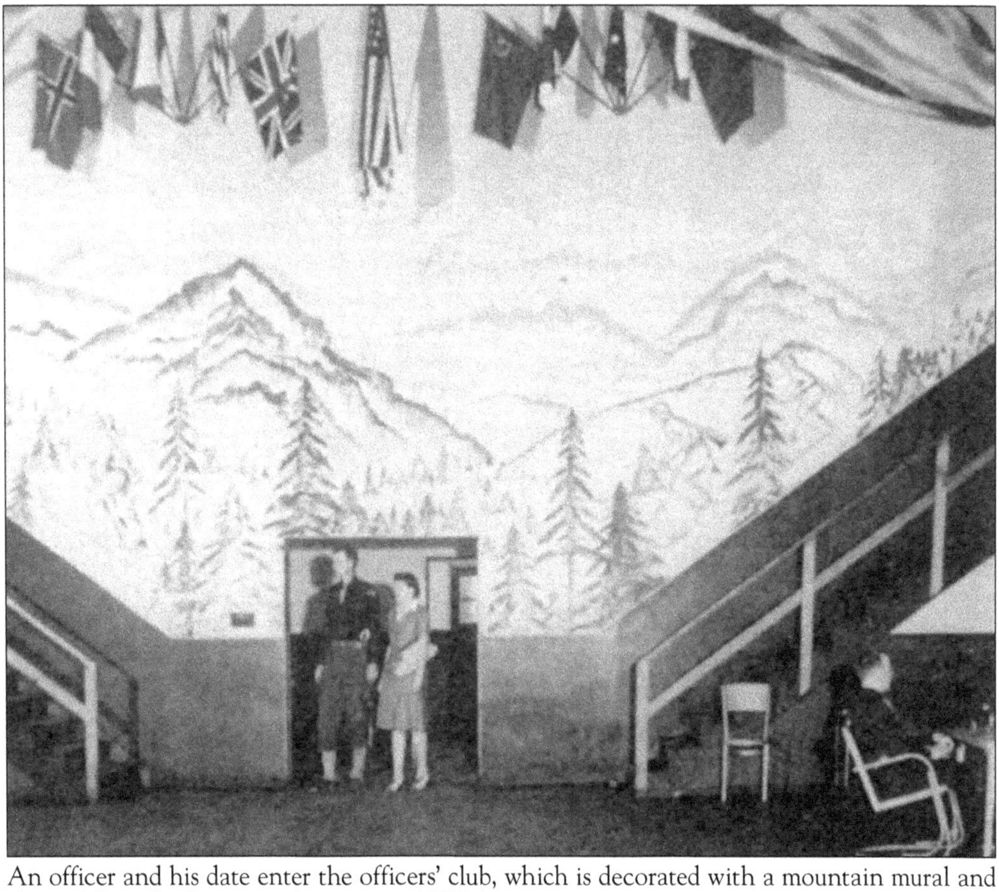

An officer and his date enter the officers' club, which is decorated with a mountain mural and flags of the Allied nations. (Courtesy of DPL.)

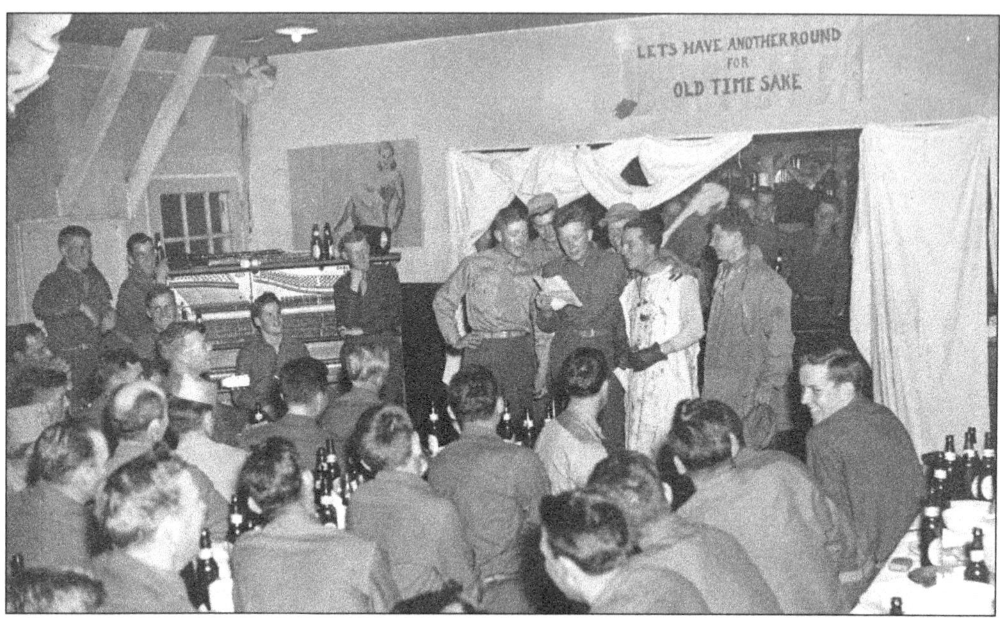

Plenty of smiles, songs, and beer were the order of the day at this enlisted men's party. To many of the soldiers, being in the 10th was like belonging to a college fraternity. (Courtesy of DPL.)

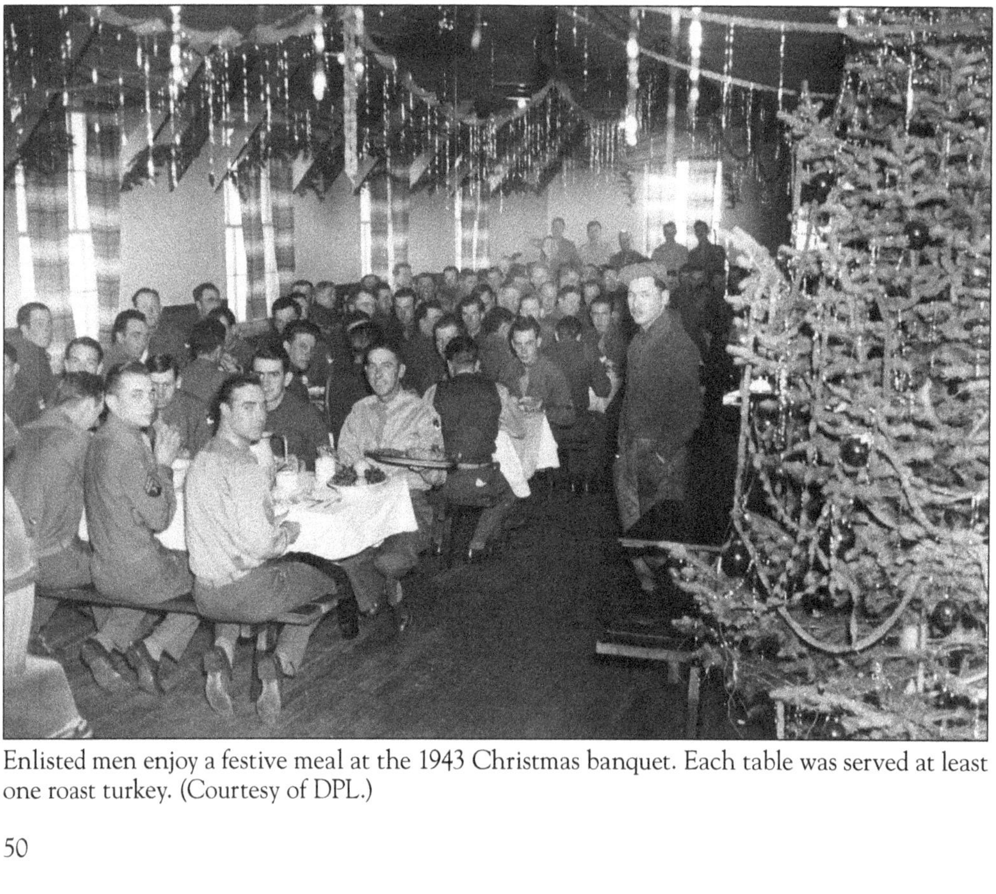

Enlisted men enjoy a festive meal at the 1943 Christmas banquet. Each table was served at least one roast turkey. (Courtesy of DPL.)

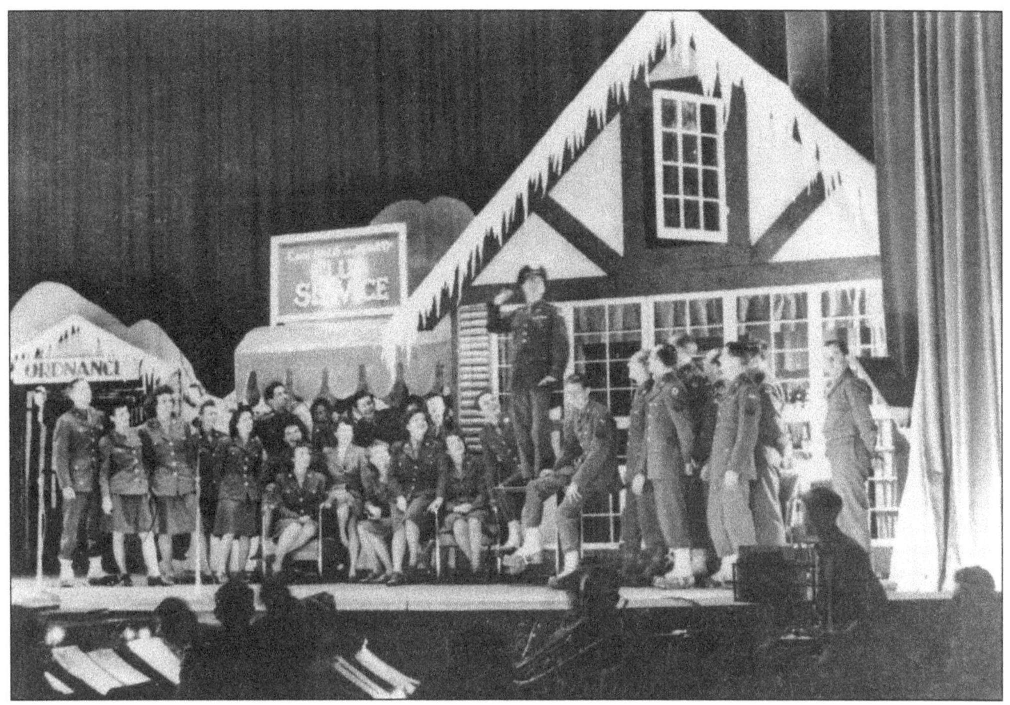

In April 1943, soldiers and members of the Women's Army Corps (WAC) detachment stage a musical review, *Camp Hale and Hearty*, the biggest and most expensive production ever staged at the field house. Here, an actor standing on a chair gets a laugh with his parody of Hitler. (Courtesy of DPL.)

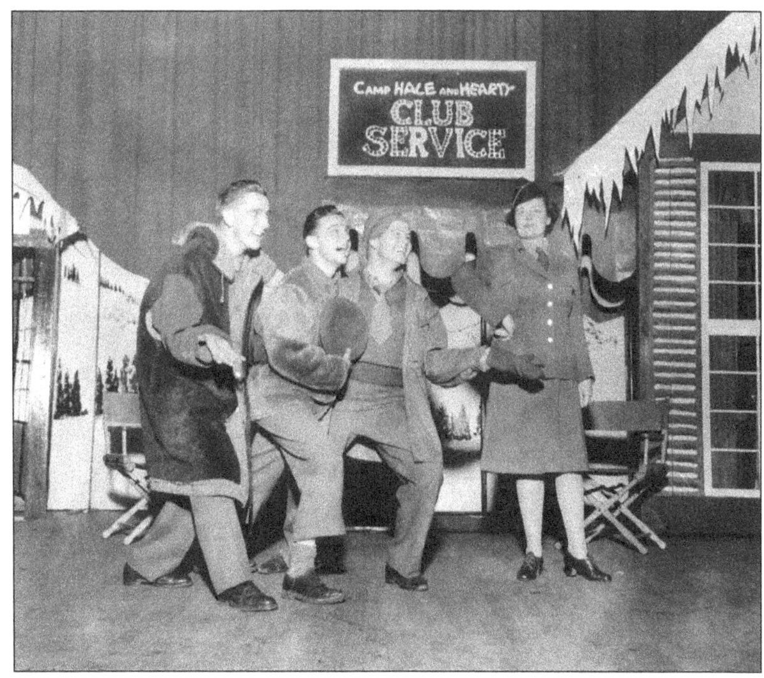

Three soldiers and a WAC ham it up in the musical *Camp Hale and Hearty*. Many of the cast members had performed in theatrical productions in high school and college. (Courtesy of DPL.)

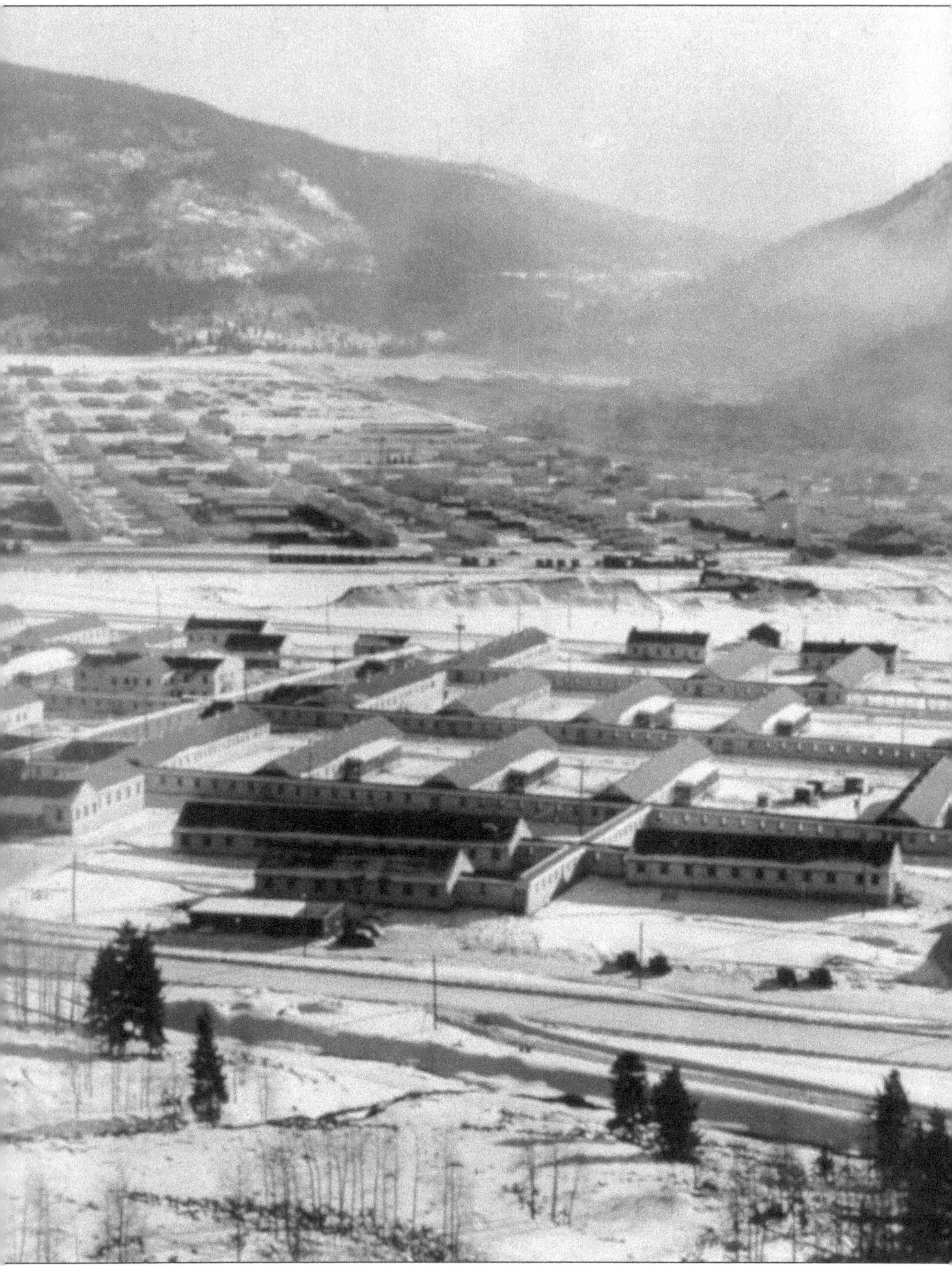

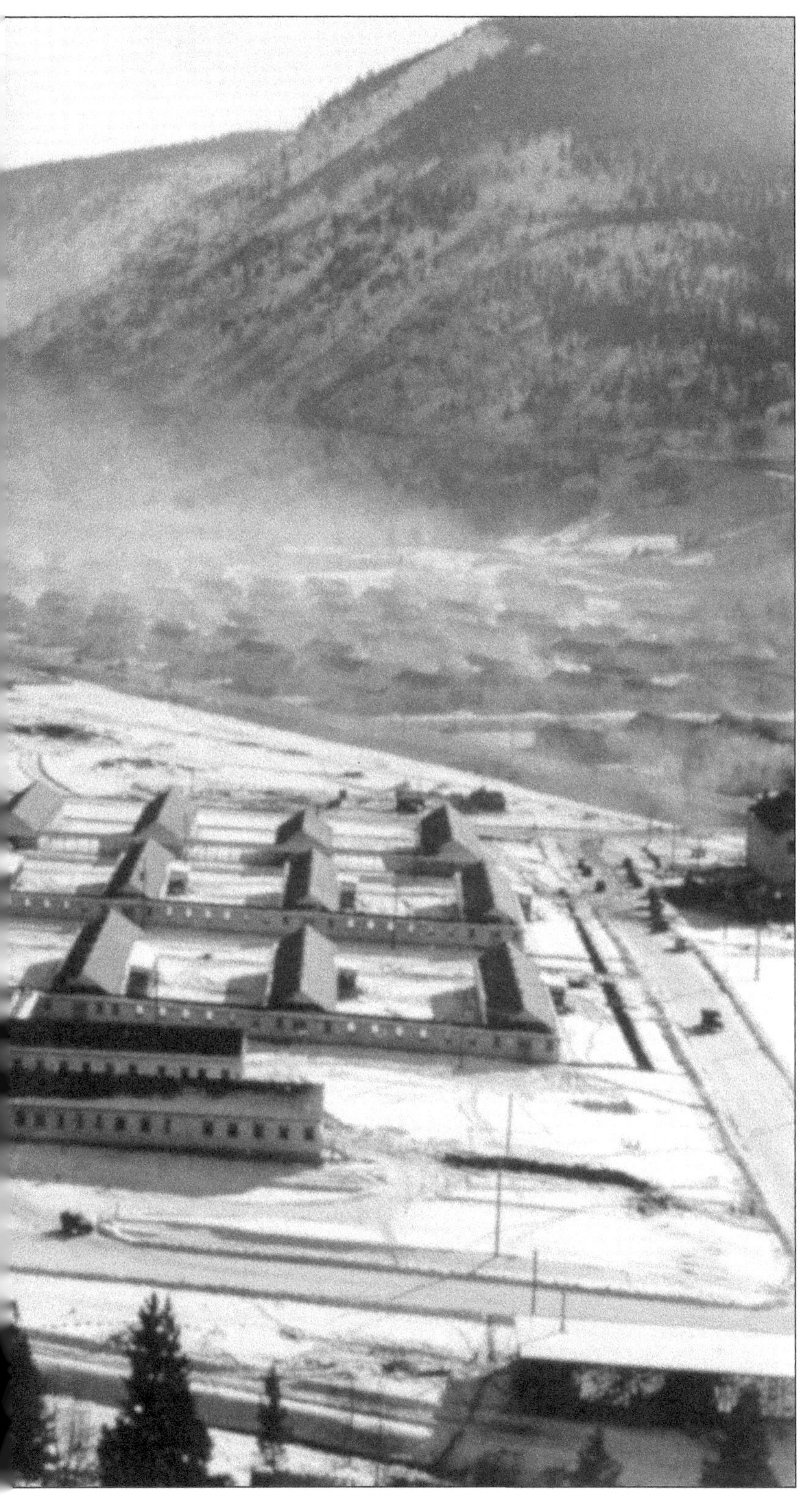

Here, a high-angle view of the 676-bed Camp Hale hospital complex at the north end of the valley shows enclosed walkways connecting the various wards. Also visible is a pall of smoke drifting over the camp—a major health concern at the camp due to its 9,250-foot elevation. Many soldiers came down with a lung condition the men dubbed the "Pando Hack," and some needed to be transferred out of the division because of it. The medical staff also cared for soldiers who were injured in training accidents—scrapes, burns, gunshot wounds, broken bones, vehicle accidents, frostbite, and snow-blindness. When the division was sent overseas in early 1945, many of the doctors and dentists accompanied the troops, but the nurses did not. (Courtesy of DPL.)

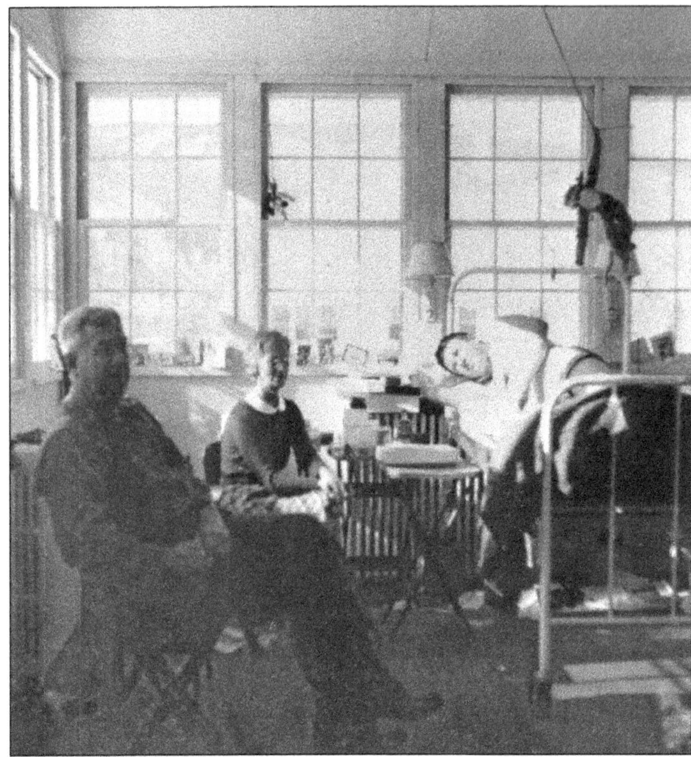

An injured soldier is visited by his parents in the Camp Hale hospital. Skiing and climbing accidents were common, and many soldiers also became ill from breathing the camp's polluted air. (Courtesy of DPL.)

Three dentists work on the teeth of two soldiers and a WAC at the camp's dental clinic. The Army's doctors and dentists voluntarily gave up their civilian practices to serve their country. (Courtesy of DPL.)

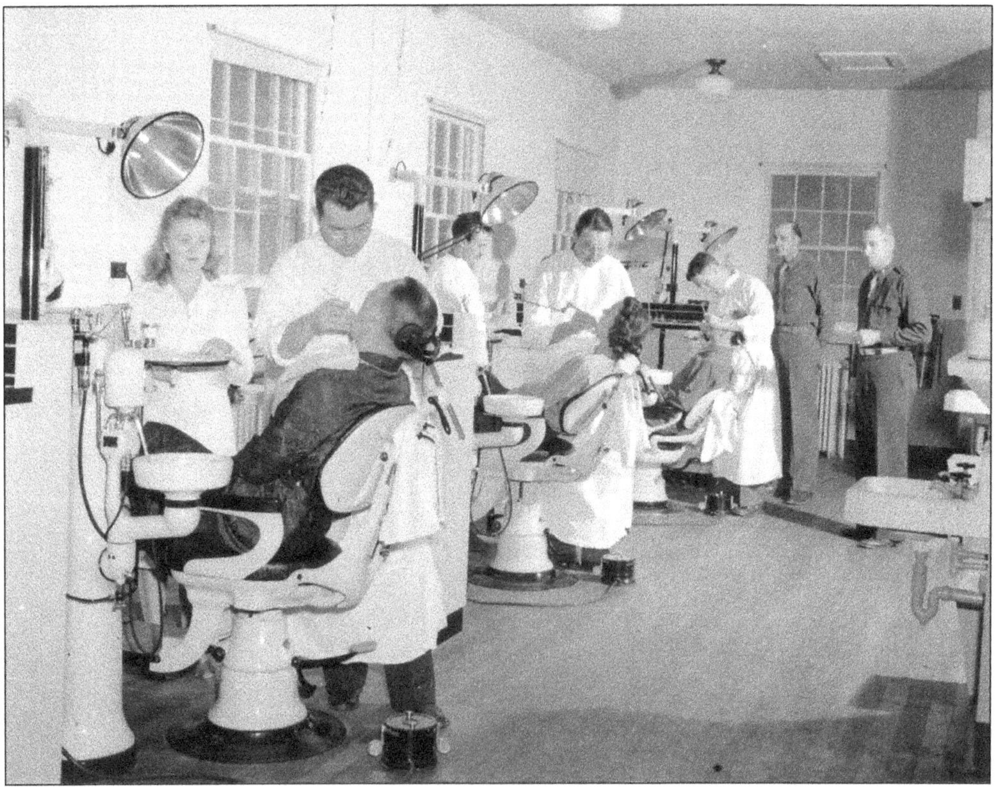

Camp Hale had five interdenominational chapels for the spiritual benefit of personnel at the post. A number of weddings between 10th troopers and their girlfriends were held in the chapels. (Courtesy of DPL.)

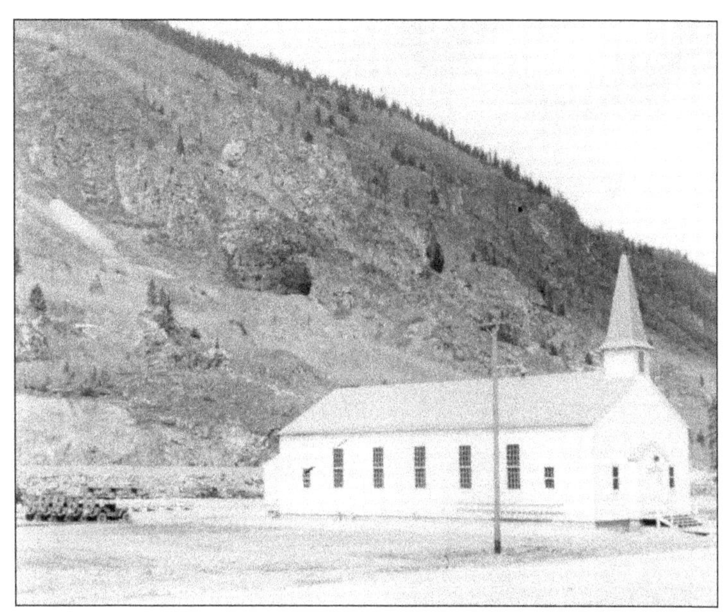

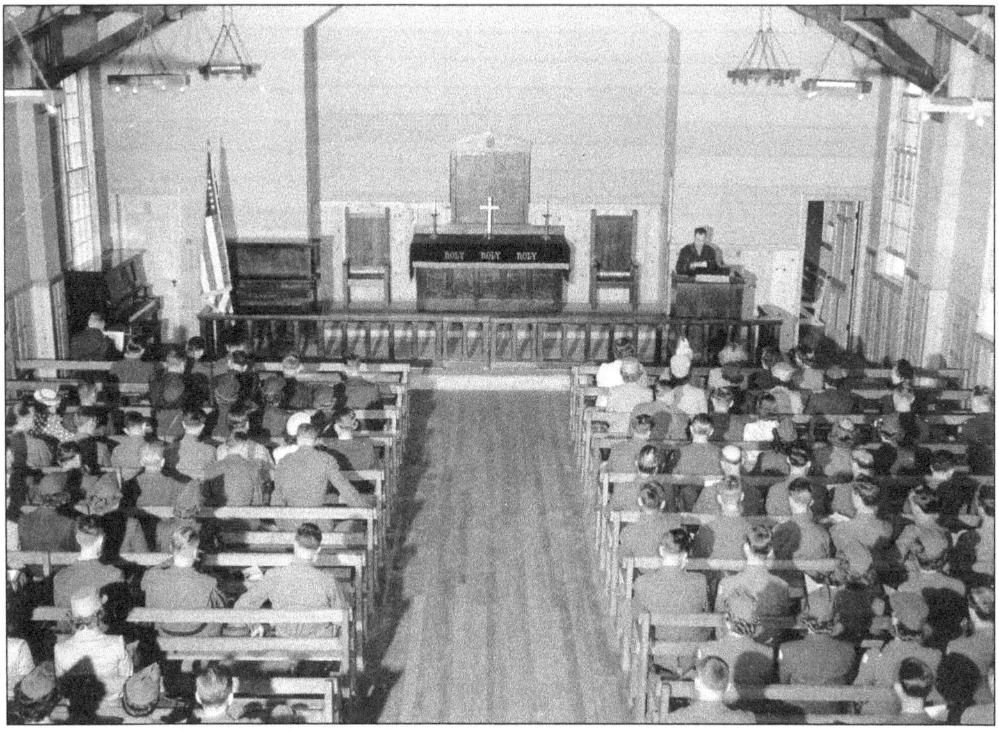

A chaplain conducts a well-attended worship service for men and WACs in one of the camp's chapels. Soldiers relied on chaplains to get them through difficult emotional situations. The 10th had four to twelve chaplains—Catholic, Protestant, and Jewish. (Courtesy of DPL.)

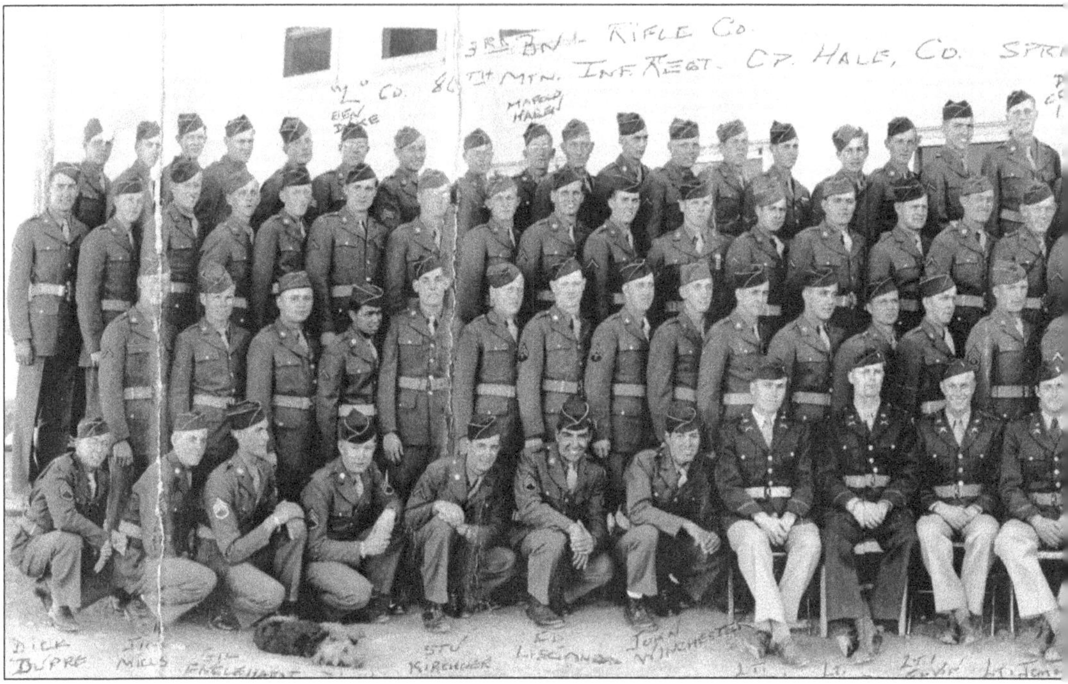

An infantry company in World War II had 12 rifle companies, each with an authorized strength of roughly 200 men. Here, F Company, 3rd battalion, 86th Mountain Infantry Regiment, poses

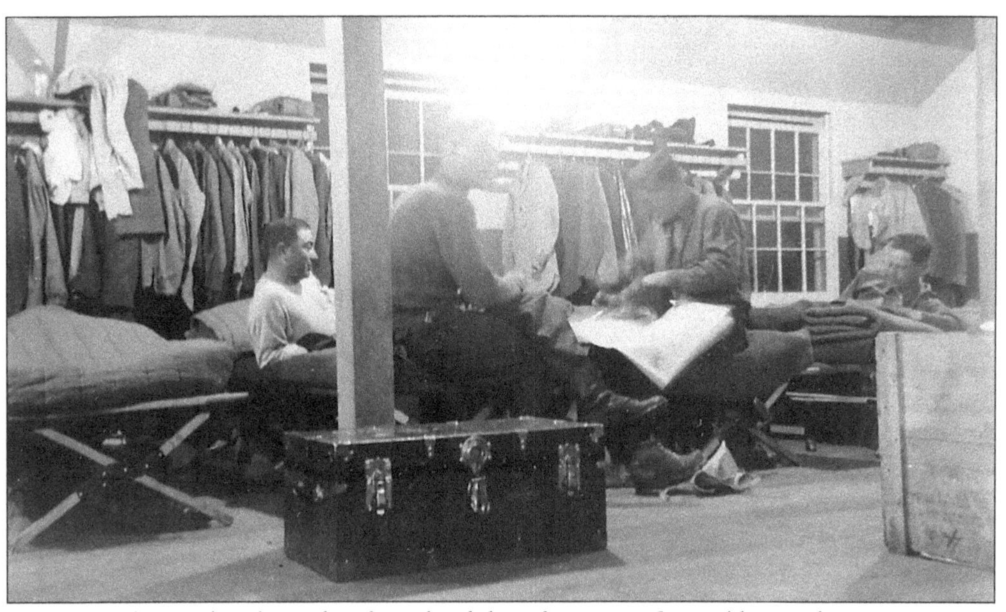

Four men relax in their barracks after a hard day of training. One soldier, with a newspaper in his lap, polishes his boots while the man at right reads a book. All of a soldier's possessions had to be either hung on a bar or stored in his footlocker. (Courtesy of DPL.)

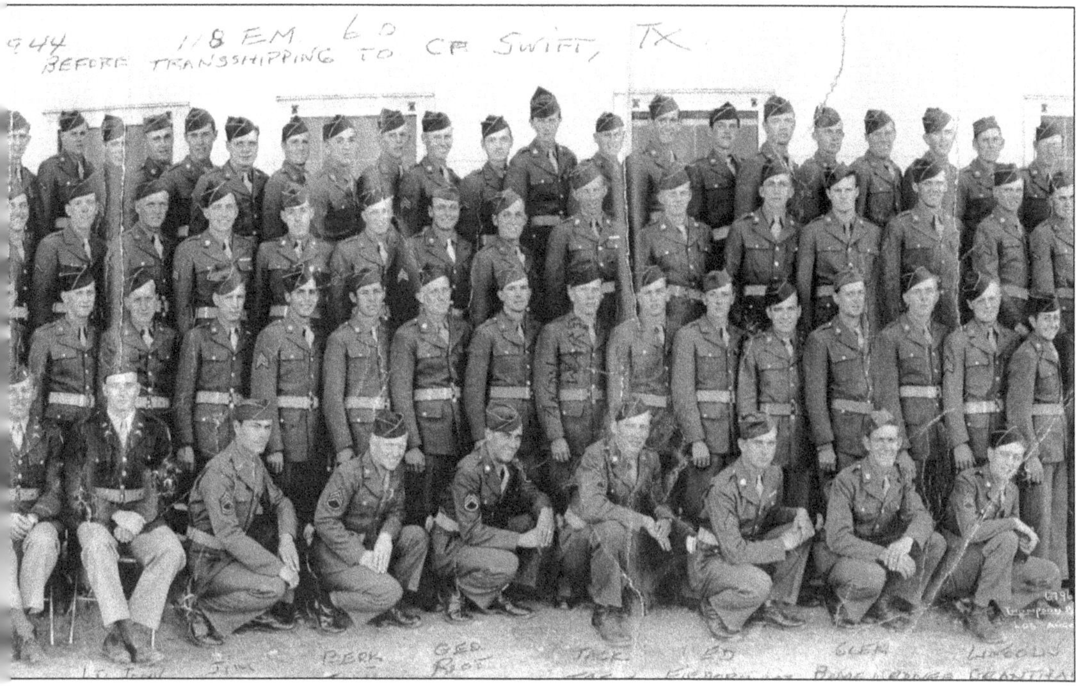

for a unit photograph. (Courtesy of David J. Little)

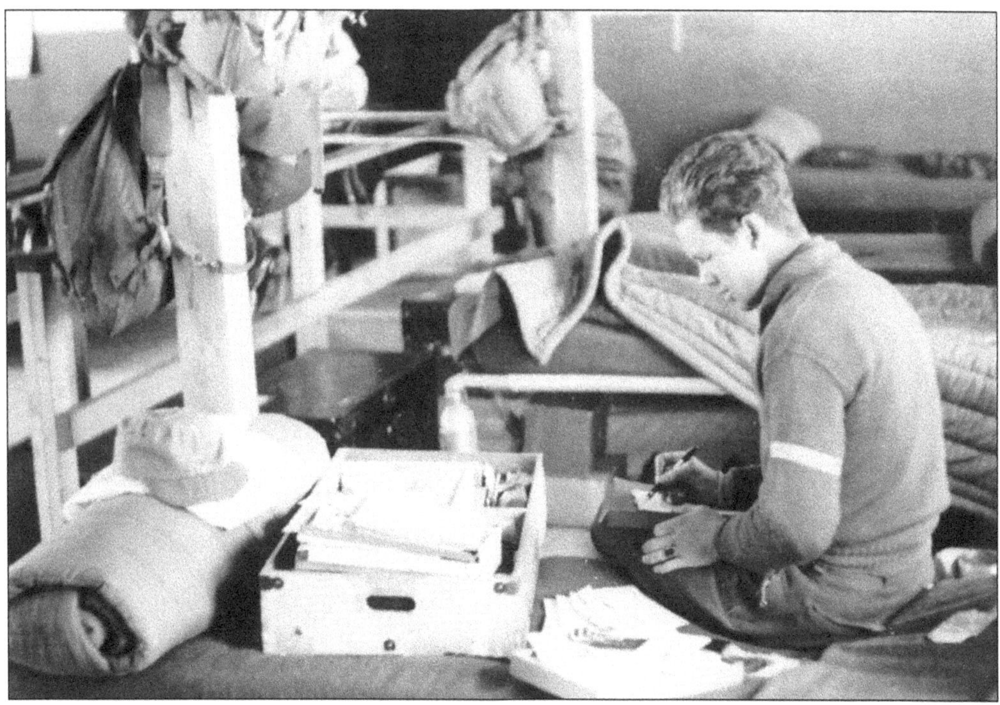

In an era before instant communication, most soldiers kept in touch with friends and family through letters that could take a week or more to arrive. Here, a soldier writes a letter while sitting on his bunk. The tray from his footlocker is in front of him. (Courtesy of Rouene Brown.)

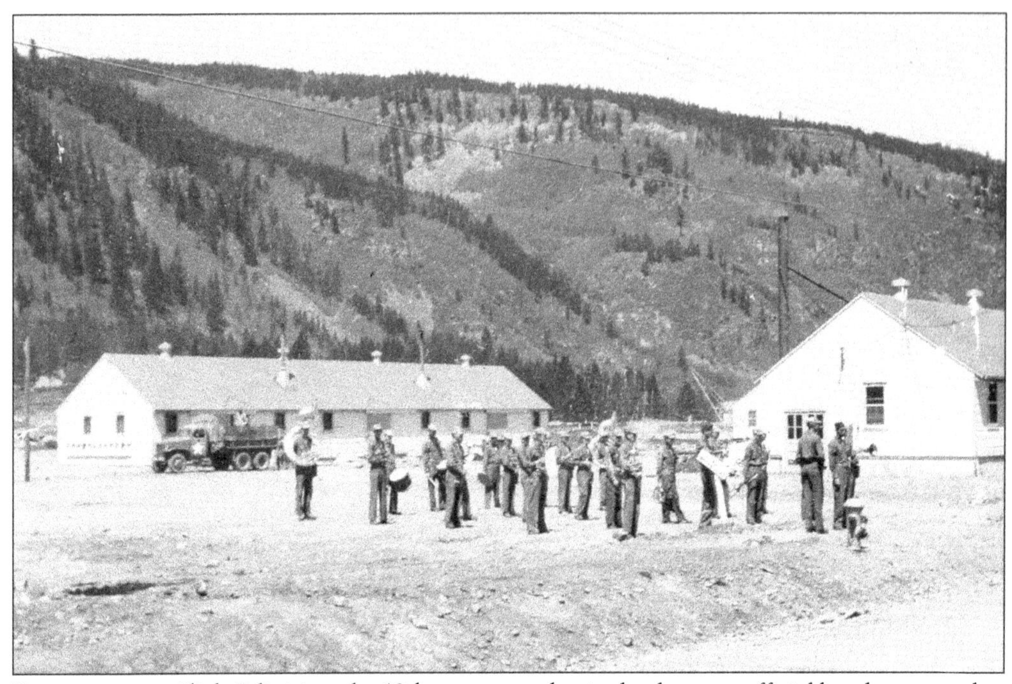

Because it was a "light" division, the 10th was not authorized to have an official band, so a number of musically inclined soldiers formed their own. Here, the 86th Mountain Infantry Regiment Band rehearses in an open field. (Courtesy of DPL.)

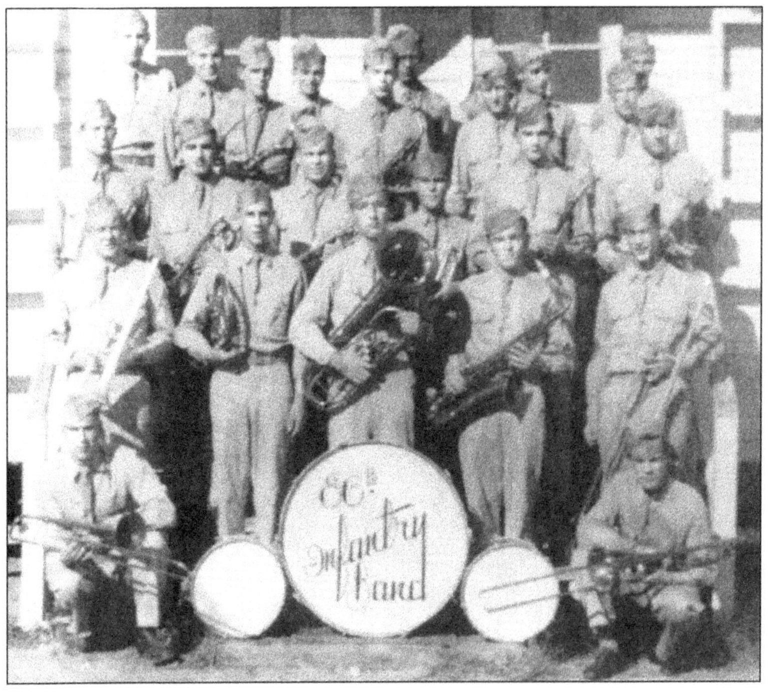

Some of the members of the band pose for a photograph. In addition to providing marching music, band members also played the popular big band music for dances at the Service Club. (Courtesy of DPL.)

Five

Winter Training

The training of mountain troops in Colorado commenced in November 1942, even as more soldiers were reporting for duty at Camp Hale. In addition to the 87th Mountain Infantry Regiment, which had just arrived from Fort Lewis, Washington, the 85th and 86th Mountain Infantry Regiments were in the process of forming. Maj. Gen. Lloyd E. Jones was the 10th Light Division's first commander.

Georgiana Contiguglia, former head of the 10th Mountain Division Resource Center at History Colorado, wrote, "The 10th consisted of some 300 experienced skiers and veteran mountaineers, about 6,000 younger skiers who were primarily volunteers, 3,000 draftees who had to be taught how to ski, and 3,000 non-skiing support personnel such as administrators, medics, mule skinners (drivers), horse wranglers, and artillery specialists. About 500 of the volunteers were foreigners, many of whom became naturalized citizens."

In addition to the 10th, a 900-man battalion of native Norwegians—designated the 99th Infantry Battalion, Separate—trained at Hale with the intention of someday liberating their homeland from the German occupiers.

A War Department reporter wrote, "Skiing the Army way—a style that's based on the premise that the soldier will be carrying weapons, ammunition, and a heavy pack. Under these circumstances, he can't afford to fall. With ski training comes snow craft—practice in judging snow texture, degree of slope, probability of an avalanche, and a hundred and one bits of knowledge that distinguishes a mountain man from the lowlander."

Training continued usually for five-and-a-half days a week—skiing and snowshoeing in the winter, hiking and mountain climbing in the summer. So rigorous was the training that the 10th men were considered to be the most physically fit soldiers in the US Army.

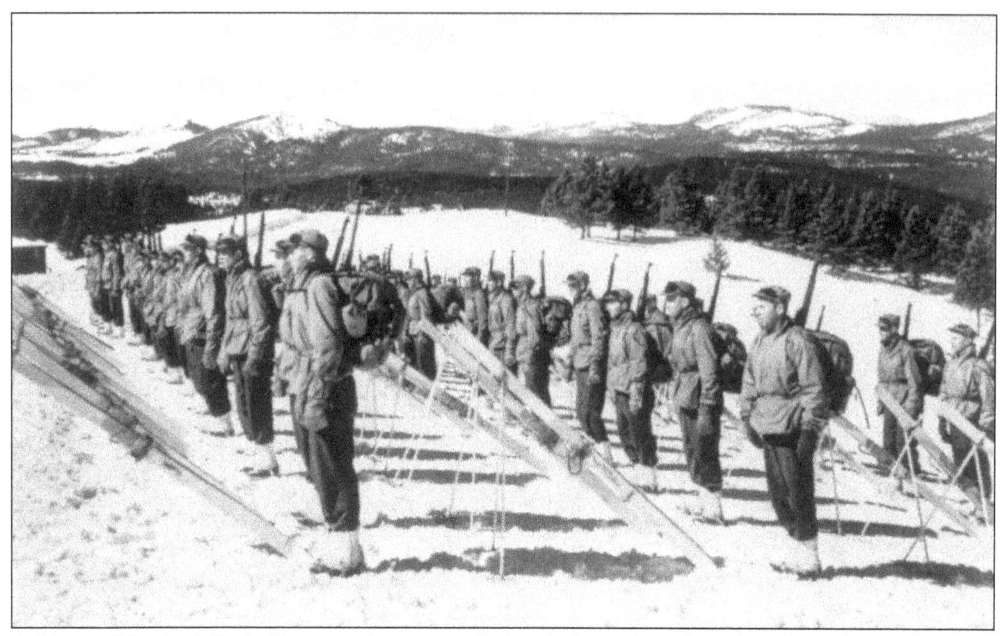

Soldiers of the 10th Light Division form up with skis, balanced on ski poles, aligned in ranks. This is a scene from the Warner Bros. recruiting film *Mountain Fighters* (see chapter nine). (Courtesy of DPL.)

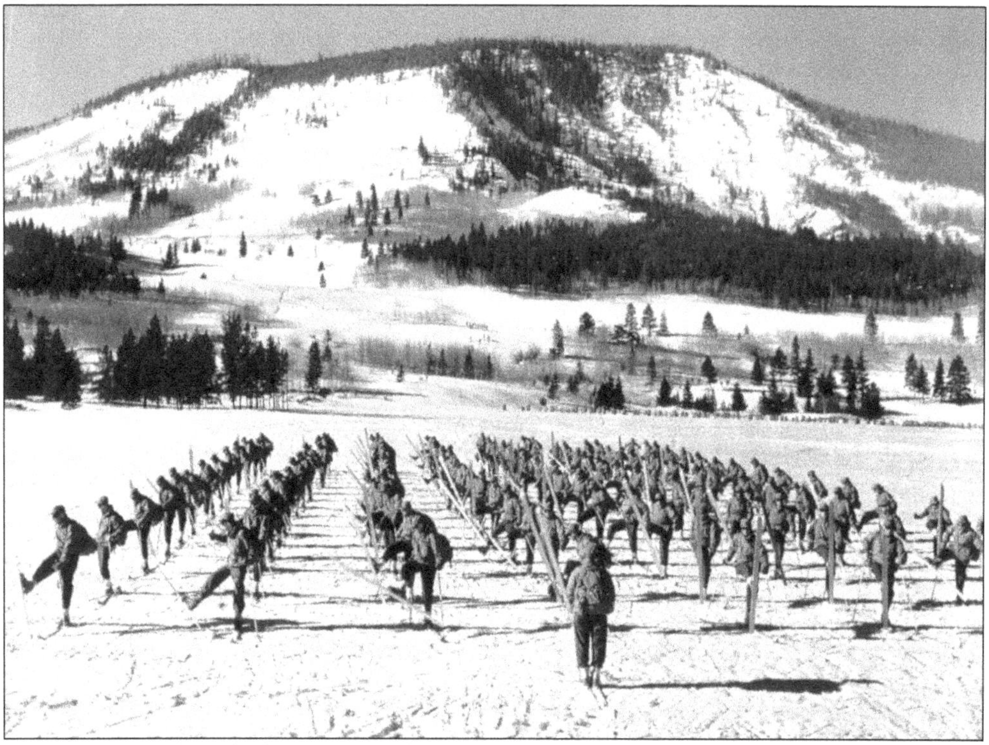

Even proficient skiers had to be re-taught how to ski in a military manner. Here, a company of soldiers is practicing the technique of making a kick turn because, on a narrow mountain slope, it might not be possible to make a wide, sweeping turn. (Courtesy of DPL.)

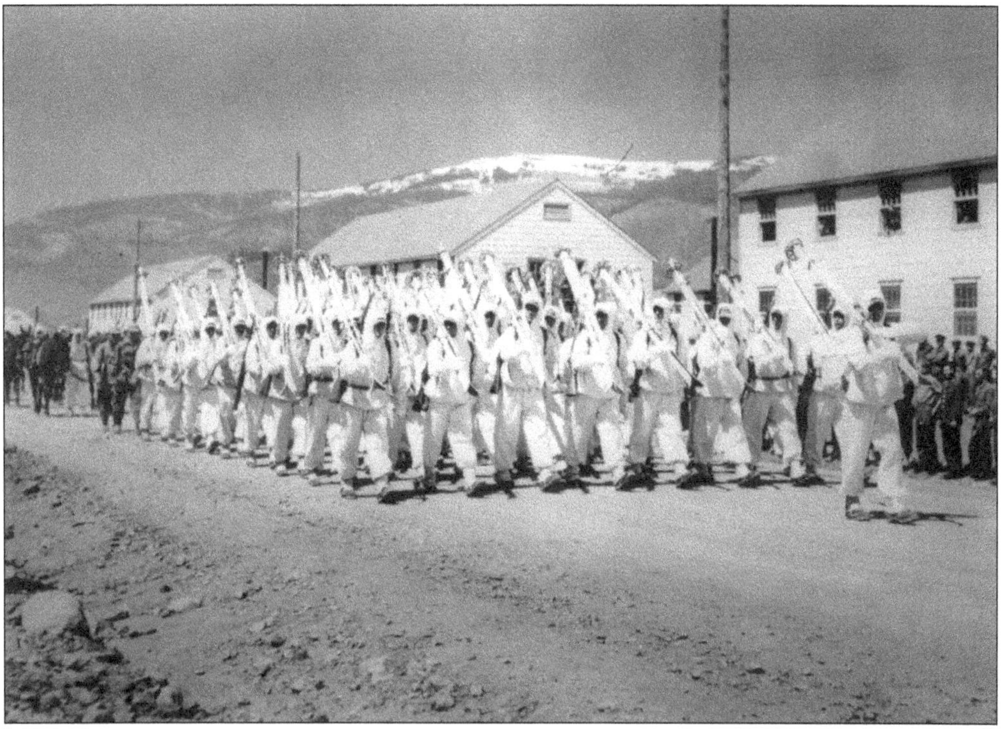

A platoon of white-clad ski troopers, followed by mules, marches down a Camp Hale street. The division often paraded in front of visiting dignitaries or, in this case, for Hollywood cameras (see chapter nine). (Courtesy of DPL.)

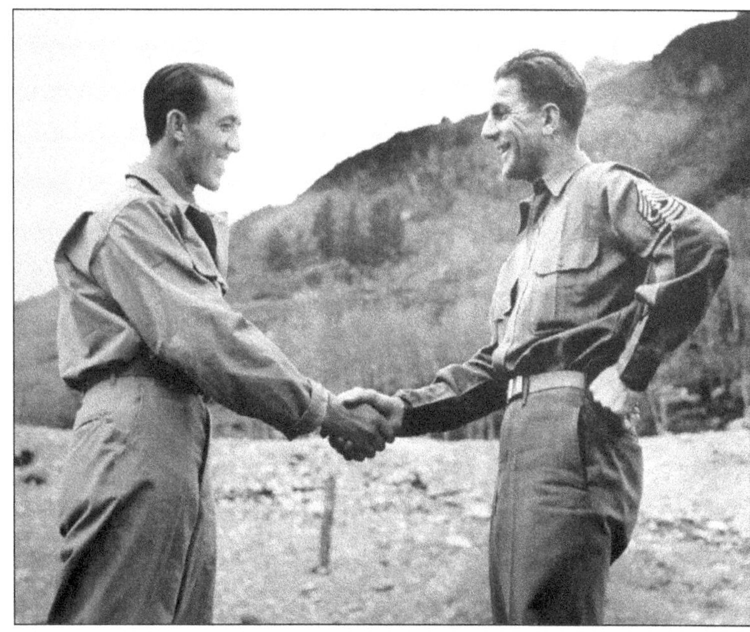

Walter Prager (right), a champion skier from Switzerland and coach of the Dartmouth College ski team, welcomes Austrian ski champion Friedl Pfeifer to Camp Hale. The 10th was studded with hundreds of world-class skiers, which added to the division's fame. (Courtesy of USS&SHOF.)

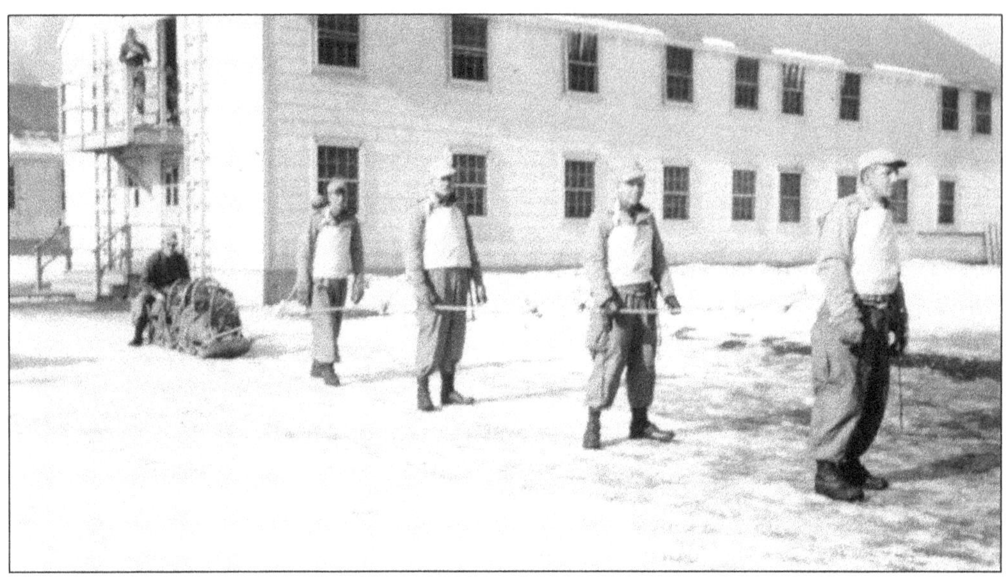

Sometimes it was necessary to pull a load rather than carry it. Here, four troopers are hitched to a heavily laden sled. (Courtesy of HC.)

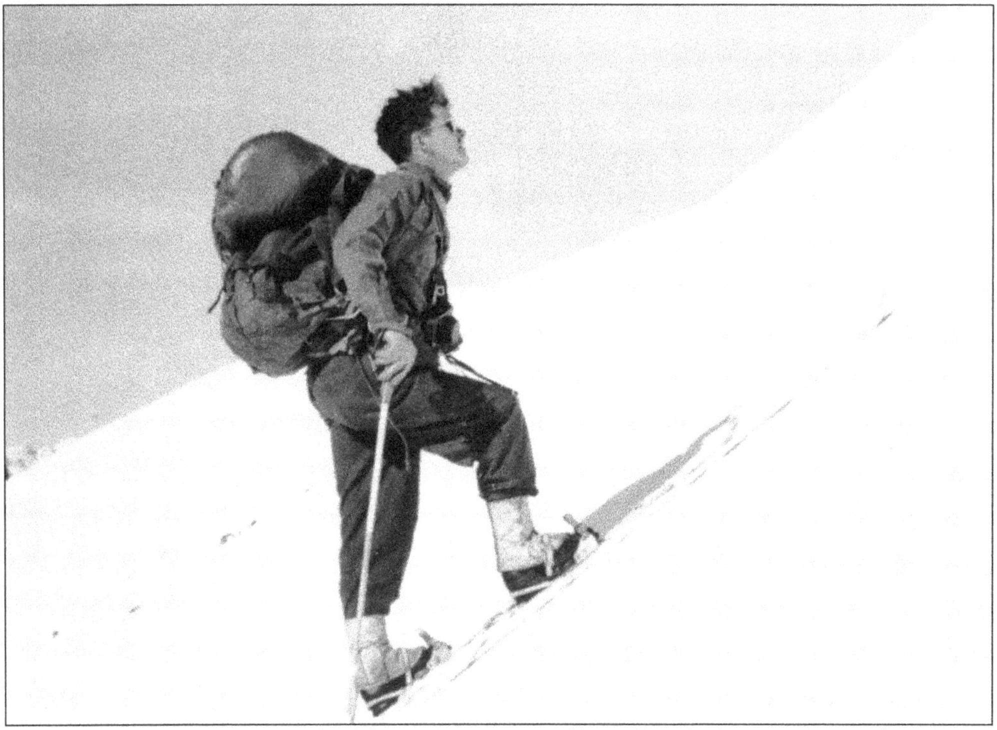

A ski trooper carrying a heavy load shows that it is possible to ski uphill—or at least walk uphill—if one has seal-skin covers strapped to the bottoms of the skis to provide traction. (Courtesy of Rouene Brown.)

Skis had to be kept in perfect condition at all times. Here, a technician mounts bindings on a pair of skis. (Courtesy of DPL.)

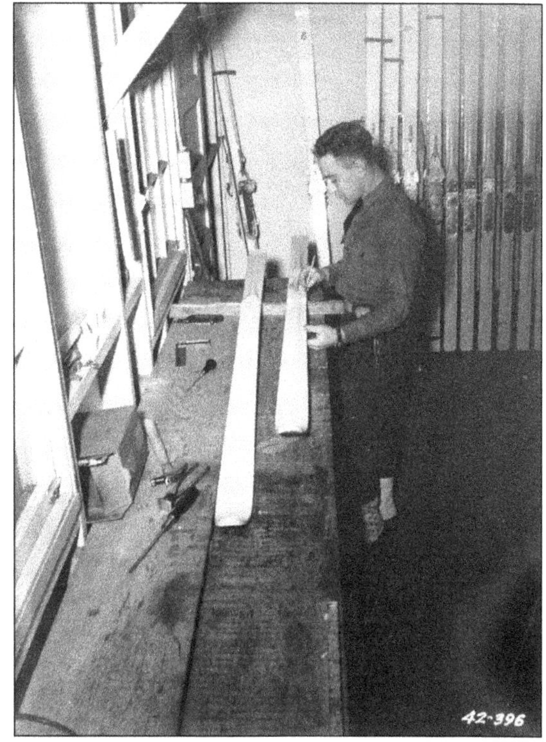

Even on the trail, skis had to be correctly waxed to adapt to changing snow temperatures and conditions. Here, one skier is helping out another. (Courtesy of DPL.)

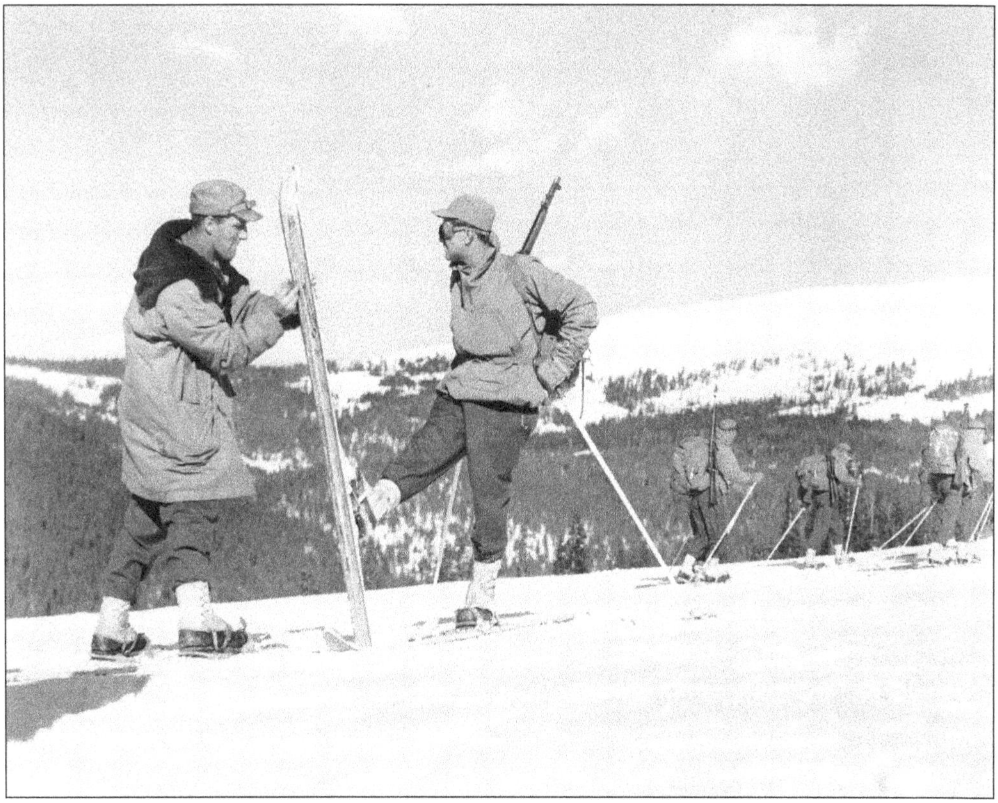

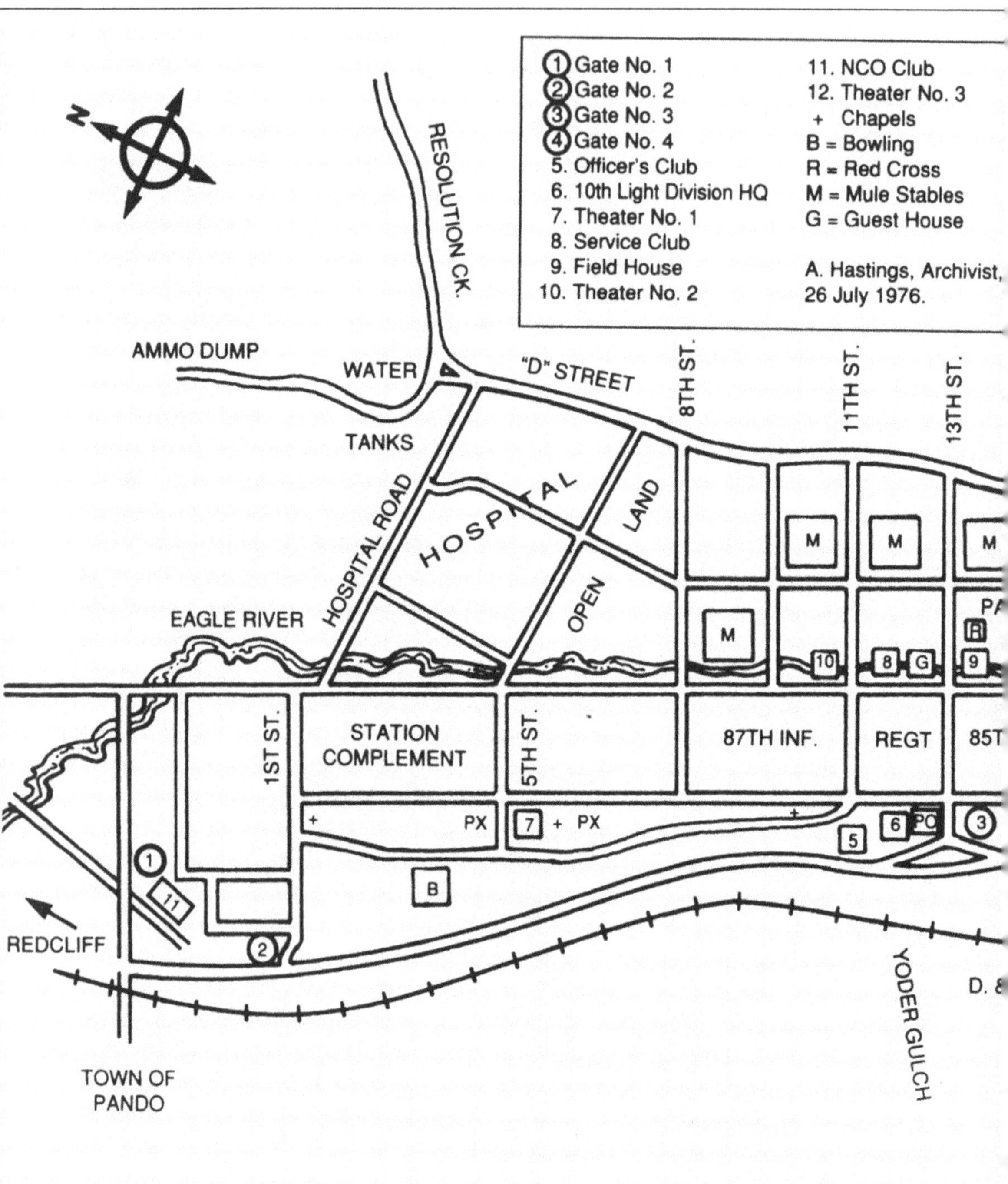

This schematic drawing shows the layout of Camp Hale after it was completely built out. The entire camp, including the artillery range, combat village, and two ski areas, encompassed almost

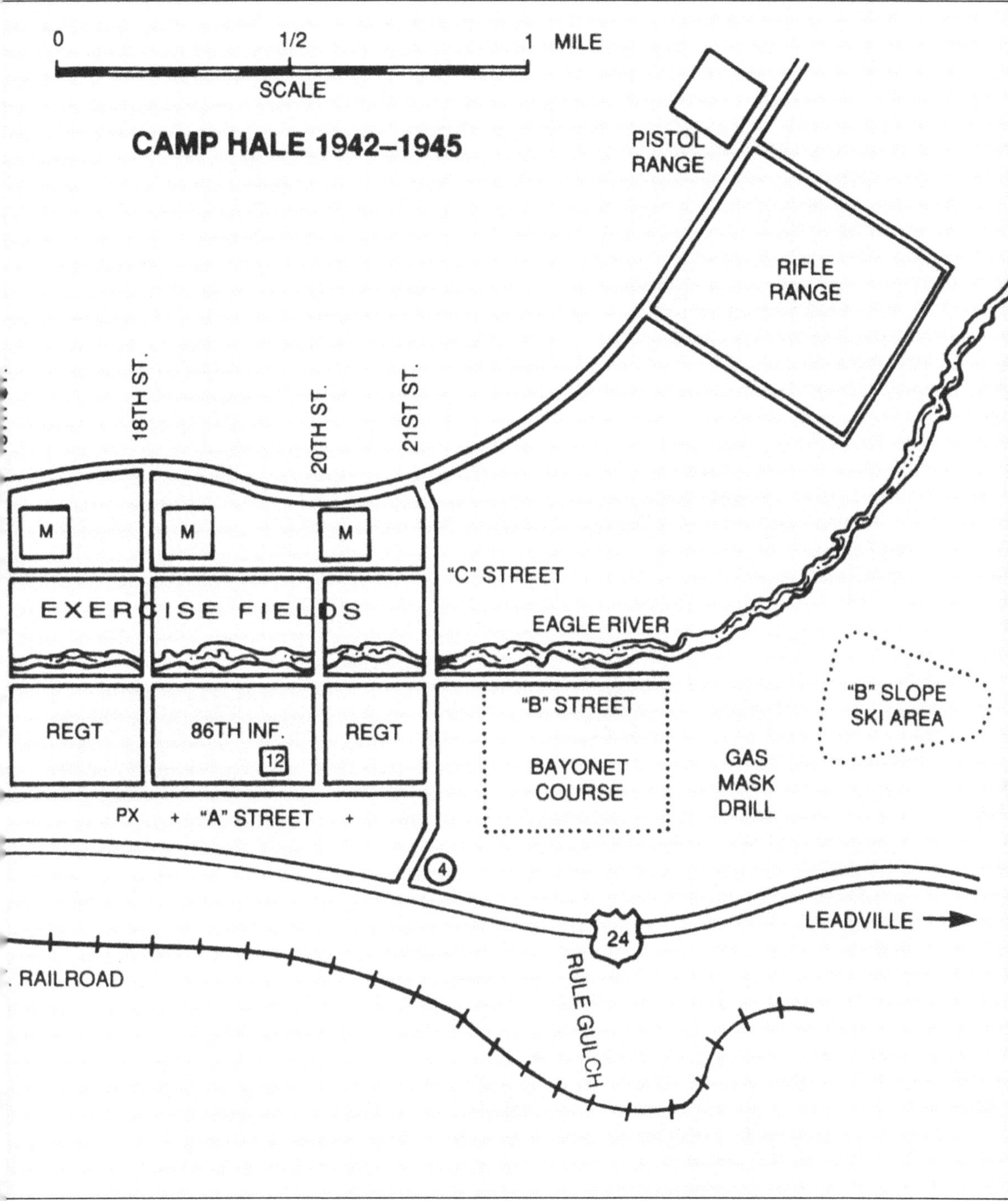

250,000 acres. (Courtesy of Andy Hastings.)

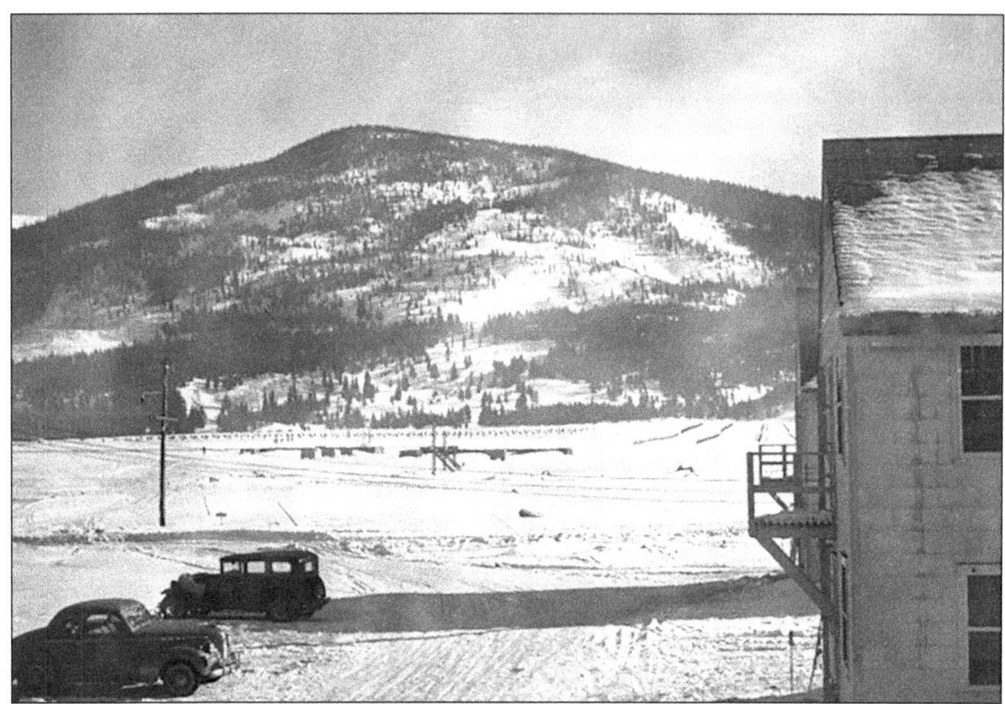

This image looks south down B Street toward the B Slope, Camp Hale's training hill for novice skiers. Over 3,000 men learned to ski on this slope before graduating to the advanced ski training at Cooper Hill, some seven miles to the south. (Courtesy of HC.)

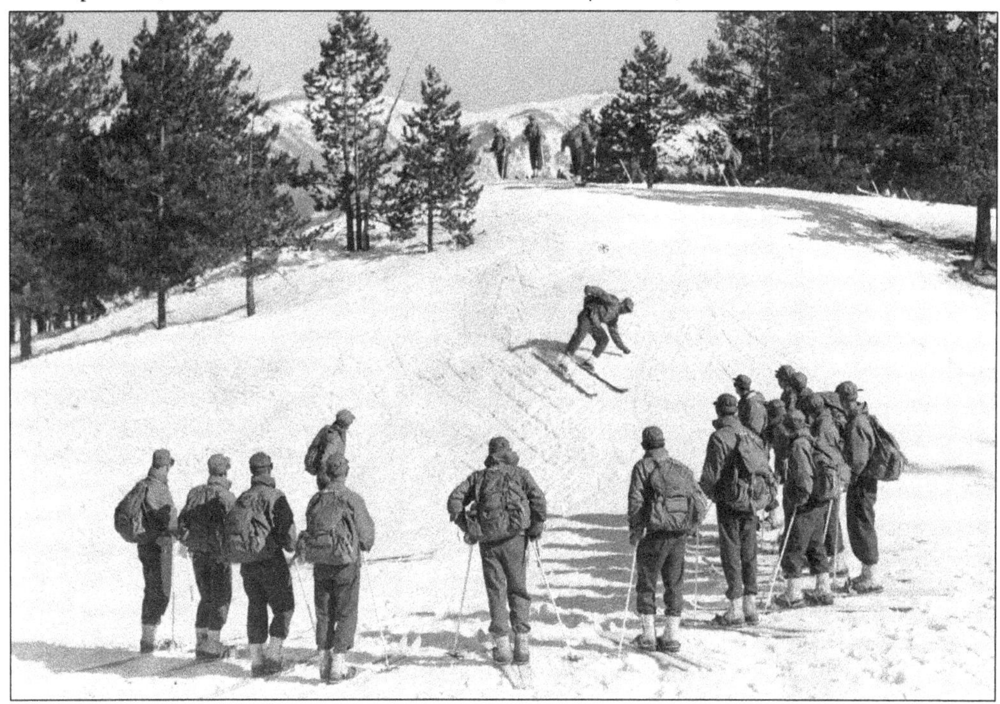

Beginning skiers watch as a demonstrator on the B Slope shows the proper technique for making a turn. (Courtesy of DPL.)

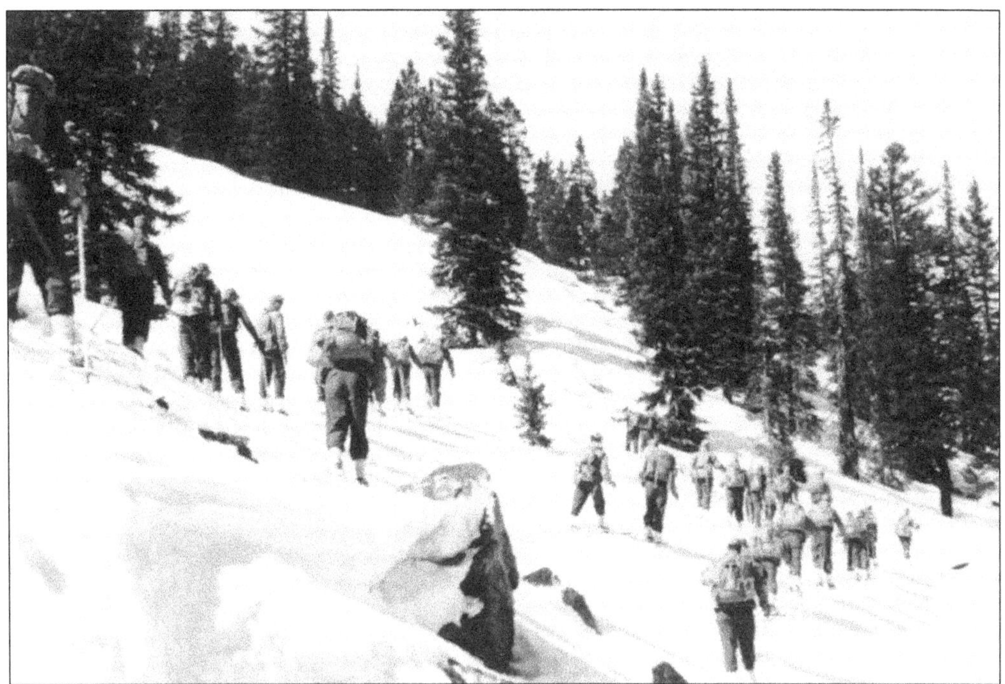

A large group of 10th men begin a cross-country trek through the backcountry. The same skis were used for both downhill and cross-country, depending on the position of the cable bindings, also known as Kandahar or bear-trap bindings. (Courtesy of Rouene Brown.)

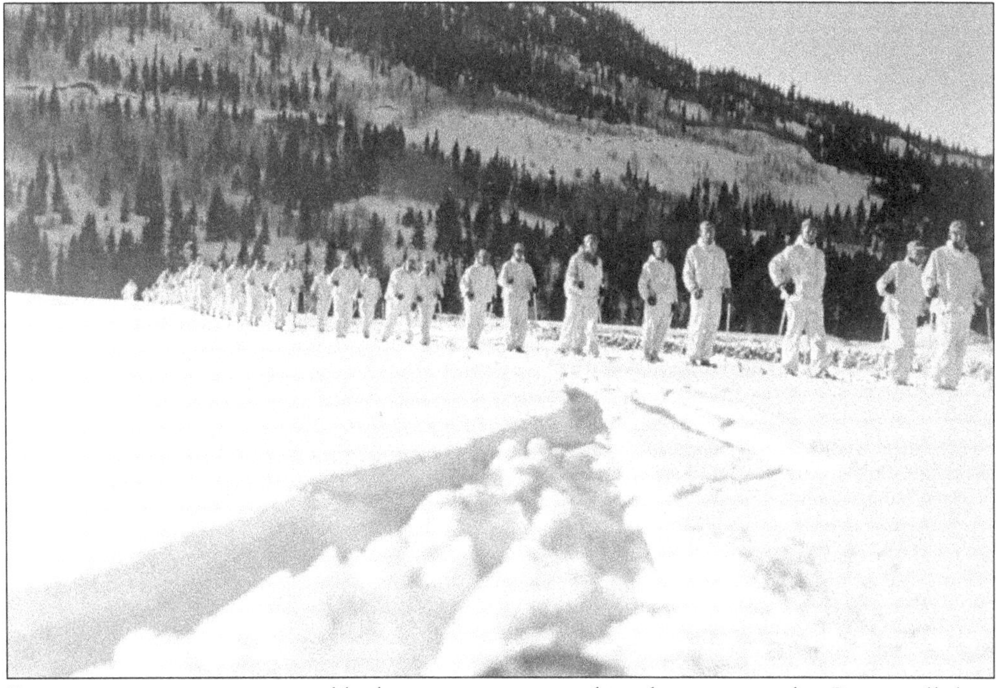

Few activities were more enjoyable than a cross-country ski trek on a sunny day. Despite all their ski training, after being deployed to Italy in January 1945, the troops were seldom on skis, except for a few early patrols. (Courtesy of DPL.)

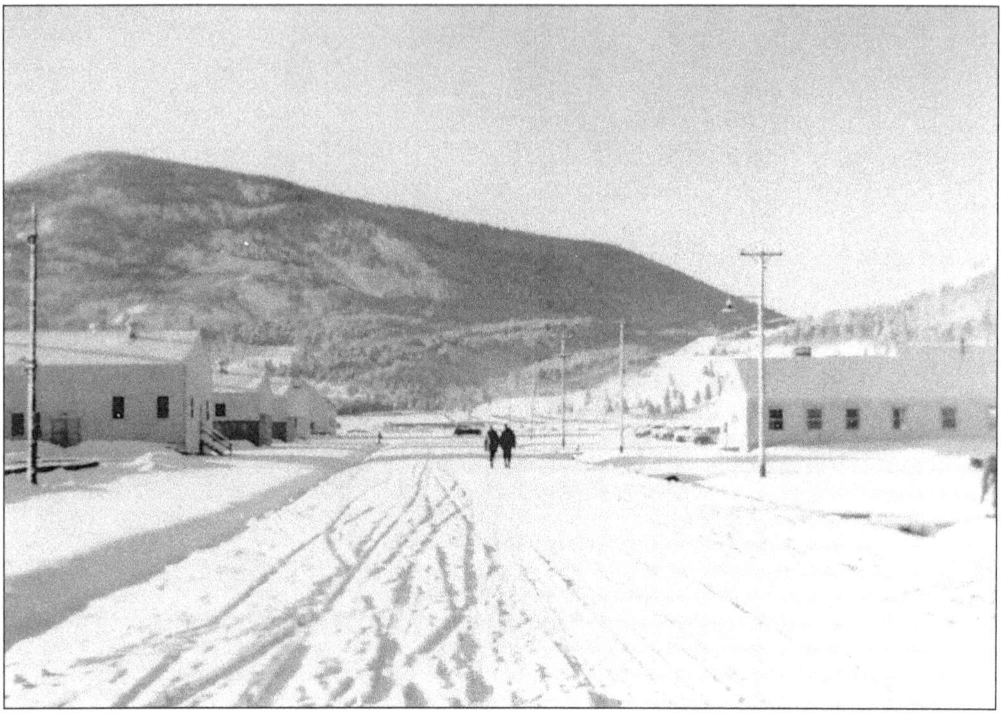

Two soldiers walk down one of the camp's snow-covered streets. In the winter, temperatures often dropped to well below zero degrees Fahrenheit. (Courtesy of DPL.)

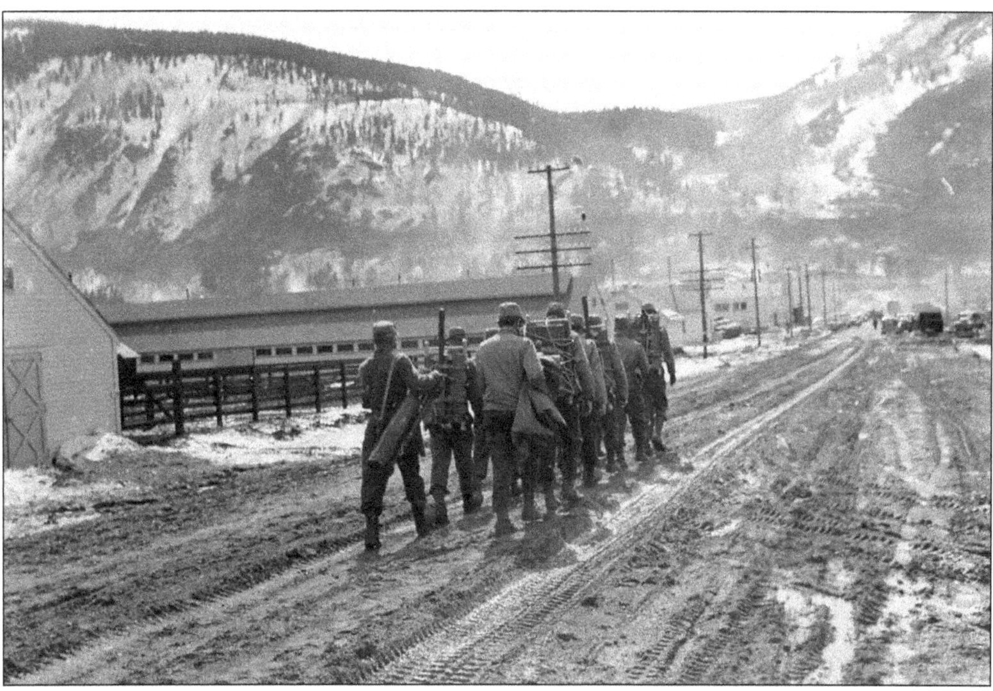

With the arrival of spring also came the start of the "mud season," as these soldiers marching past the mule barns are discovering. (Courtesy of DPL.)

A soldier's favorite day of the month was payday, when the payroll officer doled out the cash. A private earned $21 a month—the equivalent of $375 today. (Courtesy of DPL.)

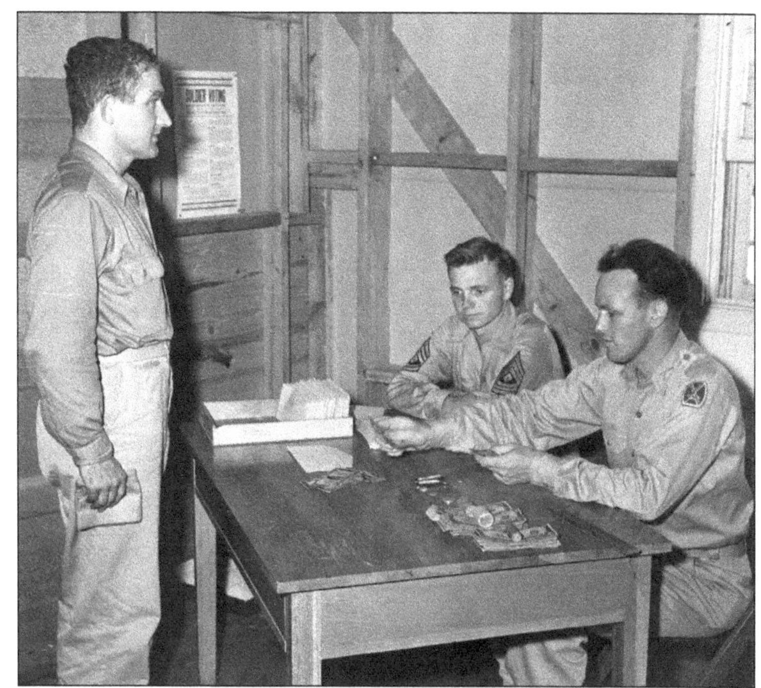

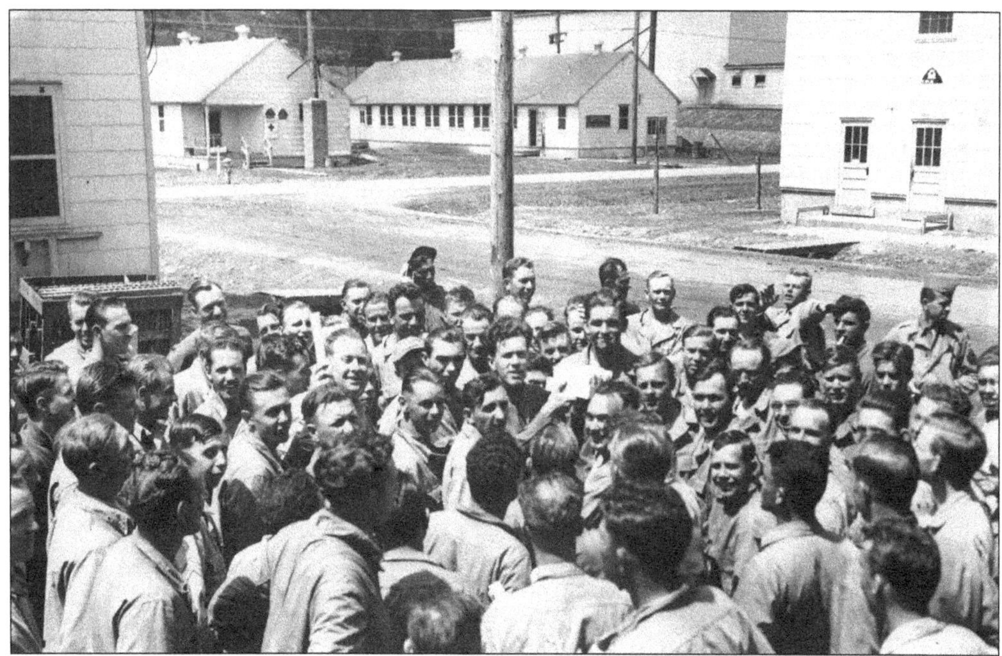

And a soldier's favorite moment of the day was mail call. Here, soldiers gather around the company mail clerk as he distributes letters and packages from home. (Courtesy of DPL.)

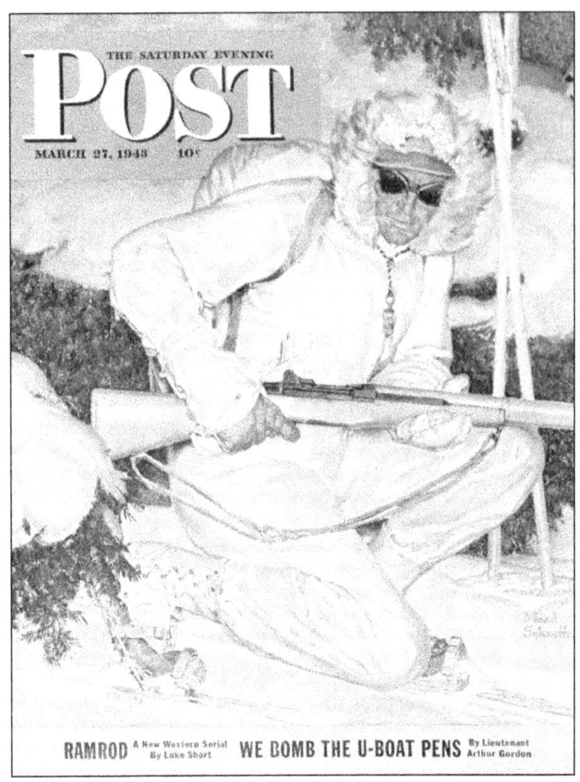

Due to their unique nature, the 10th received considerable publicity while training at Camp Hale. Here, *Saturday Evening Post* cover artist Mead Shaeffer depicts a ski trooper in all whites (including his white-washed rifle, which was never done in practice). (Courtesy of HC.)

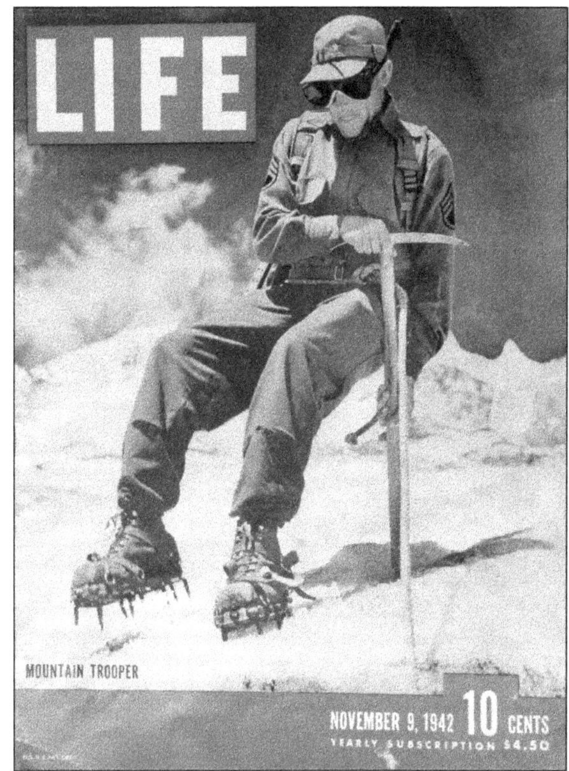

The November 9, 1942, issue of *Life* magazine featured a photo essay on the 10th, with Staff Sgt. Walter Prager shown on the cover with an ice ax and crampons. (Author's collection.)

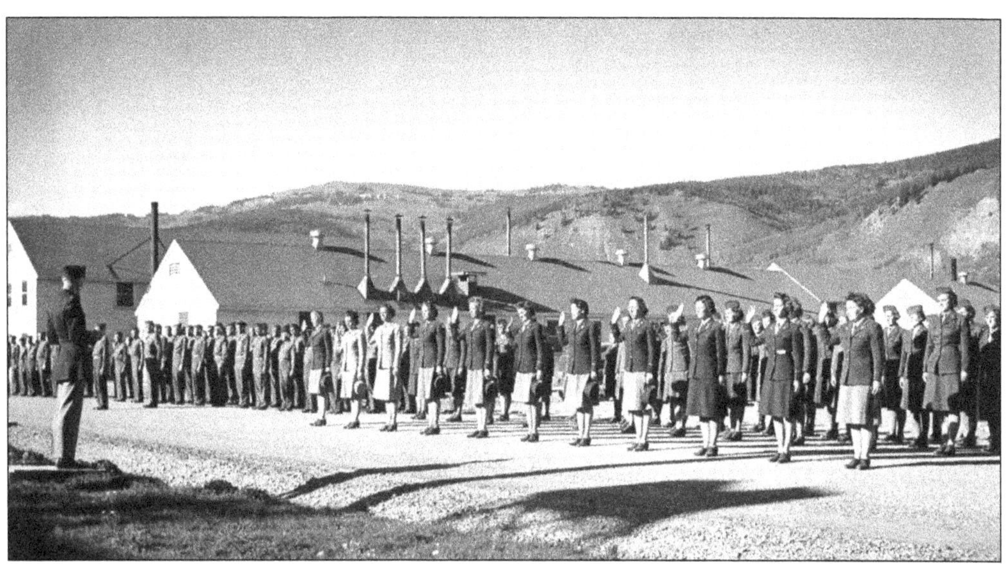

A 240-woman WAC detachment arrived at Camp Hale on May 27, 1943. They served as motor-pool drivers and mechanics, supply specialists, and secretaries, and worked in communications and accounting. Their barracks were at First and B Streets. (Courtesy of CSSM.)

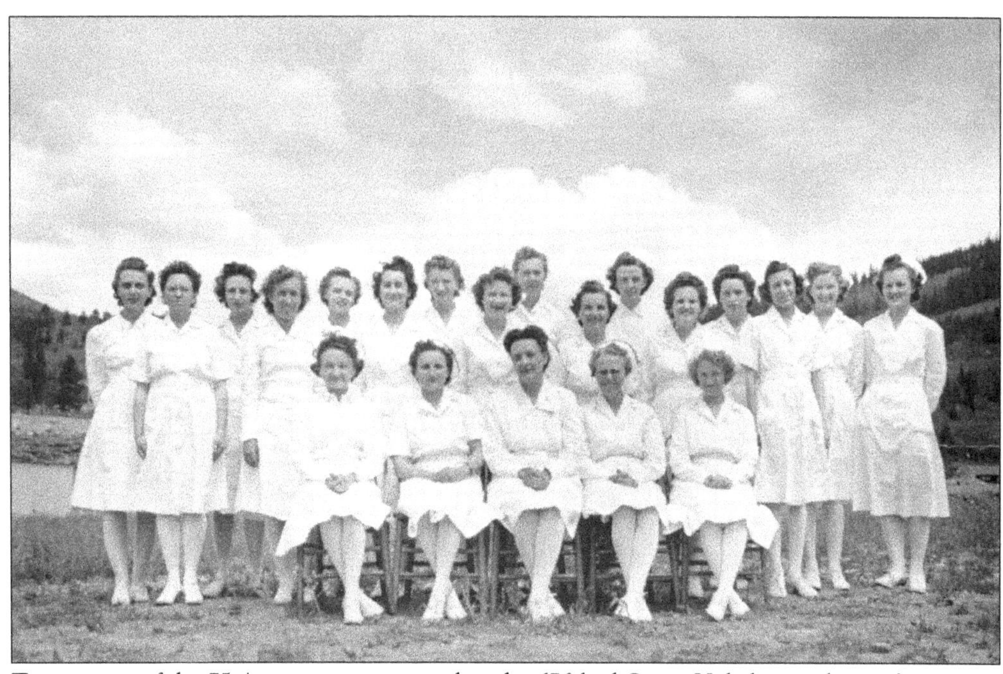

Twenty-one of the 75 Army nurses assigned to the 676-bed Camp Hale hospital pose for a group photograph. Many had numerous years of experience in the nursing profession, while some were fresh out of nursing school. All of them were commissioned officers. (Courtesy of DPL.)

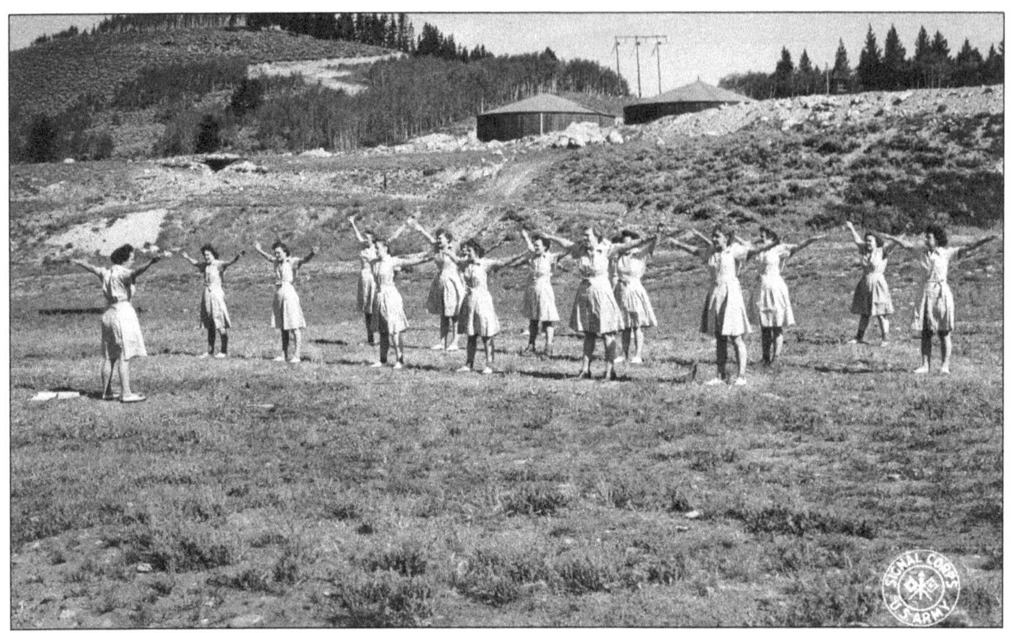

Nurses perform calisthenics near the hospital at the north end of the camp. In the background are the camp's water-storage tanks. (Courtesy of DPL.)

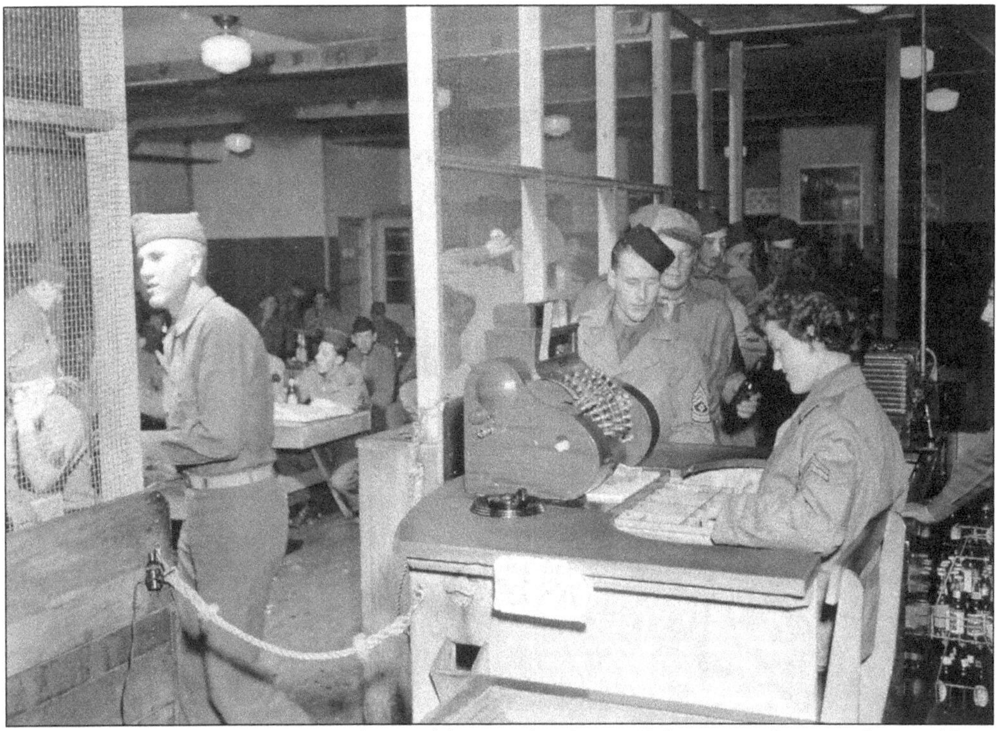

A WAC cashier collects payment from soldiers at the Camp Hale post exchange, where soldiers could buy snacks, drinks, and personal-care items during their off-duty hours. The small sign next to the cash register reads, "One Beer Per Man." (Courtesy of CSSM.)

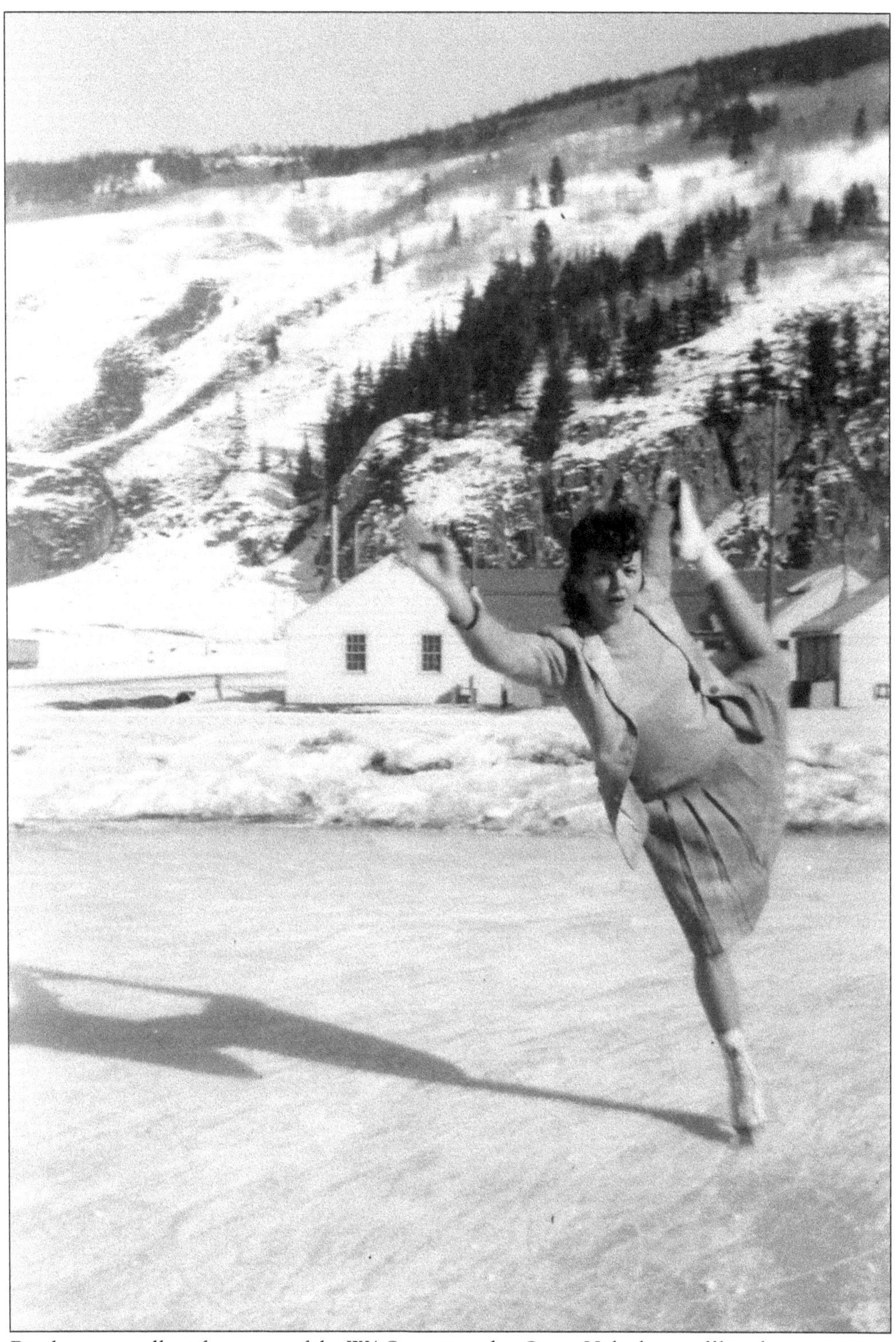

Displaying excellent form, one of the WACs stationed at Camp Hale shows off her skating prowess on a frozen pond. (Courtesy of DPL.)

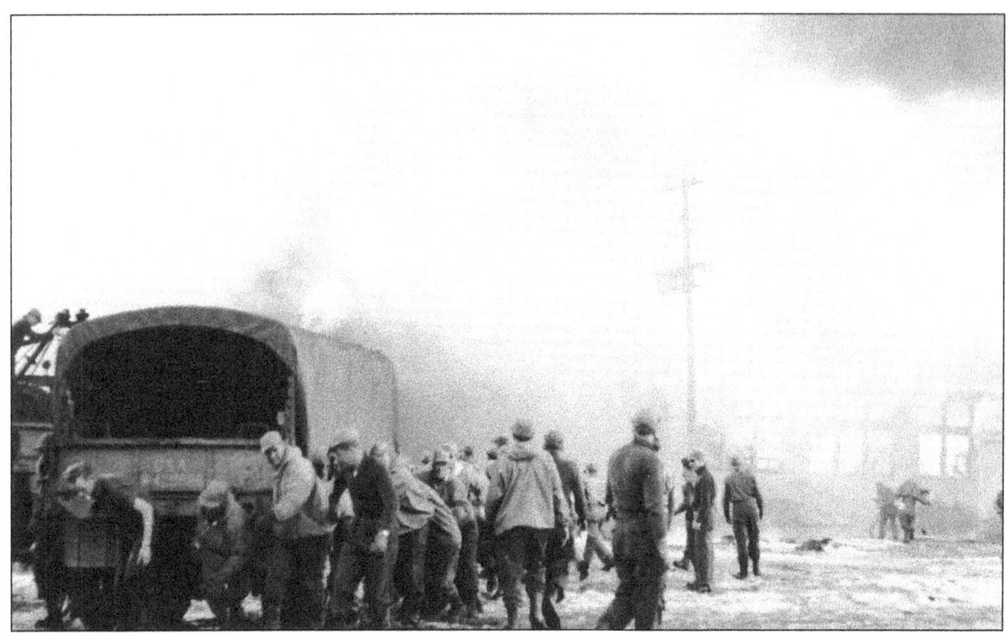

The danger of fire was always present. Here, soldiers push and pull a 2.5-ton truck away from the blazing vehicle maintenance shop. This fire on February 19, 1943, caused $150,000 worth of damage to the building and the loss of $100,000 worth of tools and equipment. (Courtesy of Rouene Brown.)

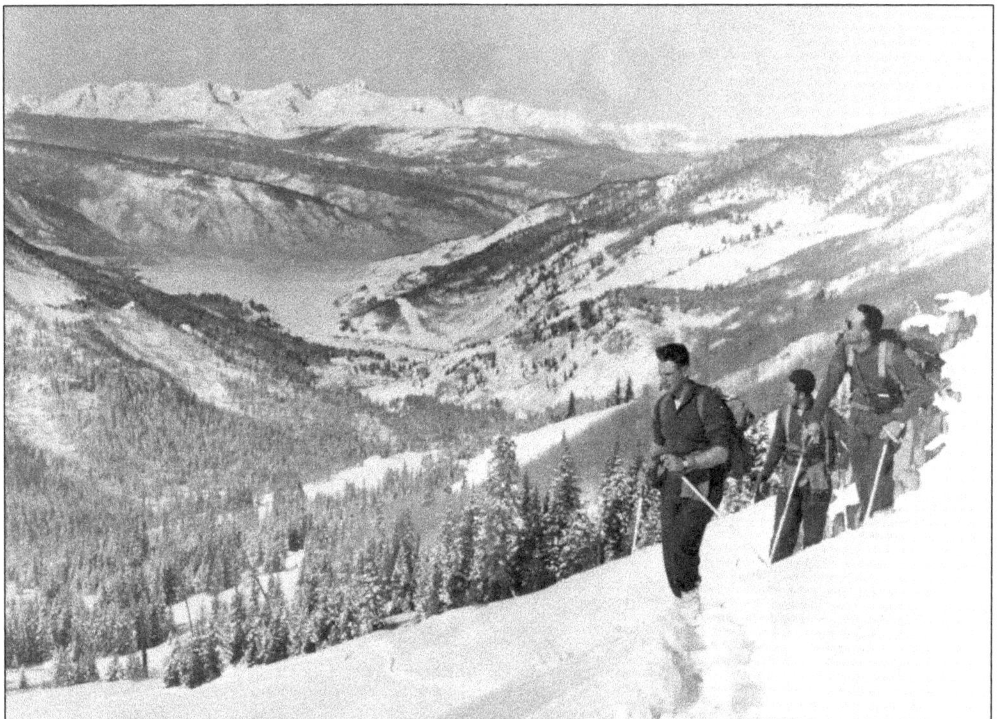

Three cross-country skiers, enjoying a sunny day off, cut through the powder high above the camp, which is just barely visible under the smog in the valley below. (Courtesy of DPL.)

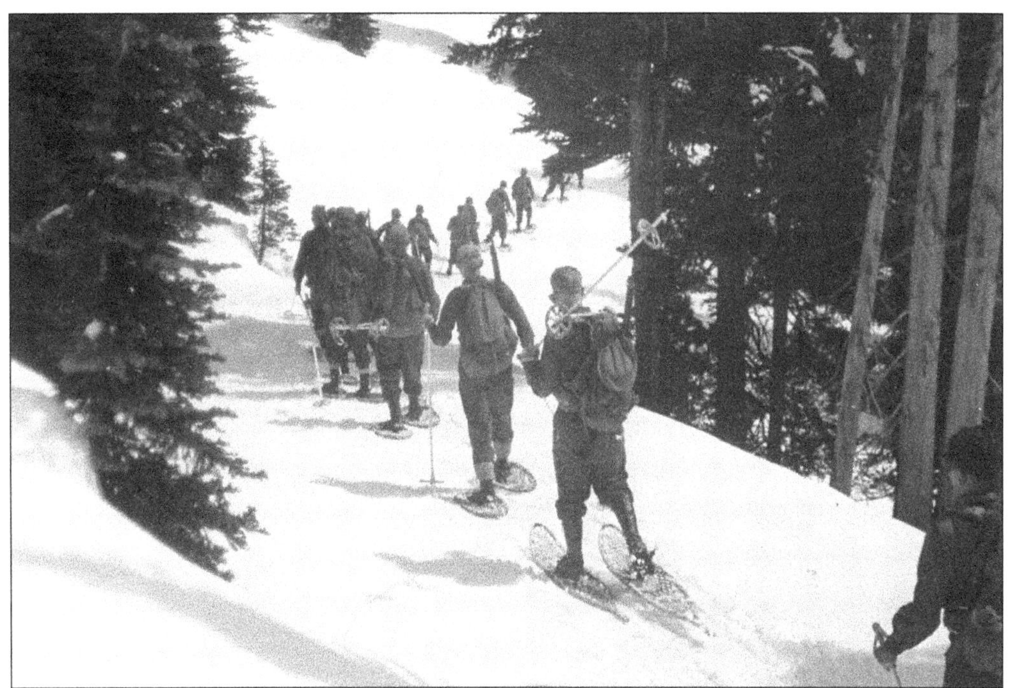

A platoon on snowshoes sets out on a trek above Camp Hale. The soldier with the pole on his shoulder is on long-tail snowshoes, while the man in front of him is on shorter bear-paw snowshoes. (Courtesy of DPL.)

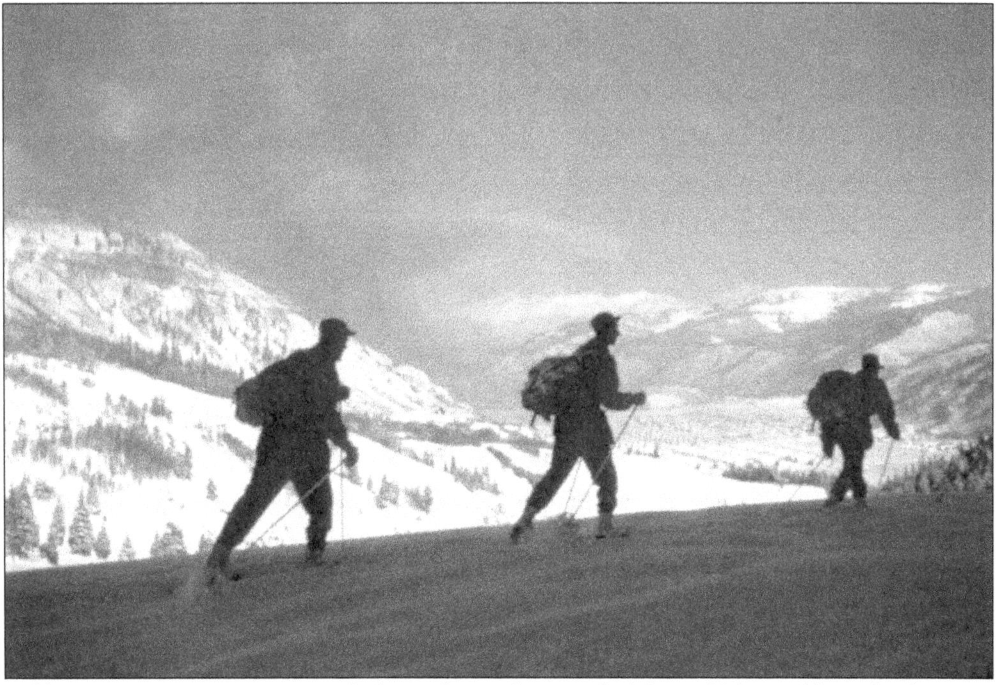

Soldiers are on a cross-country trek above the southern end of Camp Hale, visible in the distance. Also visible is the black cloud of smoke from hundreds of coal-burning stoves in the camp that created respiratory issues—known as the Pando Hack—for Hale's inhabitants. (Courtesy of DPL.)

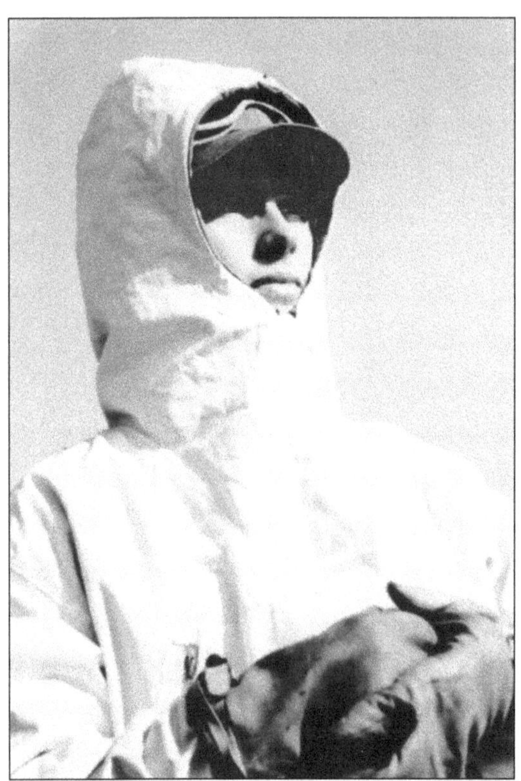

The 10th was always being used by the Army's Quartermaster Corps to test new types of clothing and equipment. This soldier is wearing the unlined, reversible cotton shell anorak, white side out. His cotton ski cap and goggles are visible under the hood. (Courtesy of Rouene Brown.)

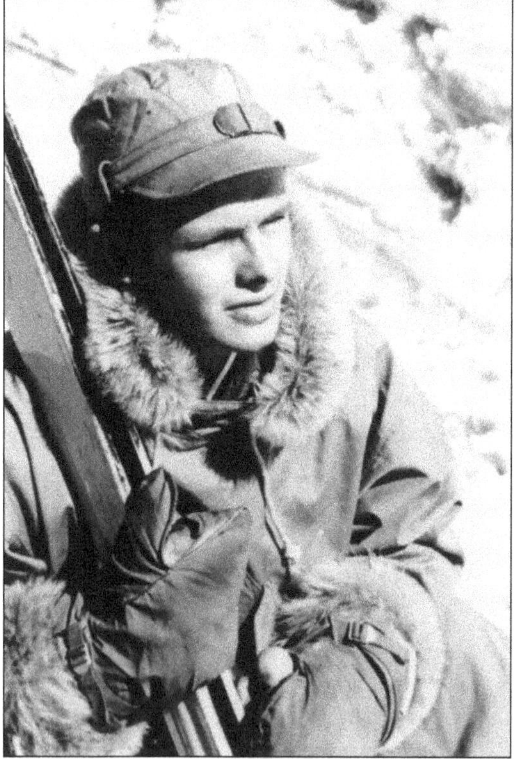

This soldier is wearing the reversible cotton shell parka, olive-green side out, with wolf-fur trim around the collar and cuffs. Note that he is also wearing mittens with a trigger finger so that he can fire his rifle without removing them. (Courtesy of Rouene Brown.)

Decked out in their fur-trimmed snow-camouflage parkas and white overpants, these two men appear ready to hit the slopes. In front of them is their rucksack, under a white cotton cover. (Courtesy of DPL.)

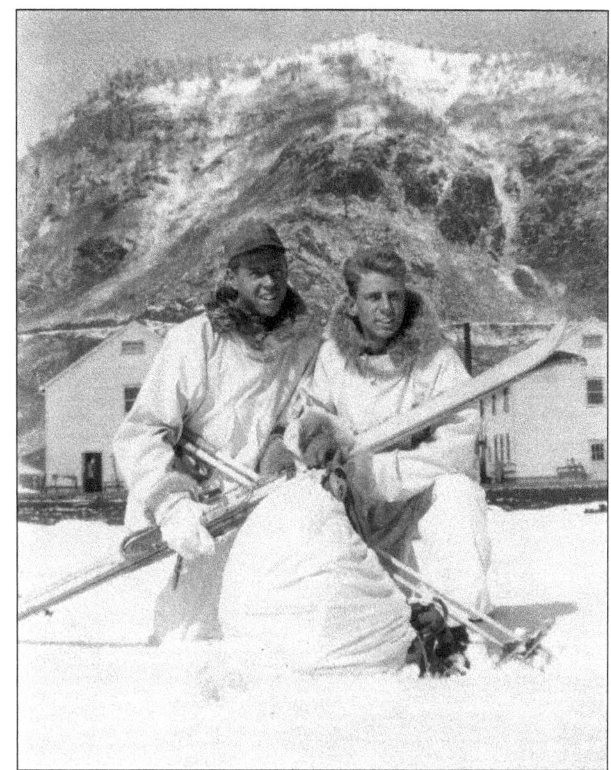

Soldiers prepare to mount the T-bar lift at Cooper Hill and ride up to the top of 10,500-foot Chicago Ridge. At 7,000 feet in length, the Cooper Hill "Constam" T-bar was the longest in the world. (Courtesy of HC.)

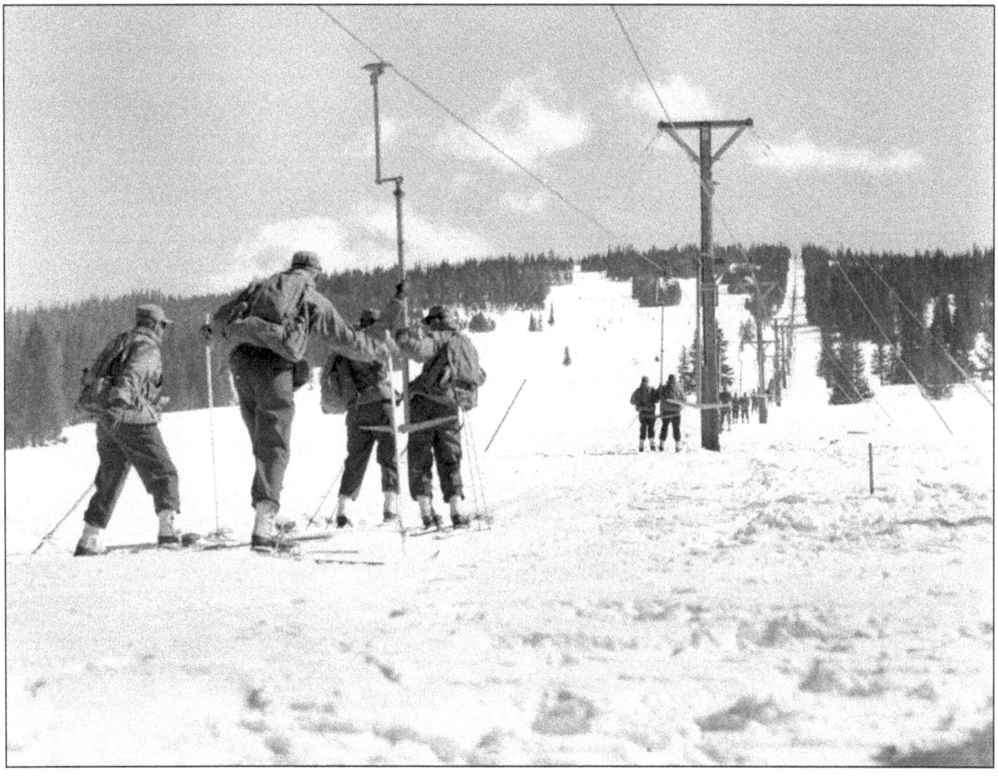

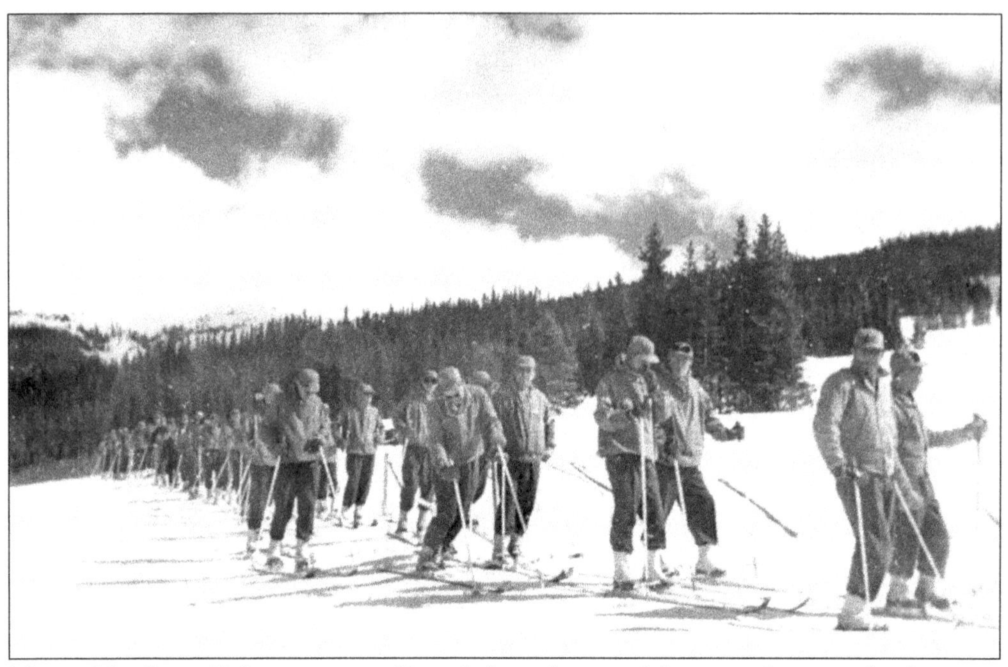

Many of the Camp Hale troopers could not believe their good fortune at being in the ski troops and being paid to ski when a lift ticket at most New England resorts cost as much as $3 a day. (Courtesy of HC.)

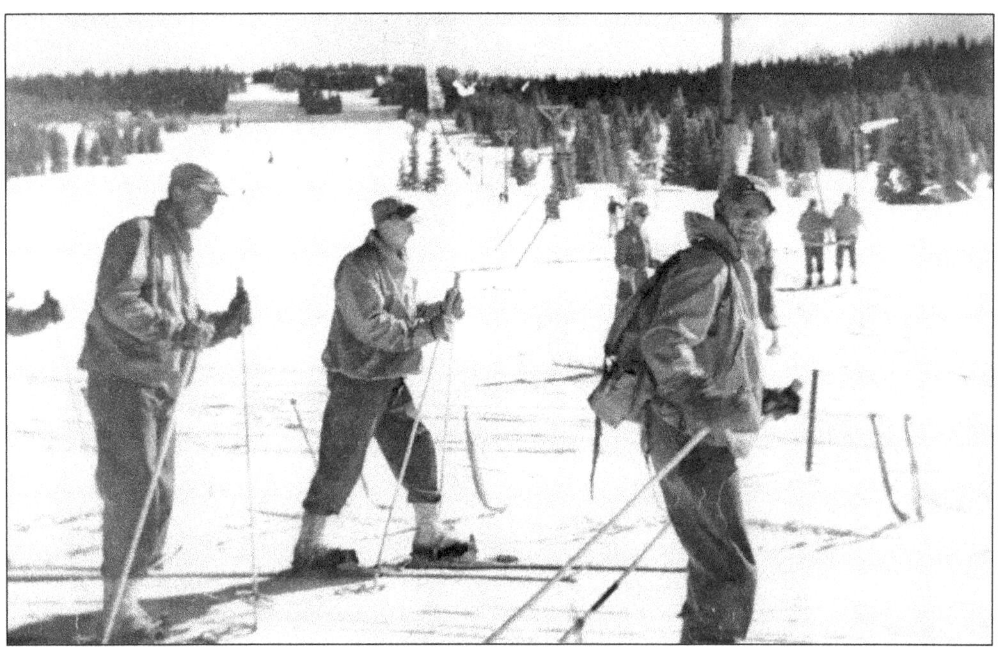

While the vast majority of men in the 10th were glad to be there, others—mostly non-skiers from the South—did not enjoy it and went so far as to ski under logs in hopes of breaking a leg and being transferred out of the 10th and re-assigned to another unit. (Courtesy of HC.)

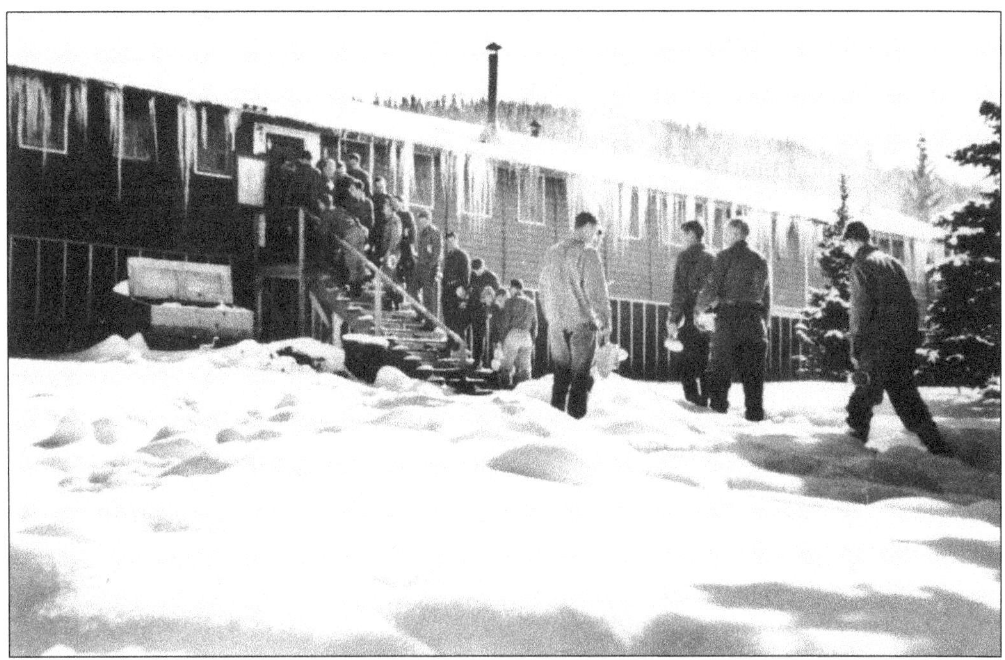

With mess kits in hand, soldiers line up for lunch outside the Cooper Hill mess hall, which is festooned with icicles. (Courtesy of Rouene Brown.)

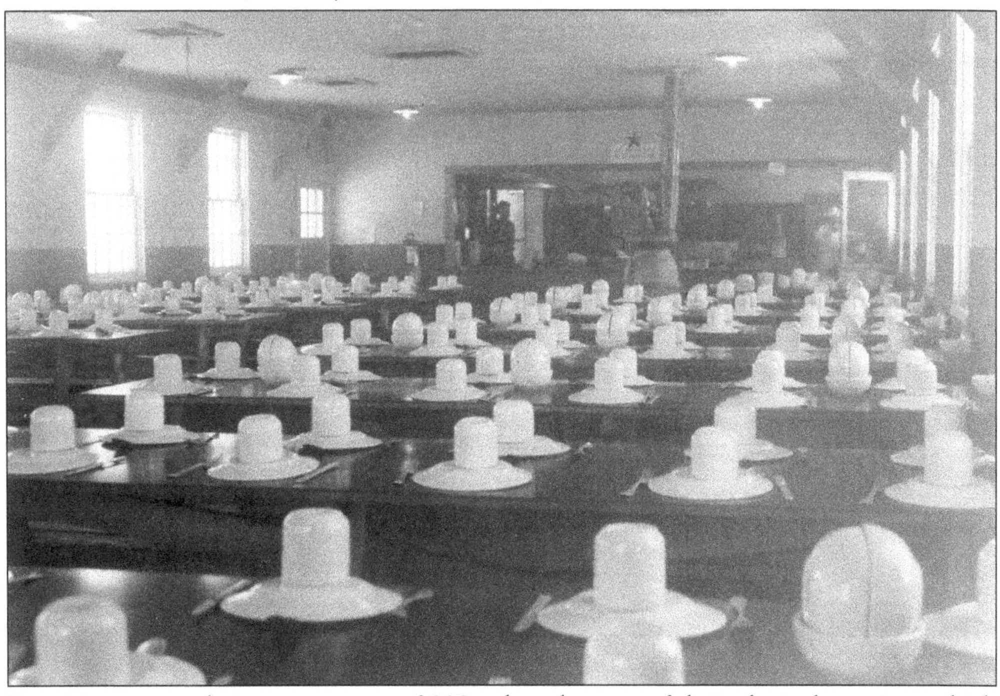

Requiring extra calories—as many as 6,000 a day—because of their physical exertion at high altitudes, the soldiers of the 10th ate especially well. Here, table settings at a Camp Hale mess hall suggest a more formal meal. The sign at the end of the room reads, "Take all you want but eat all you take," a phrase found in mess halls throughout the US military to discourage wasting food. (Courtesy of DPL.)

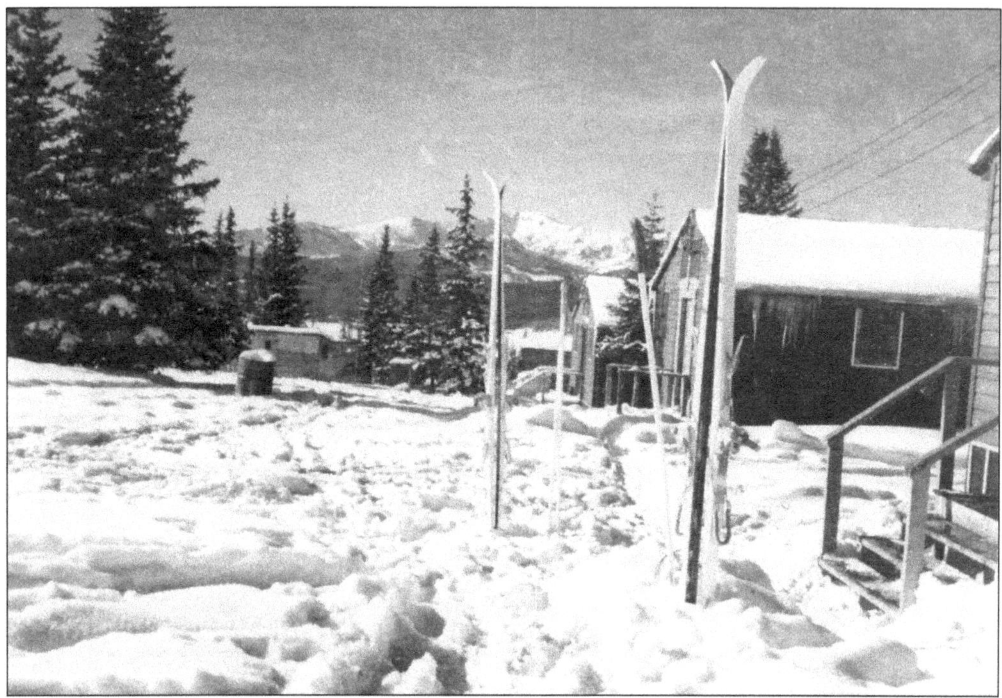

Light, fluffy snow—Colorado's famous "champagne powder"—covers the one-story buildings at Cooper Hill. After the war, the ski area opened to the public, changed its name to Ski Cooper, and has been in operation ever since. (Courtesy of DPL.)

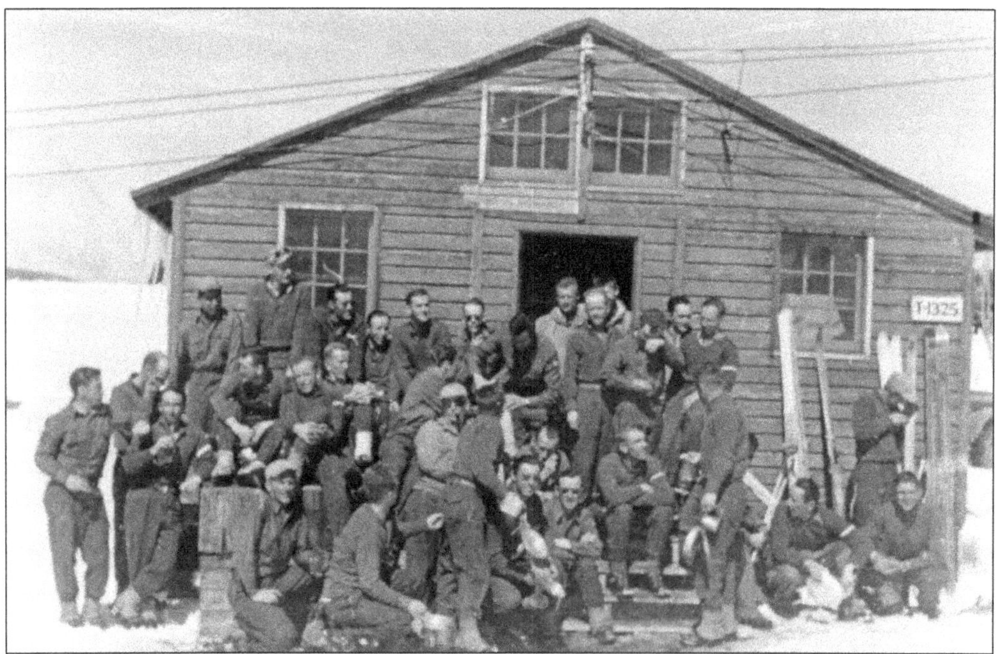

The 32 ski instructors with the Mountain Training Group—some of the finest skiers in the world—gather for a group picture outside the Cooper Hill mess hall. (Courtesy of DPL.)

Six

Summer Training

The short summer season at 9,250 feet was packed with training activities. The men of the 10th put away their skis and snowshoes and learned how to climb the steep and rugged cliffs along the camp's west side, building confidence with each step.

In addition to scaling the cliffs that flanked the east side of the camp, there were long conditioning hikes both on the road and in the wilderness. Soldiers were also given instruction in various weapons (rifles, pistols, machine guns, anti-aircraft guns, hand grenades, rocket launchers—known as "bazookas"—and more).

Ironically, when the 10th went into combat in Italy, only a few patrols were conducted on skis because of their arrival in early spring. Their climbing skills, however, proved invaluable when tackling their first combat assignment—Riva Ridge, in the Northern Apennines—and other steep, challenging places.

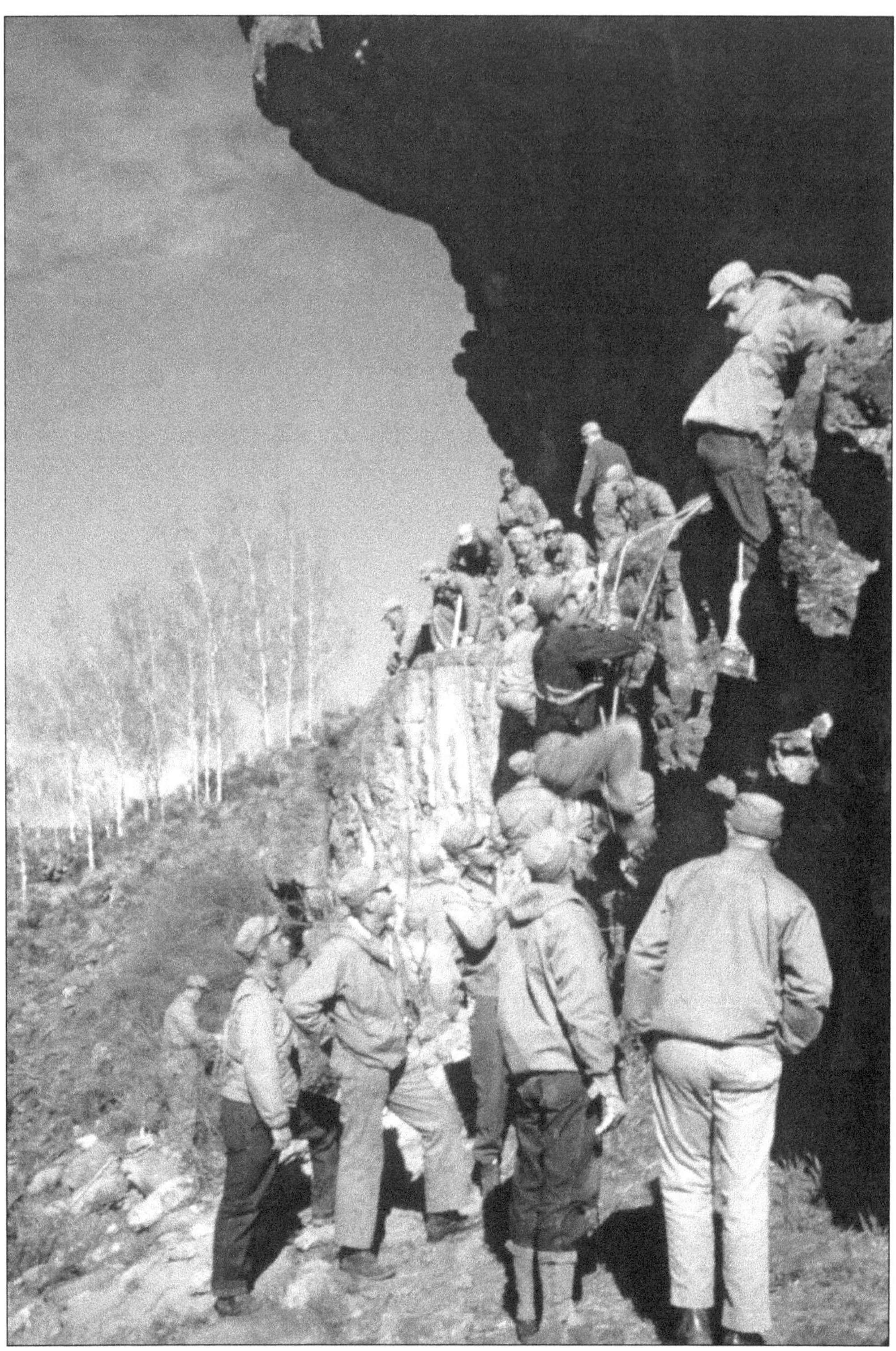

Troopers of the 10th Light Division, wearing a variety of uniforms, get their first taste of rock climbing close to the ground at the cliffs on the east side of the cantonment area. (Courtesy of DPL.)

Men with a fear of heights soon learned to conquer their fear with the help of skilled instructors who guided their every step until they became proficient climbers. (Courtesy of AHS.)

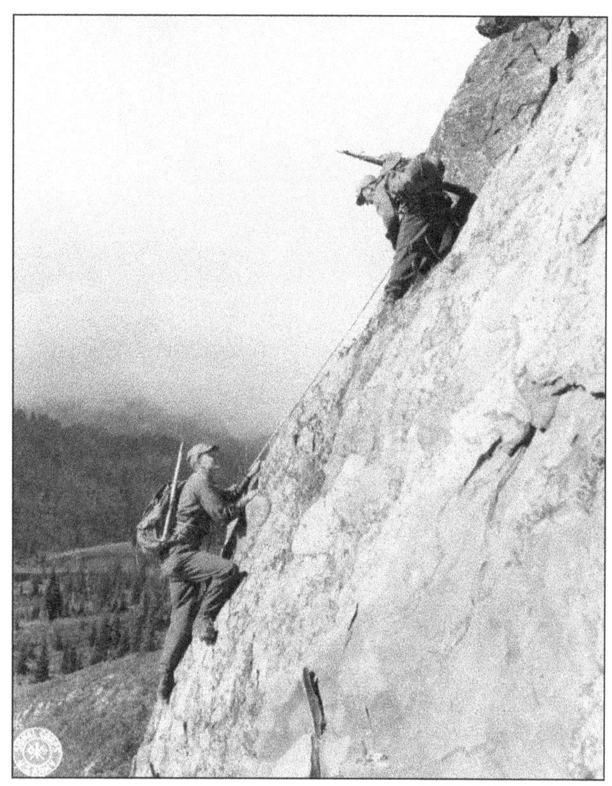

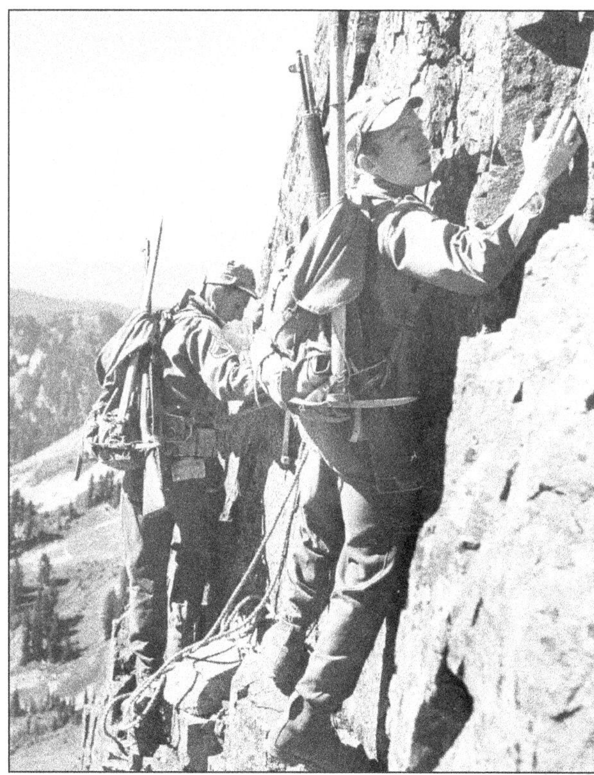

Two experienced climbers, outfitted with rucksacks, climbing ropes, rifles, and ice axes, work their way along a sheer rock face high above the camp. When the 10th first went into combat in Italy in February 1945, their climbing skills were much more important than their skiing abilities. (Courtesy of DPL.)

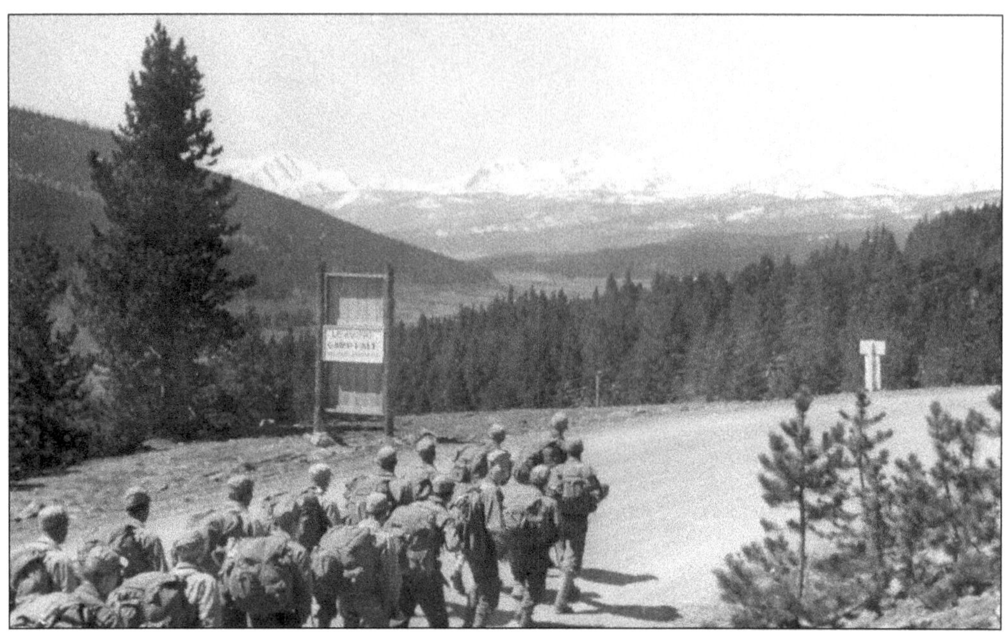

A platoon of 10th men with full packs leave the Camp Hale boundary and head south on a summer training hike along US Highway 24. Mt. Elbert (left) and Mt. Massive (right) are visible in the distance. (Courtesy of DPL.)

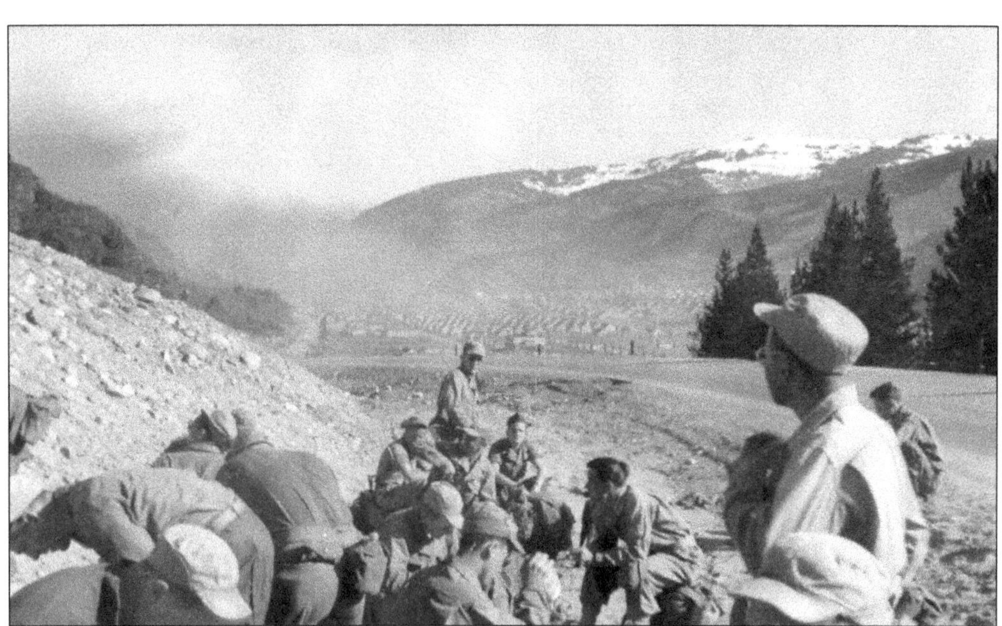

Taking a short break on their hike, the troopers look back at smog-shrouded Camp Hale. Getting out of the polluted valley was usually a welcome treat. (Courtesy of DPL.)

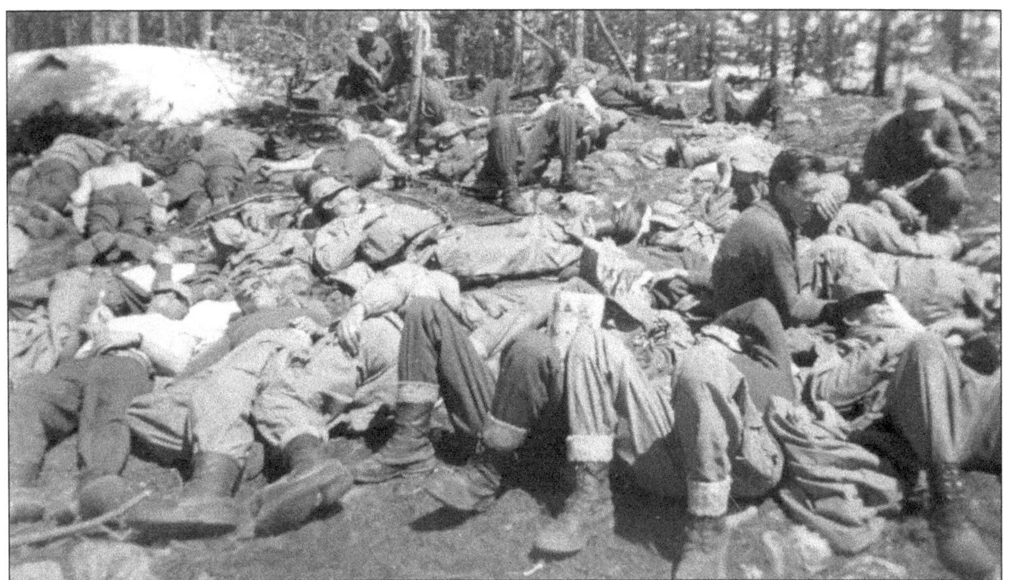

"Fall out and take five!" was always a welcome command while on a long hike of 20 miles or more at high altitudes. (Courtesy of DPL.)

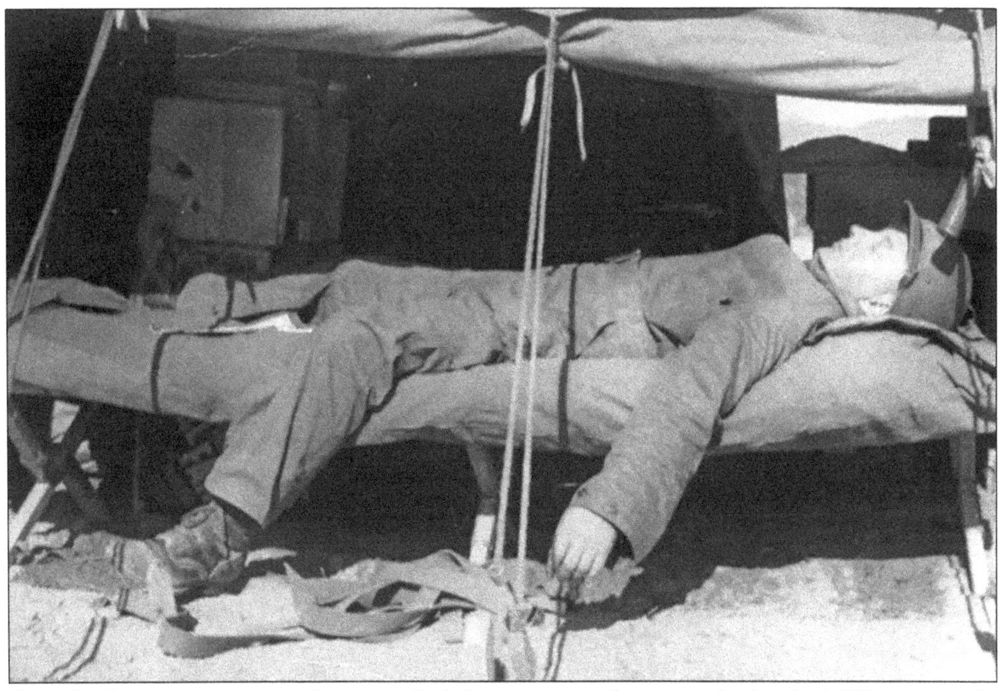

Once back in camp, a pooped trooper finds his cot as soothing as a feather bed. When properly conditioned, a soldier has more confidence in his abilities. (Courtesy of DPL.)

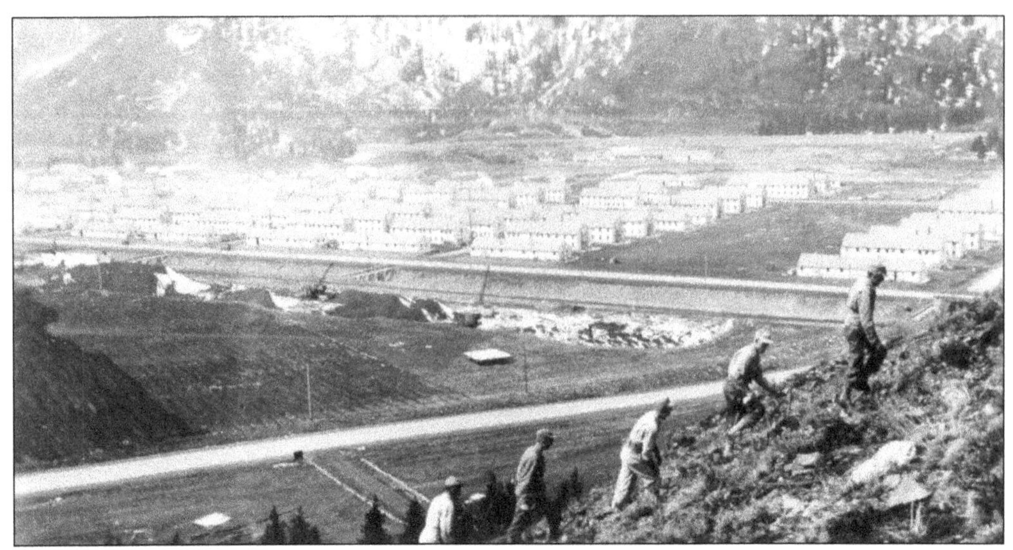

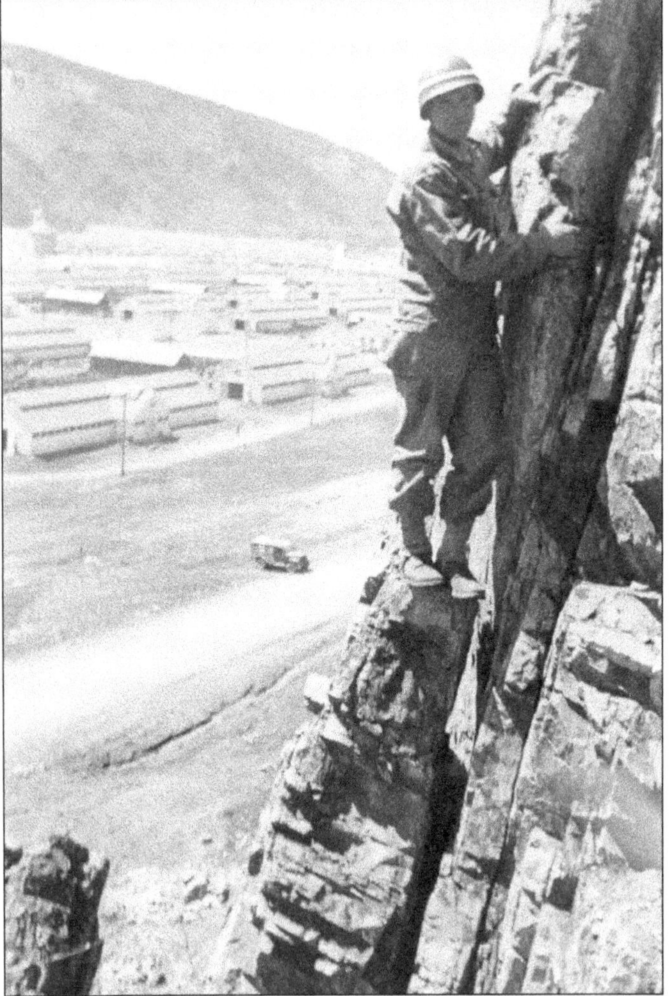

Soldiers take a hike up the hills at the camp's northern end. The dark area to the left is the camp's coal yard. (Courtesy of DPL.)

A mountain trooper does his impression of a mountain goat on a rocky ledge on the cliffs east of the camp. Note the military ambulance far below. After reaching a high vantage point, soldiers could look down on their camp, contemplate their future, and wonder when—or if—they might be going into combat. (Courtesy of DPL.)

During communications training, a 10th soldier uses semaphore flags to signal a message to a distant unit. When field radios and telephones were unavailable or inoperable, messages could still be sent by runner, dog, or semaphore. (Courtesy of DPL.)

Playing war games in a remote Colorado valley when most American divisions were overseas fighting the enemy sometimes began to wear on the soldiers, who were eager to get into combat and prove what they could do. Here, two troopers armed with M1 Garand rifles smile while taking part in maneuvers. (Courtesy of Rouene Brown.)

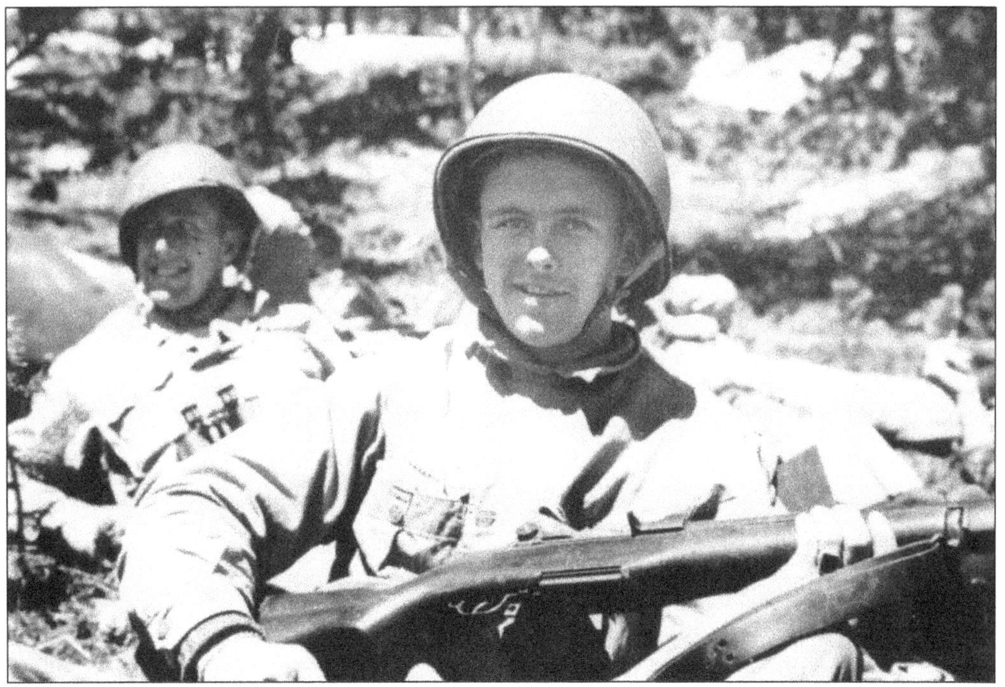

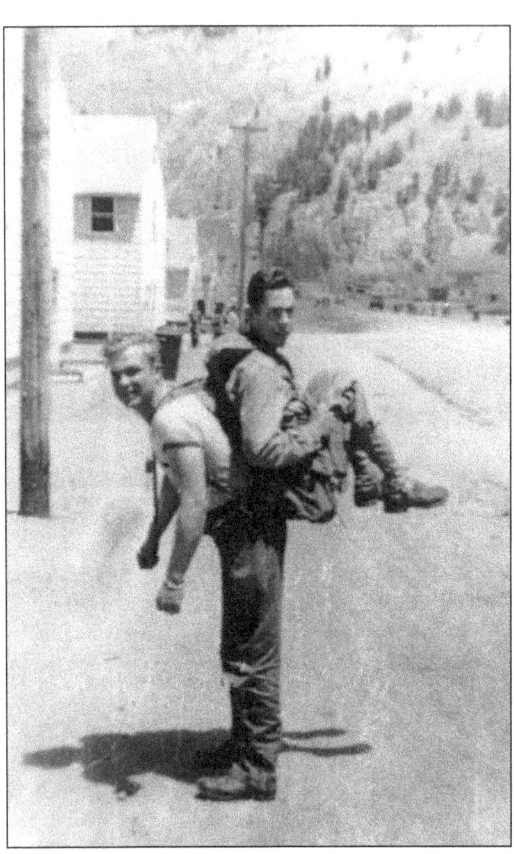

Posing for a comical photograph to send home, one trooper gives his backpack buddy a "lift." (Courtesy of DPL.)

A Type 3600 2-8-8-2 locomotive of the Denver & Rio Grande Western Railroad heads north above the white-painted buildings of Camp Hale during the summer of 1943. Many of the soldiers down below wished that they were on a train to a port of embarkation so that they could get into combat. (Courtesy of DPL.)

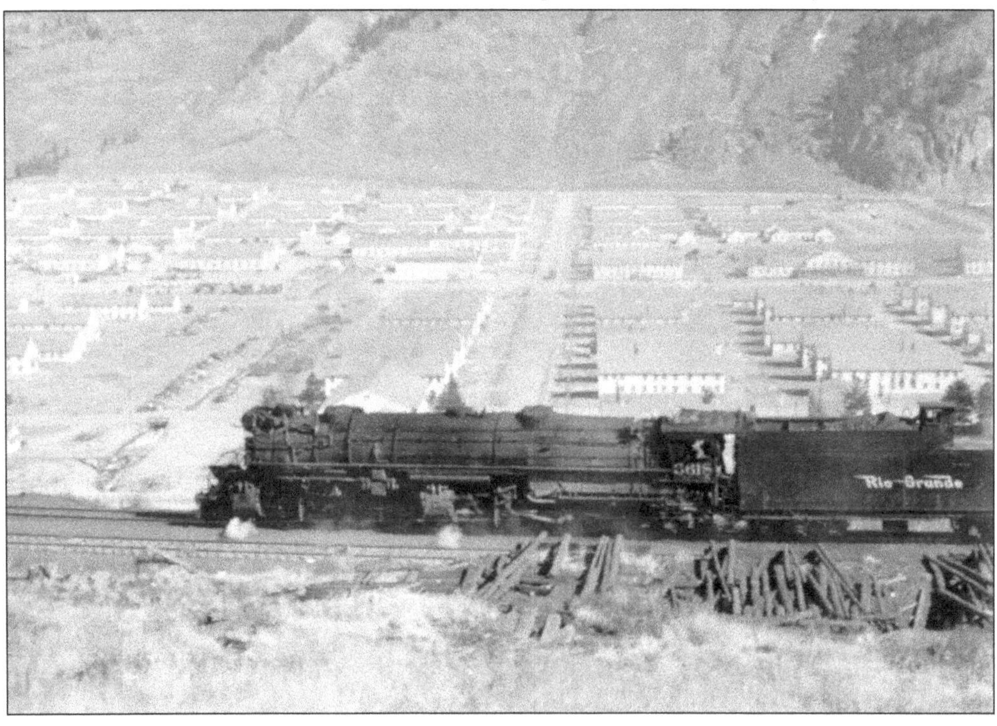

Seven

Men, Mules, and Machines

Because the 10th was designated a "light" division, it did not have the usual complement of trucks and jeeps that a regular infantry division had. Supplies and even the components of a 75mm pack howitzer had to be loaded onto six mules and carried into the high country where roads did not exist. Rodeo cowboys and mule skinners were recruited to train the animals to accept heavy loads and even riders.

Although they could be stubborn and cantankerous at times, the mules, once trained, were smart and hard-working. Unfortunately, when the division left for Italy in January 1945, the mules stayed behind in the United States, and the Army was forced to buy Italian mules that were much smaller and could not carry heavy loads.

Horses, too, were part of the division, and not just for ceremonial purposes. The 10th had a horse-mounted reconnaissance platoon. (Once in Italy, it conducted the US Army's last horse-mounted cavalry charge in battle.)

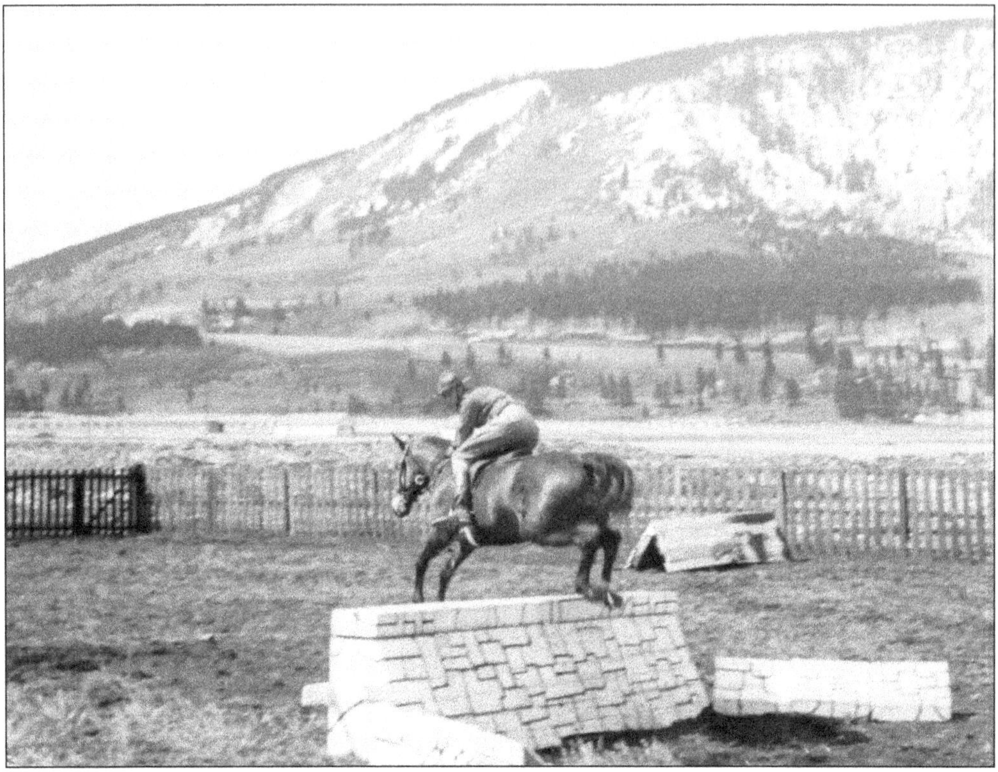

A number of 10th personnel were skilled equestrians, cowboys, mule skinners, and rodeo cowboys. Here, Col. Onslow Rolfe, 87th Mountain Infantry Regiment commander and a former cavalry officer, expertly guides his mount over a jump. (Courtesy of DPL.)

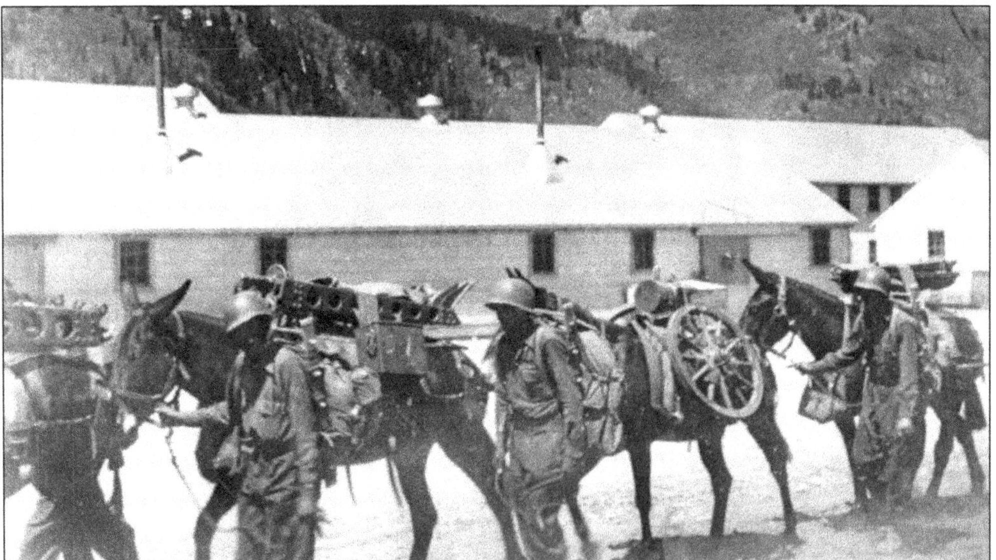

The 10th's units requiring the greatest number of mules were the three artillery battalions. A 75mm pack howitzer could be disassembled into six major components and loaded onto six mules. Here, members of an artillery battery lead a mule train with components of a gun strapped to their backs. Each mule was capable of carrying hundreds of pounds. (Courtesy of DPL.)

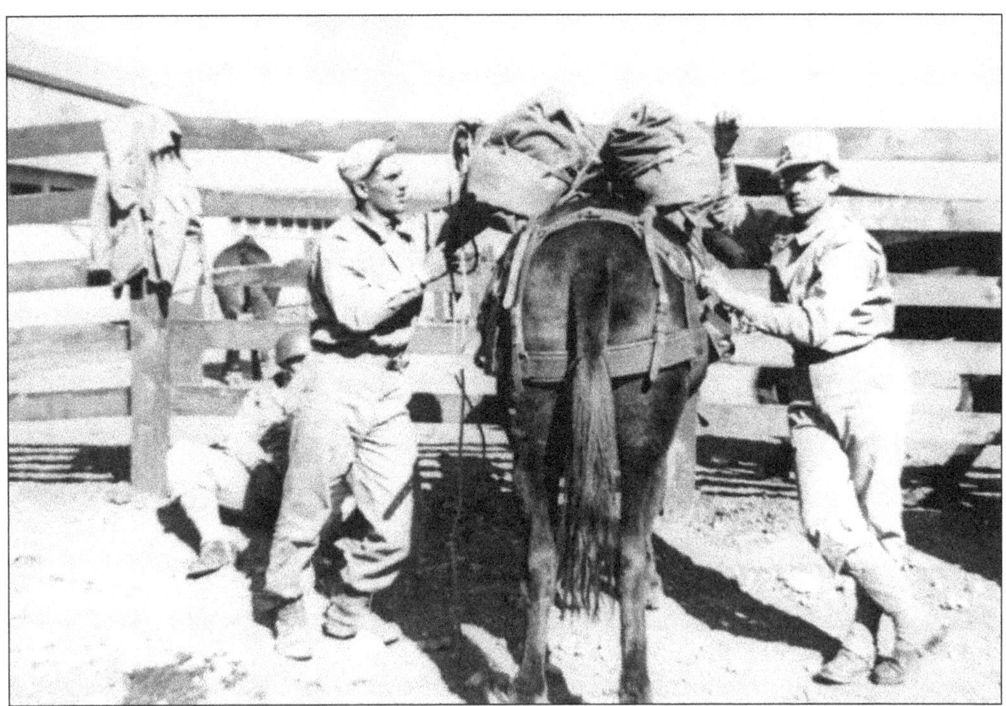

Members of the supply and artillery battalions were sent to "mule school" to learn how to handle, pack, and care for the animals. The mules were often "ornery" and resisted attempts to turn them into beasts of burden by biting and kicking their handlers. (Courtesy of HC.)

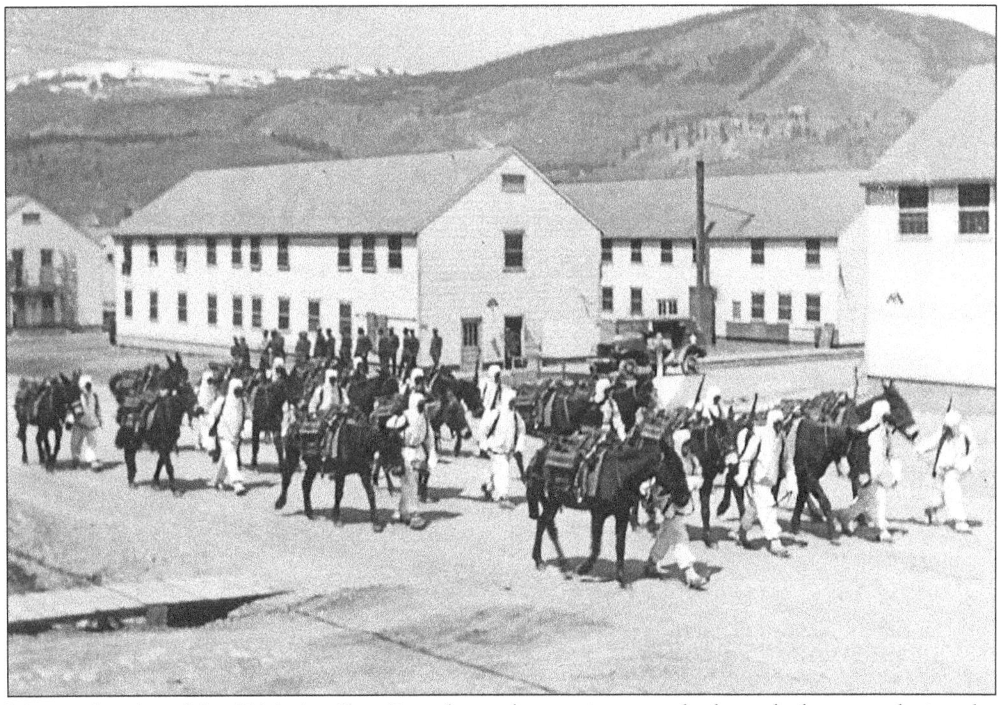

Men and mules of the 616th Artillery Battalion take part in a parade through the camp during the filming of *Mountain Fighters*, a recruiting film made by Warner Bros. in 1943. (Courtesy of DPL.)

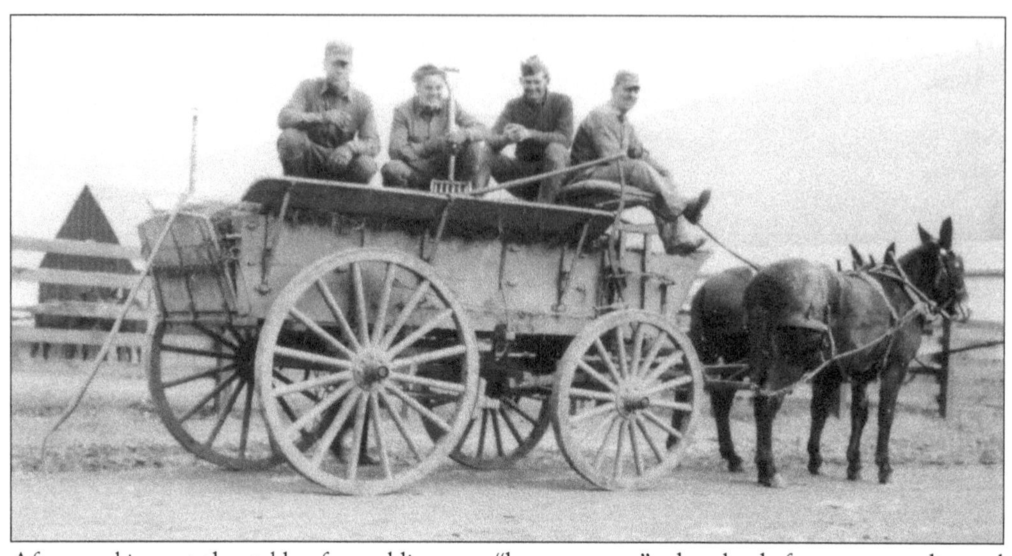

After mucking out the stables, four soldiers on a "honey wagon" take a load of manure to a disposal site. Cleaning up after the mules was a soldier's least-favorite duty. (Courtesy of DPL.)

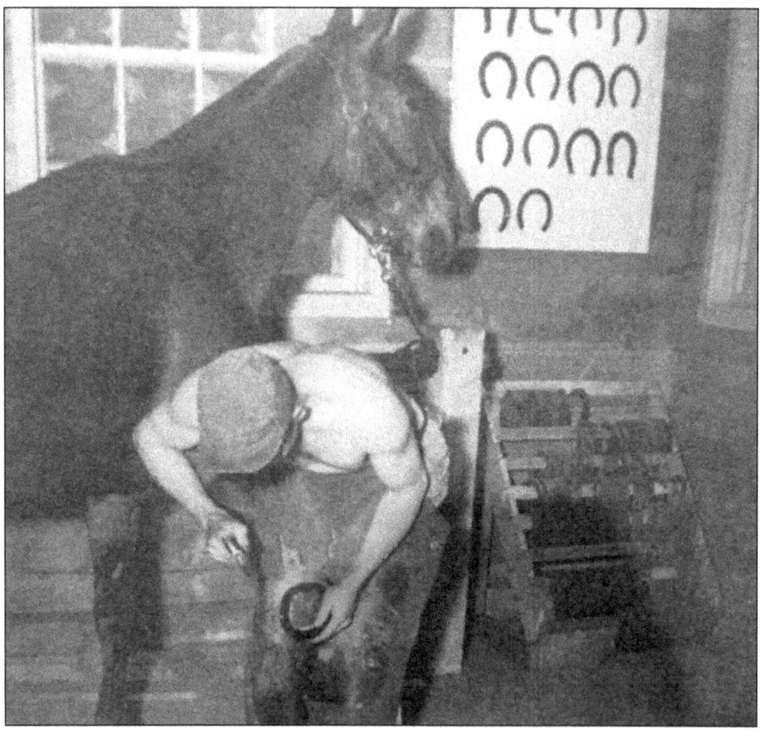

A farrier shoes a mule in the camp's blacksmith shop. With 3,000–4,000 mules and horses, the 10th's wranglers, blacksmiths, and veterinarians were kept very busy. The large number of animals was one reason why the Army had a problem deciding where to deploy the division. (Courtesy of DPL.)

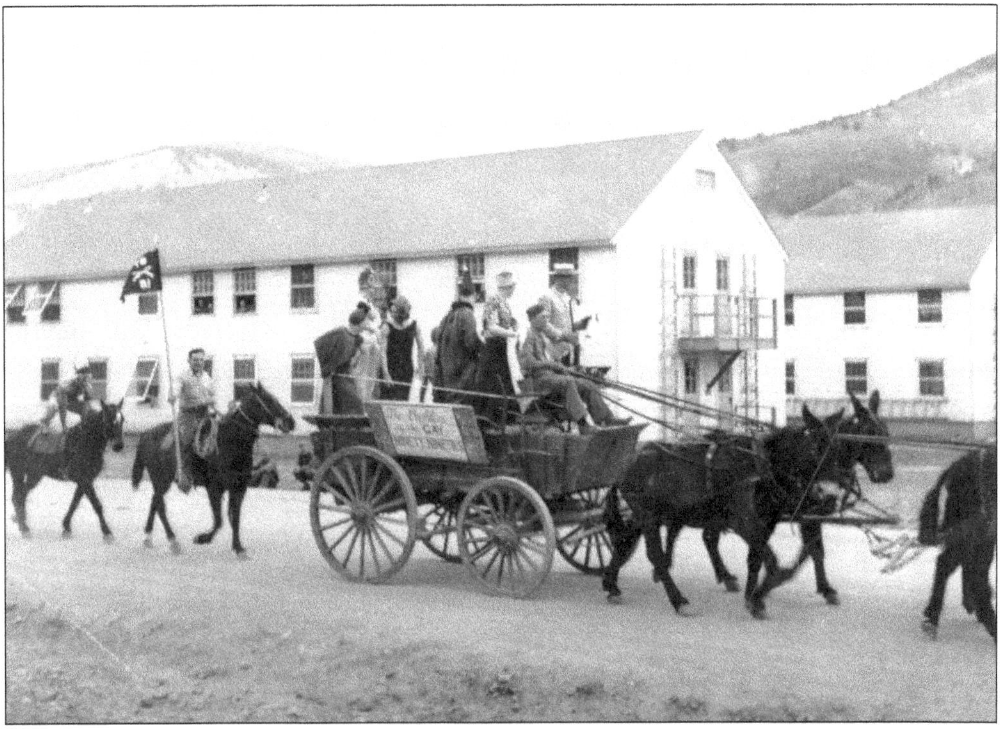

Like a scene out of the Old West, a mule team pulls a wagon full of costumed revelers of the all-Norwegian 99th Infantry Battalion during a Mardi Gras parade. (Courtesy of HC.)

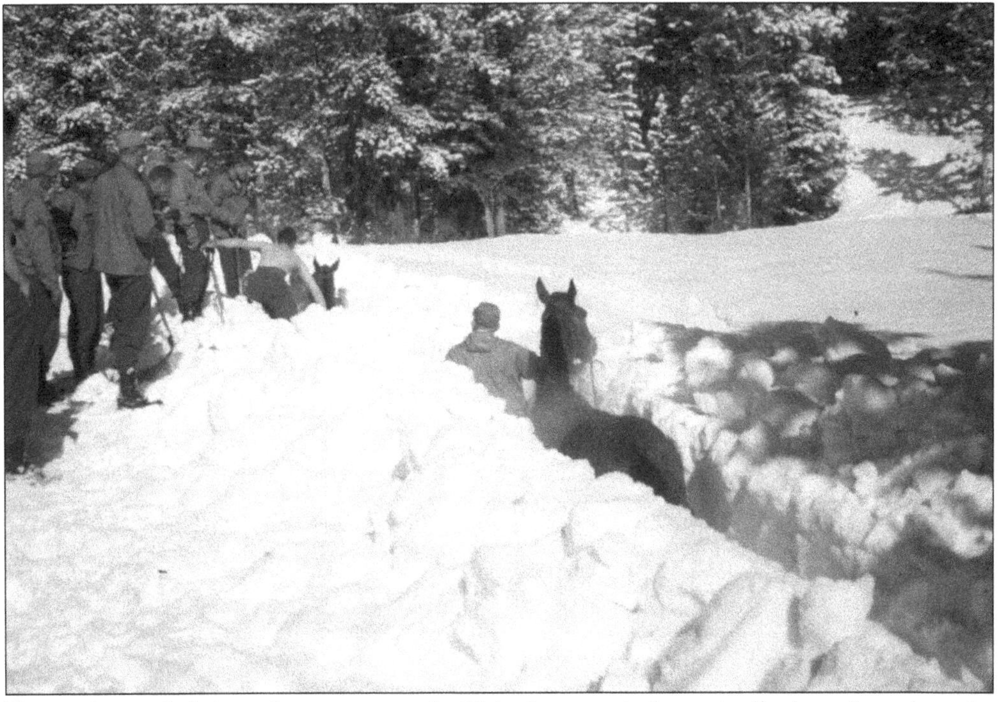

Two mules are led through a snow trench. This photograph dramatically shows how deep the snow at Camp Hale could get—an annual average of 250 inches. (Courtesy of DPL.)

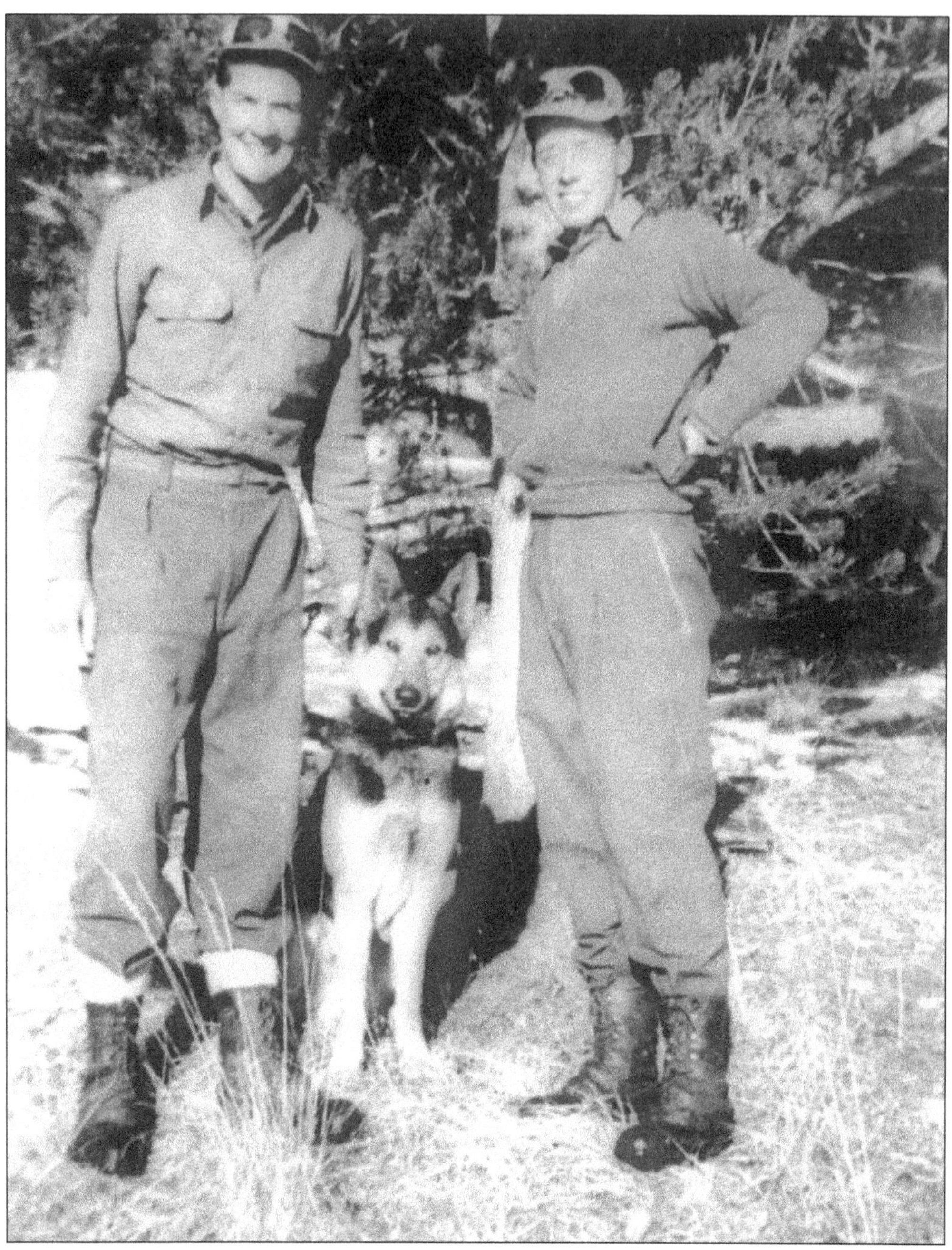

Besides mules and horses, the 10th also had scores of dogs—mostly German shepherds and huskies. The German shepherds were used for messenger, sentry, and attack duty, while the huskies were used to pull sleds. Here, two 10th men, wearing waterproof ShoePacs, pose next to their dog Monty. The dogs were loyal and made great companions, but many suffered from discipline problems. (Courtesy of HC.)

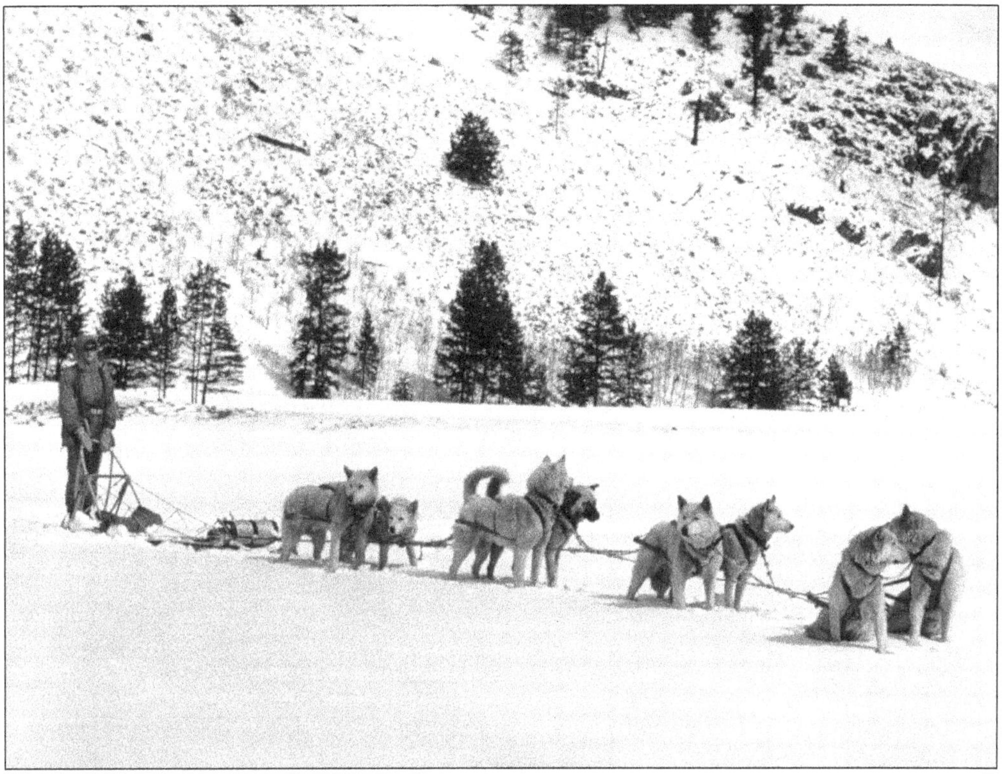

Some dogs were trained to pull sleds over the snow. Here, an eight-dog husky team waits for its handler to order them to proceed. (Courtesy of DPL.)

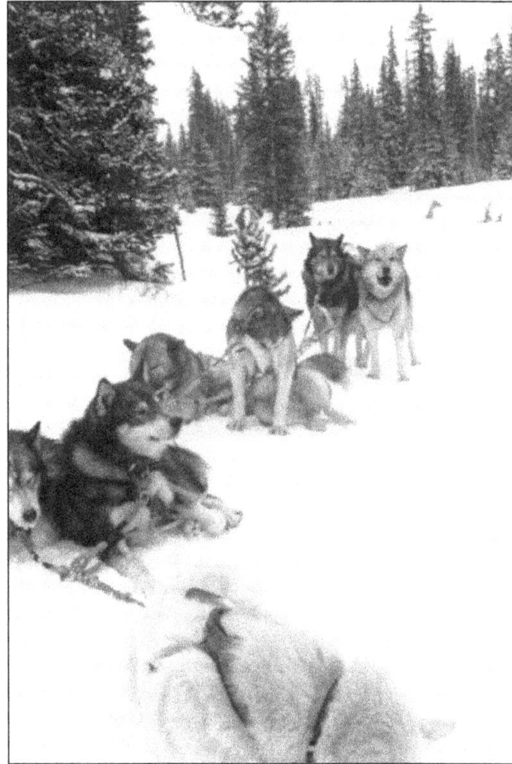

A team of huskies rest after a dash across a snow field. Like the men, the dogs needed time to acclimate to the camp's high altitude. (Courtesy of DPL.)

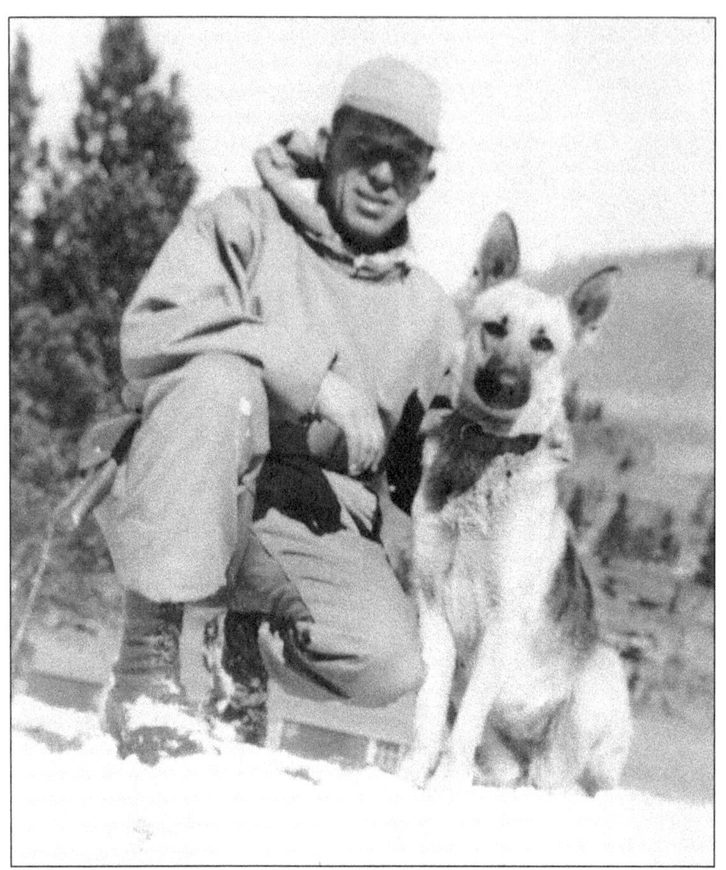

Strong bonds were forged between the dogs and their handlers, but their time together was cut short due to disciplinary problems with the animals. (Courtesy of DPL.)

Unfortunately, according to at least one trooper, the dogs hated the mules and would frequently chase them; many dogs and mules were injured in these encounters. The dogs were sent back to the military dog-training center at Front Royal, Virginia, for retraining—and never returned. (Courtesy of DPL.)

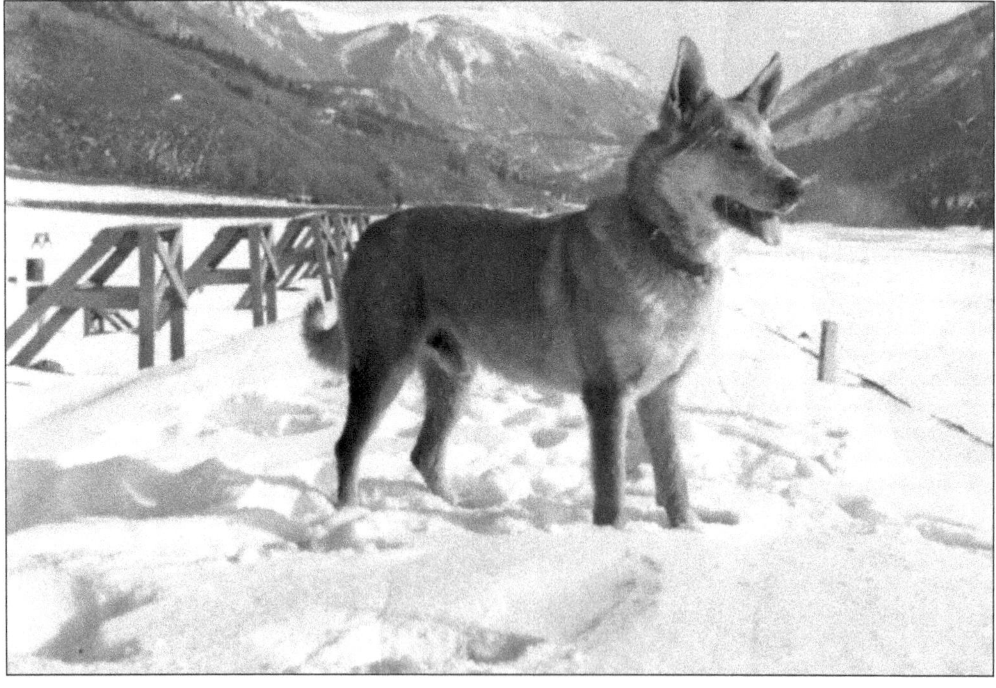

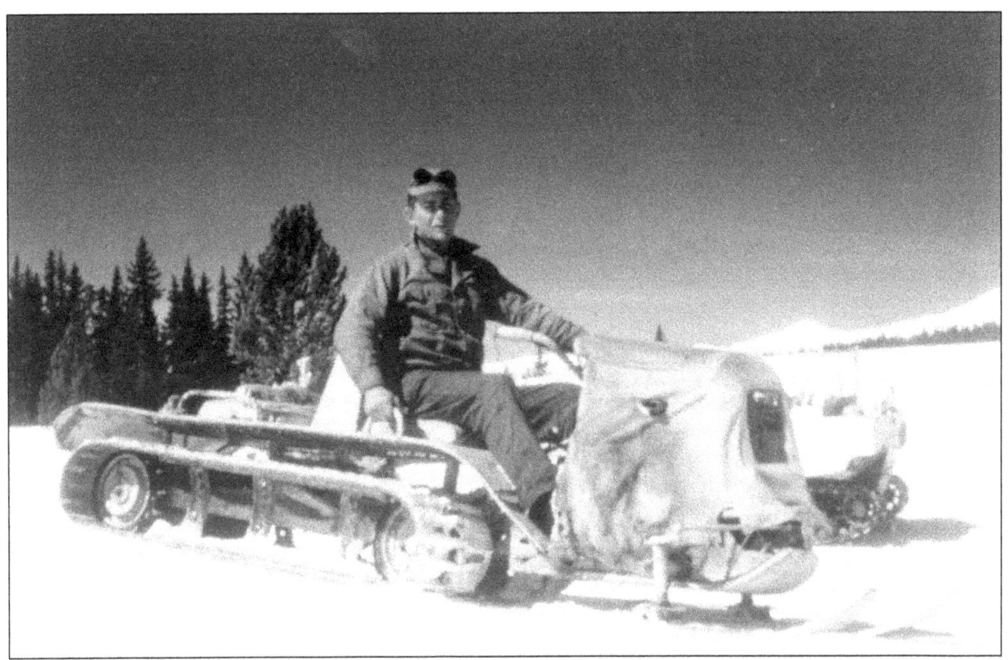

While dog teams could pull light loads over the snow, the 10th needed something capable of carrying and pulling heavier loads. The Army sent a variety of different over-snow vehicles to Camp Hale to be tested. This early experimental model of a snowmobile had wide tracks to help it glide over snow, but it was too underpowered. (Courtesy of DPL.)

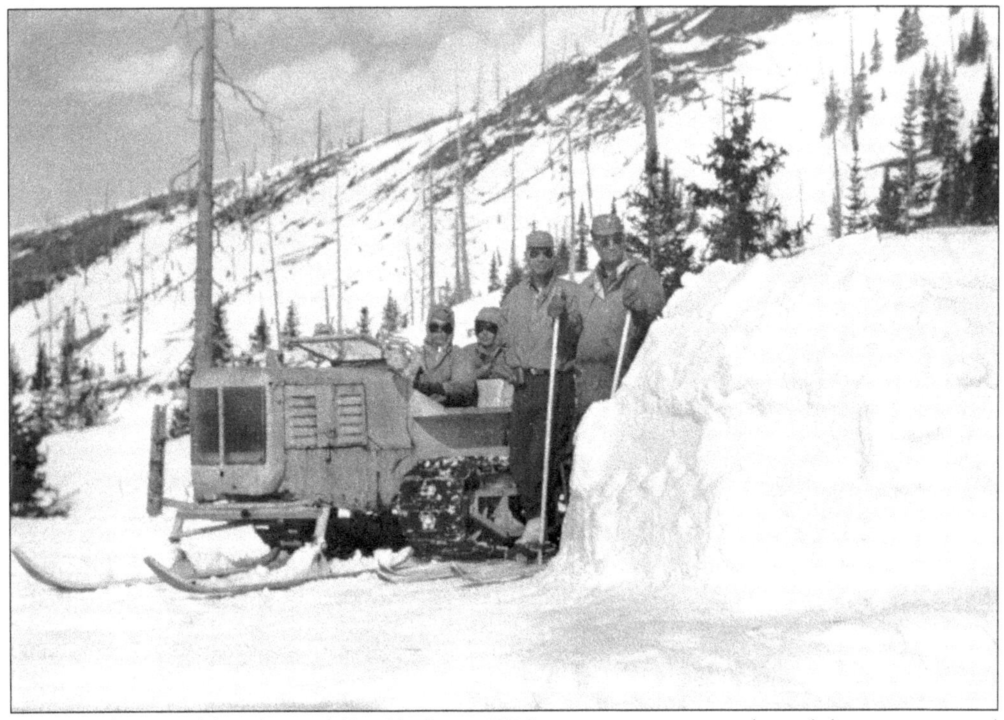

Men on skis stand beside an Allis-Chalmers T-26 snow tractor—another of the experimental vehicles that the 10th tested for the Army. (Courtesy of DPL.)

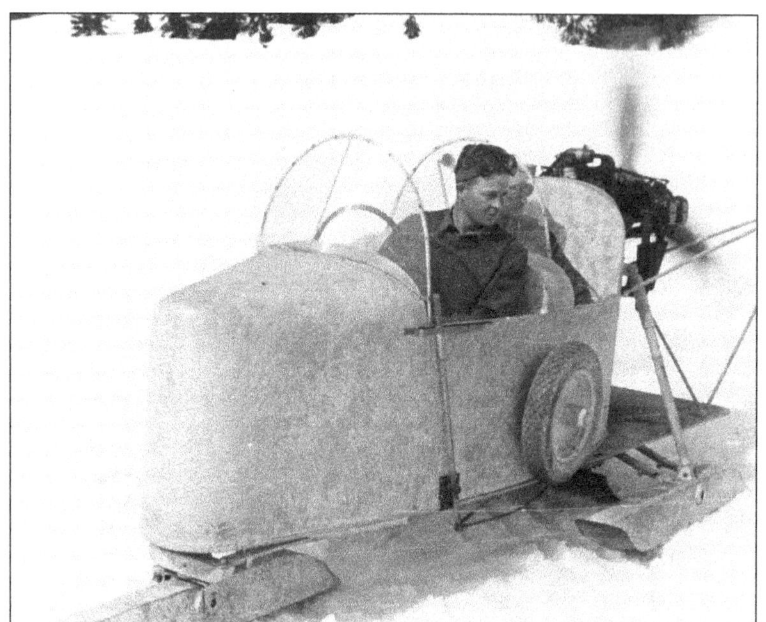

This odd contraption used a rear-mounted propeller to push it across the snow but was rejected for being too small and impractical. (Courtesy of DPL.)

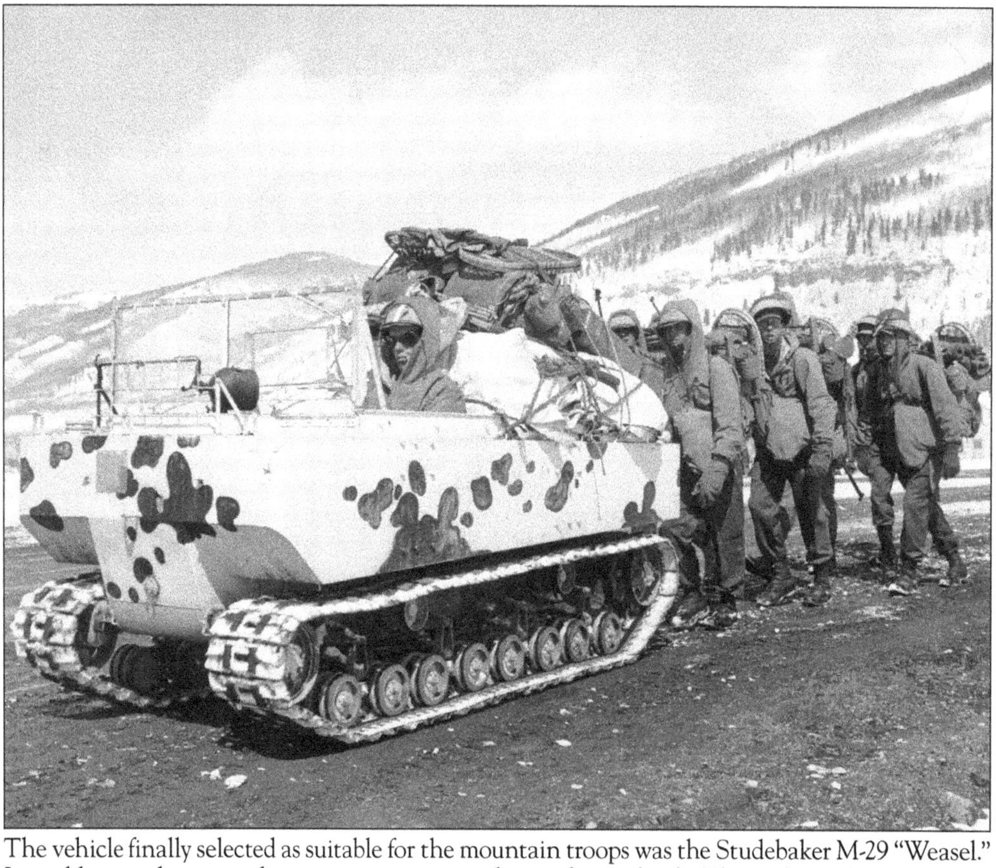

The vehicle finally selected as suitable for the mountain troops was the Studebaker M-29 "Weasel." It could carry three people, tow many more, and carry heavy loads. The wide tracks also kept it from sinking into anything less than the softest, deepest snow. (Courtesy of DPL.)

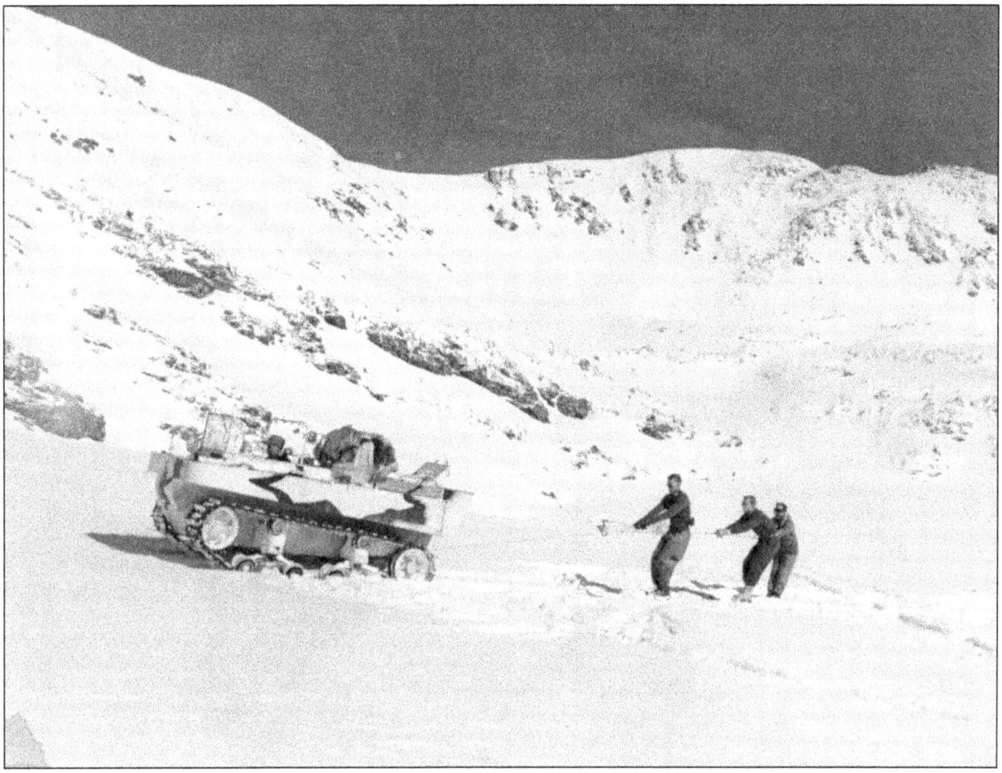

Three skiers get a lift uphill behind a Weasel. The Studebaker-manufactured vehicle had a 70-horsepower engine and a top speed of 36 miles per hour. (Courtesy of DPL.)

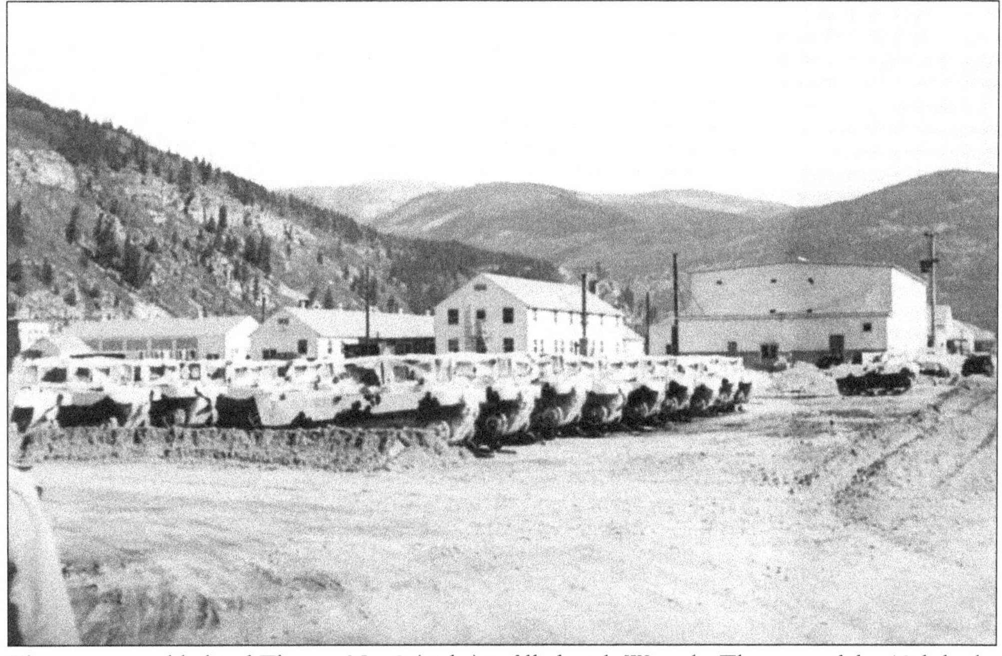

The motor pool behind Theater No. 2 (right) is filled with Weasels. The men of the 10th had a love-hate relationship with the machines—just as they did with the mules. (Courtesy of DPL.)

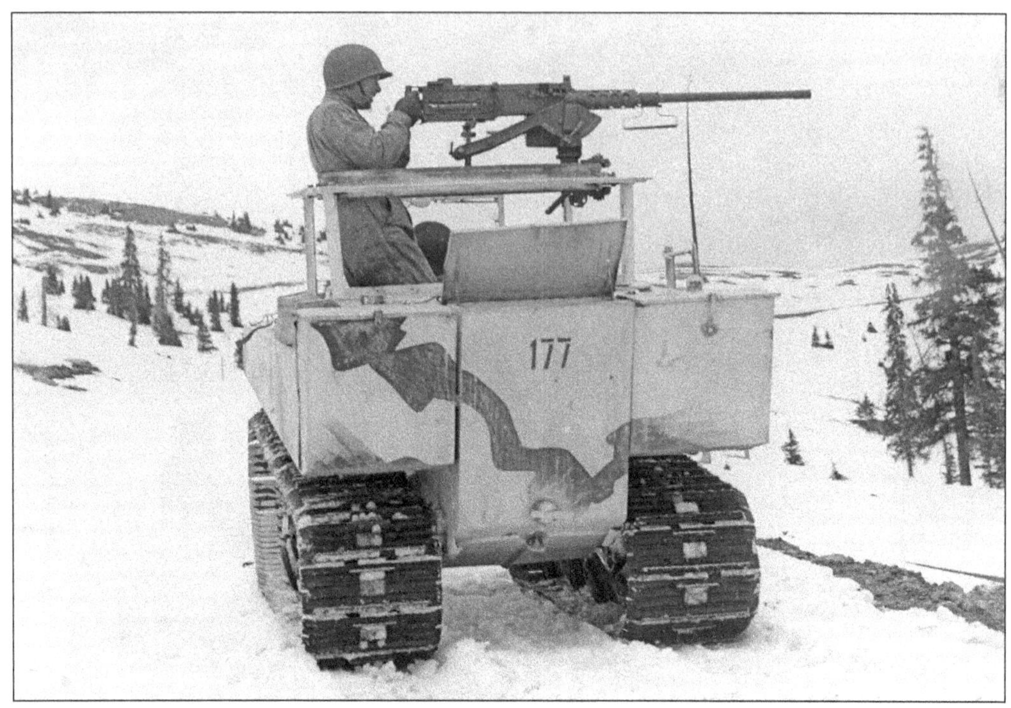

One of the Weasel's strengths was its extreme versatility. Here, an M-29 is fitted with a powerful .50-caliber machine gun, the same type of weapon that American tanks and aircraft were armed with. (Courtesy of DPL.)

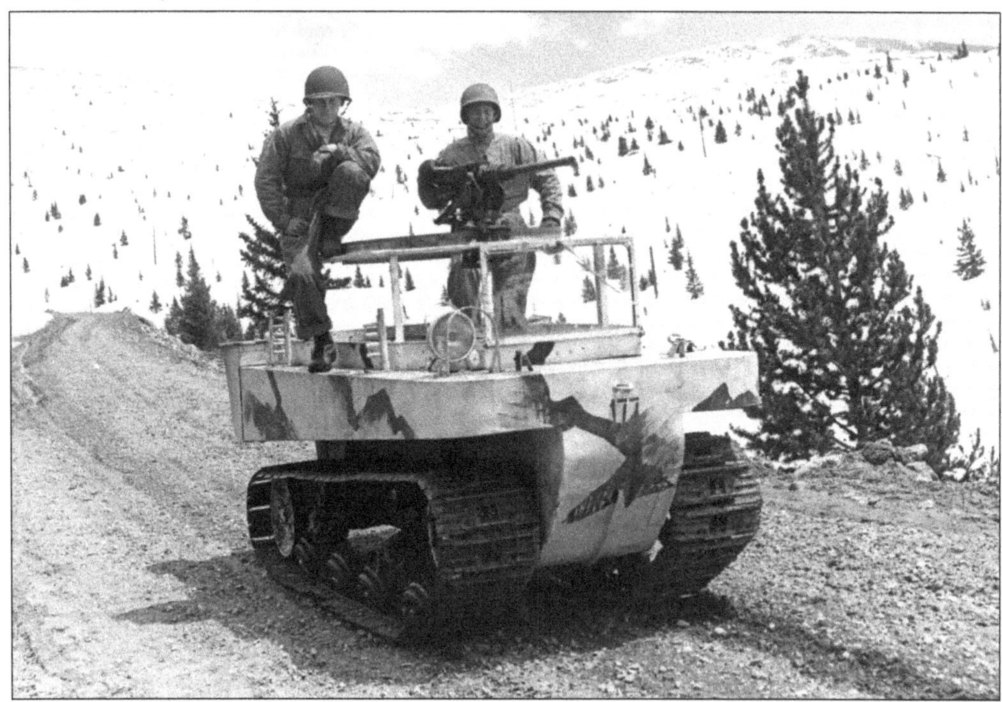

The same vehicle shown above is seen in a front view. Few, if any, Weasels were sent to Italy when the division shipped out in early 1945. (Courtesy of DPL.)

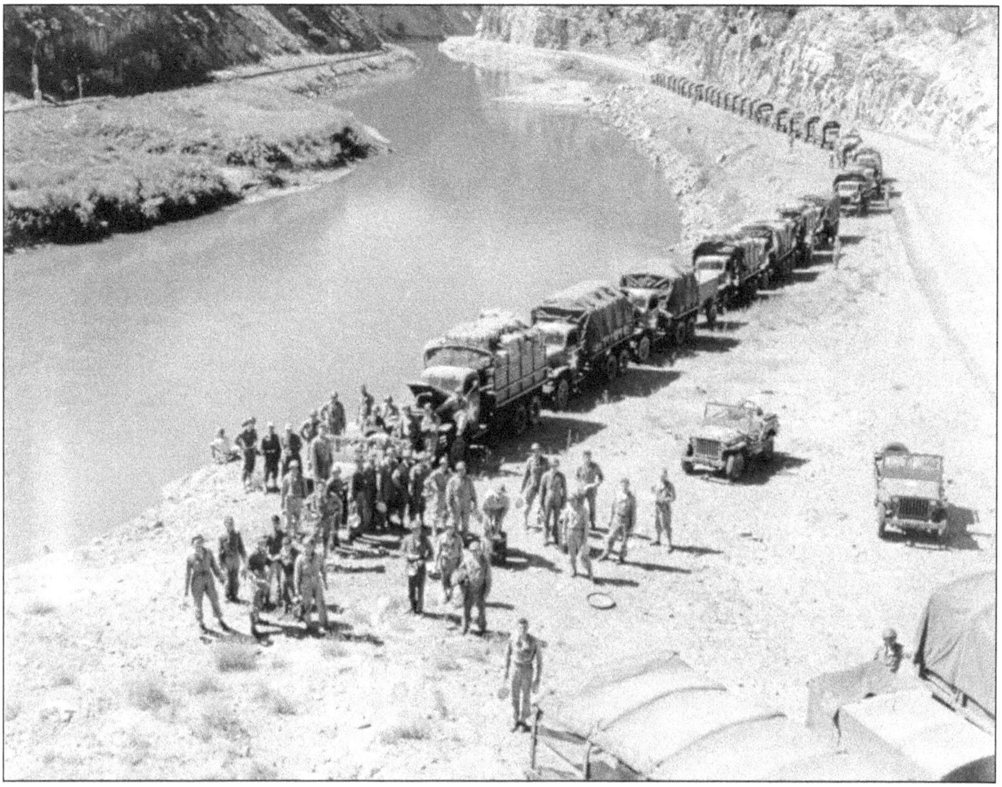

A long convoy of Army trucks from Camp Hale stop along the banks of the Colorado River in November 1943. The destination and purpose of this convoy are unknown. (Courtesy of DPL.)

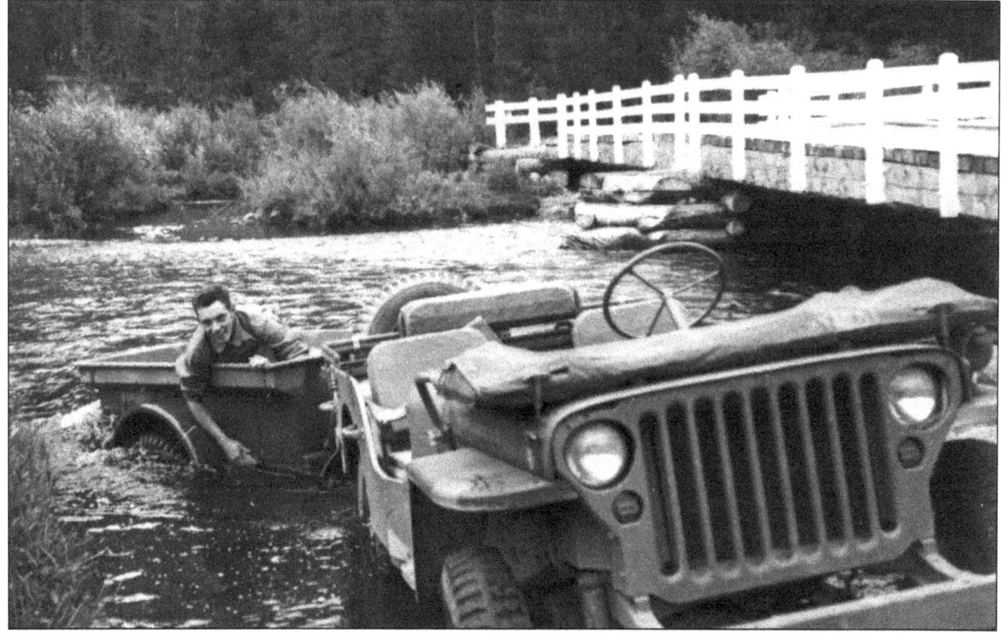

The ubiquitous jeep was also used extensively at Camp Hale. Here, a driver washes mud from his jeep and trailer in the Eagle River. (Courtesy of DPL.)

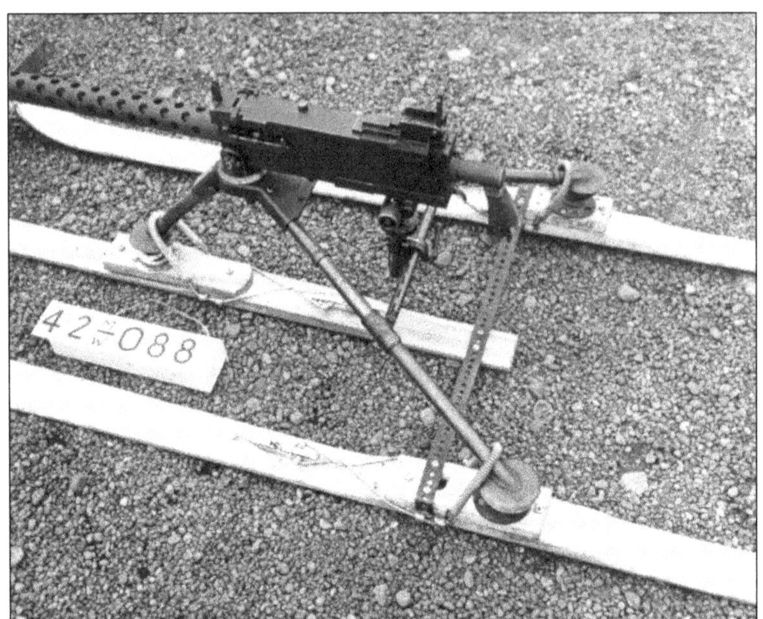

Always thinking of new and more efficient ways to operate in snow, the 10th tested the idea of mounting a .30-caliber machine gun on a sled made from three modified skis. (Courtesy of DPL.)

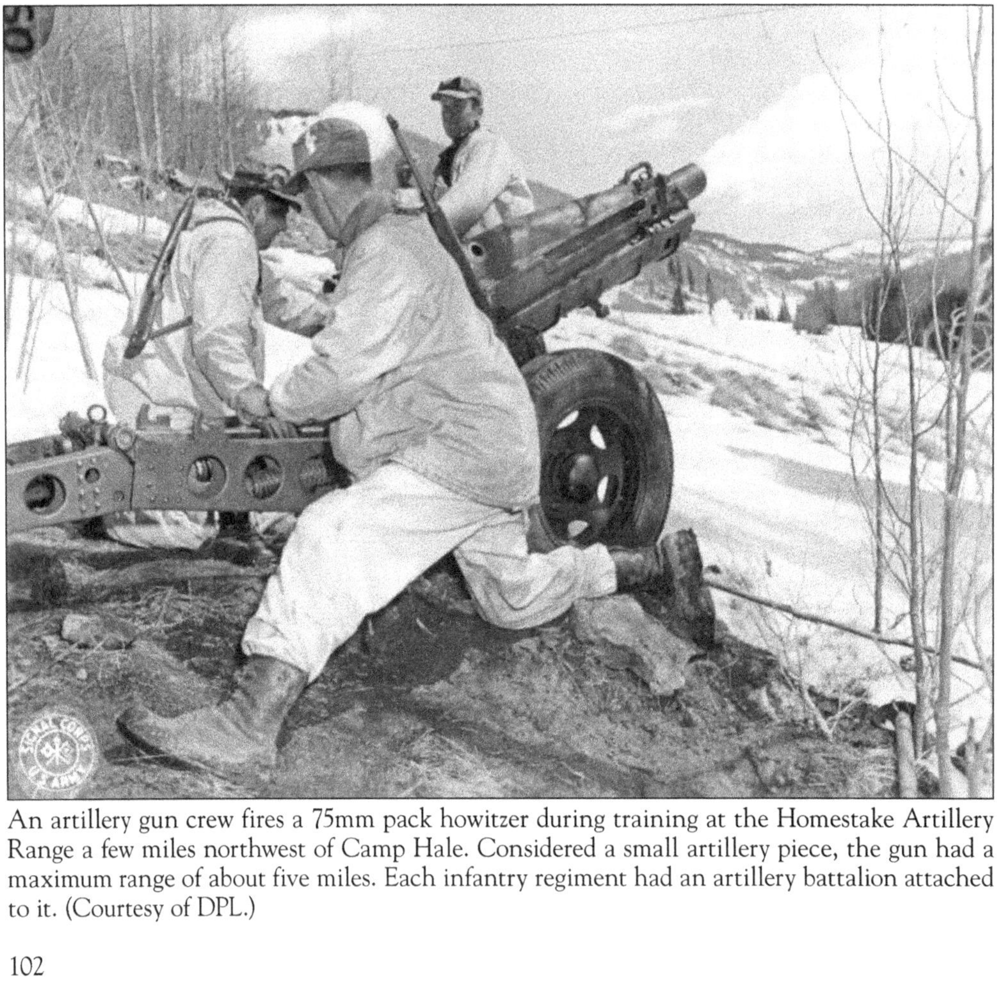

An artillery gun crew fires a 75mm pack howitzer during training at the Homestake Artillery Range a few miles northwest of Camp Hale. Considered a small artillery piece, the gun had a maximum range of about five miles. Each infantry regiment had an artillery battalion attached to it. (Courtesy of DPL.)

The 10th soldiers were trained and cross-trained in a variety of weapons. Here, two men in a snow pit adjust the sights on a 60mm mortar during maneuvers. (Courtesy of DPL.)

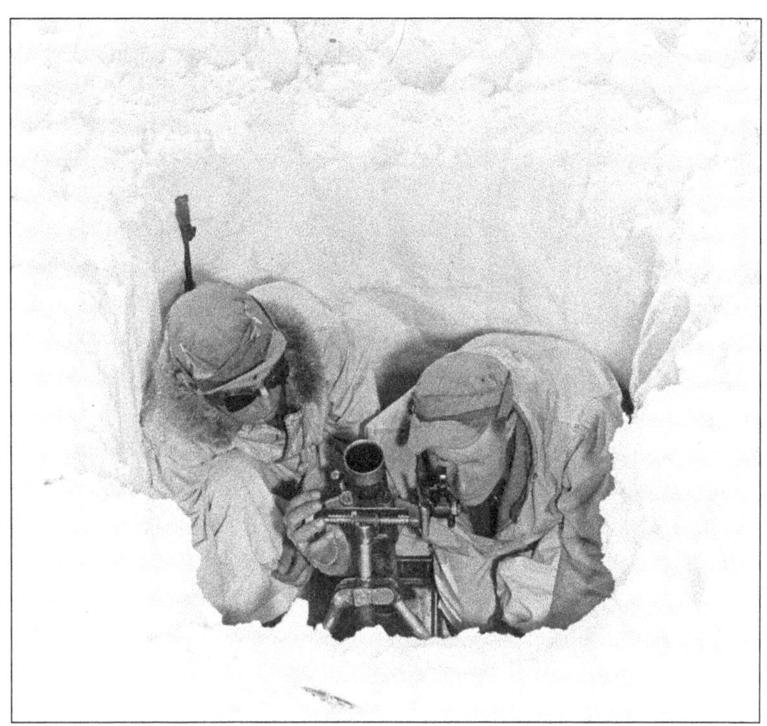

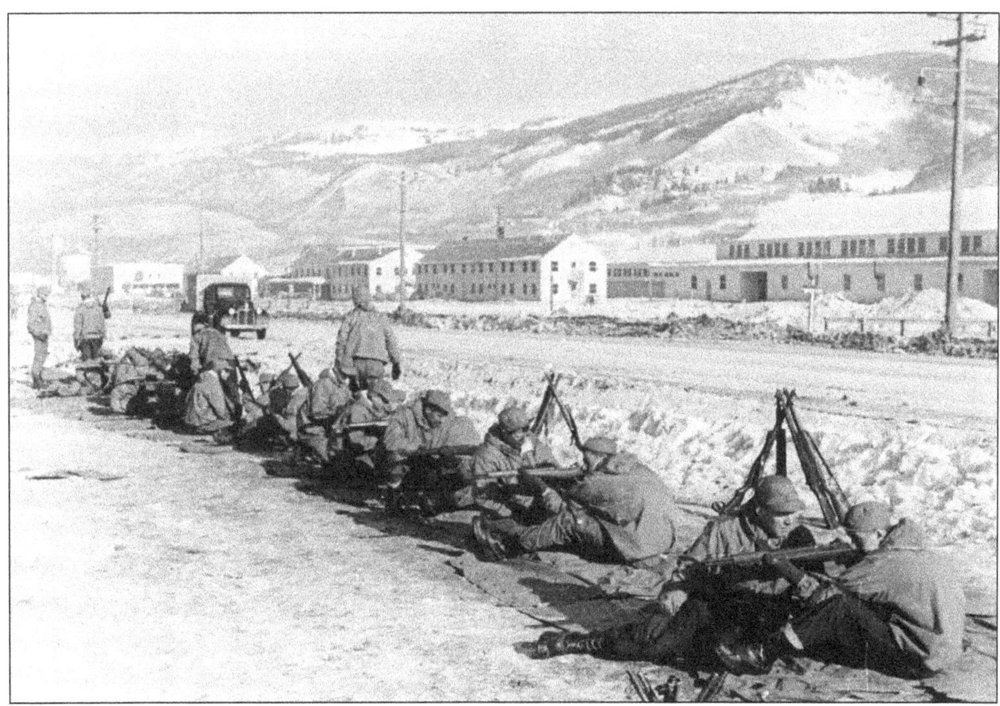

A line of mountain troopers pose for a publicity photo as though they are on the rifle range, which in reality was a mile from where this photograph was taken. (Courtesy of DPL.)

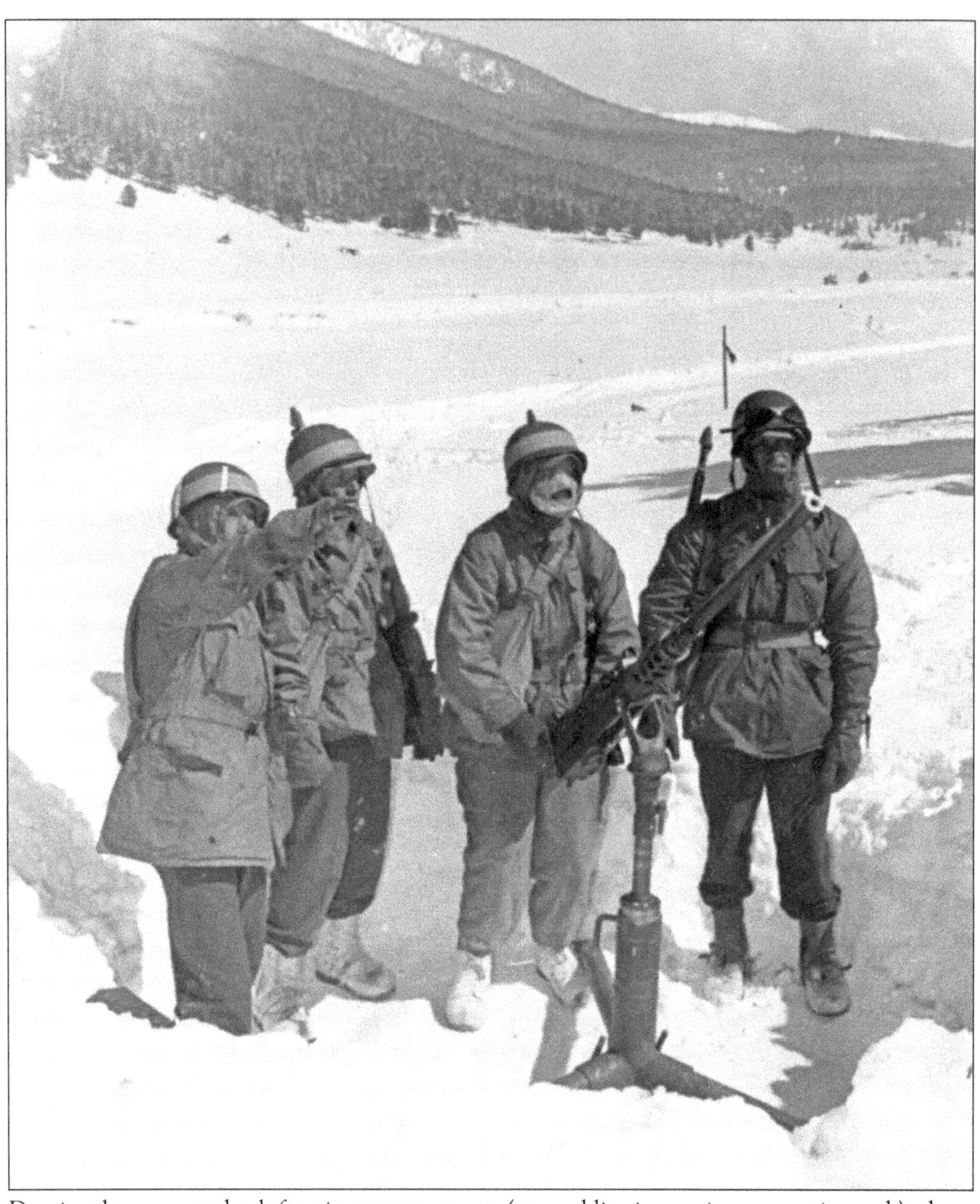

Despite the snow and sub-freezing temperatures (one soldier is wearing an arctic mask), these members of the anti-aircraft unit hone their skills. In combat in Italy, the division did not have the occasion to use their anti-aircraft training, as the German air force, the Luftwaffe, was practically nonexistent by then. (Courtesy of DPL.)

Eight

Hale's Neighbors

Besides being the highest Army post in terms of elevation, Camp Hale was also one of the most isolated. Without occasional breaks in their training routine, soldiers can quickly suffer burnout. Although helpful for maintaining morale, the recreational facilities at Camp Hale did not compensate for the soldiers' needs to get away every now and then and enjoy a non-military environment.

Only three nearby small towns offered this chance to escape the regimentation of camp life: Leadville, Red Cliff, and Minturn. Of the three, Leadville, which had been a fabulously wealthy gold- and silver-mining town in the 1800s, was the largest. Its streets, which looked like they were from some Western movie set, were lined with saloons, and a thriving red-light district flourished on the back streets. As a consequence, the Army frequently placed Leadville off-limits—meaning that Camp Hale soldiers were subject to arrest by the military police if discovered there.

The other two nearby towns were tiny by comparison and lacked Leadville's rowdy decadence. Soldiers with weekend passes often drove or took the train into Denver, 100 miles to the east.

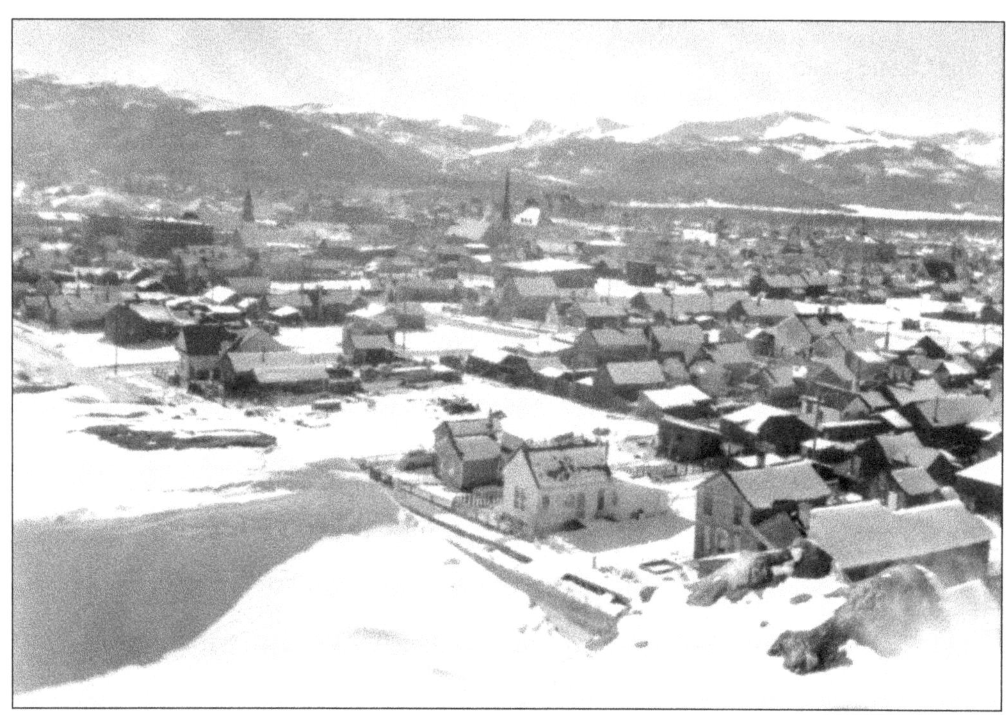

Looking peaceful under a dusting of snow, Leadville, at 10,152 feet above sea level, could be a rowdy and sometimes dangerous place. (Courtesy of LCCC.)

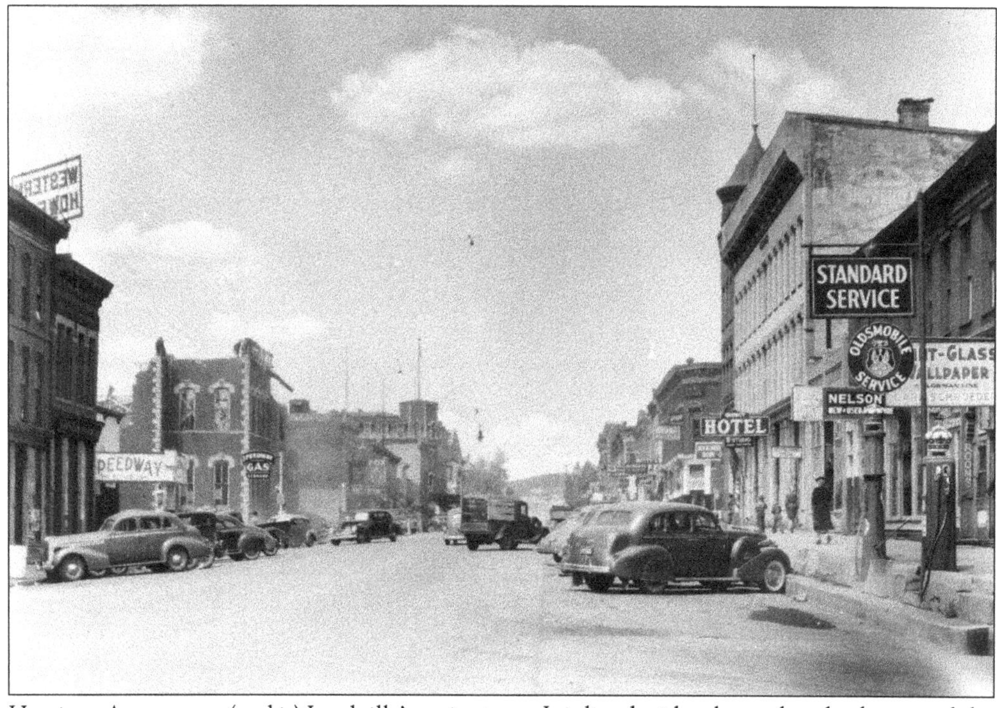

Harrison Avenue was (and is) Leadville's main street. It is lined with saloons, hotels, shops, and the Tabor Grand Opera House, a cultural landmark. At left, behind the Speedway sign, are the remains of the Lake County Courthouse that was destroyed by fire on July 3, 1942. (Courtesy of LCPL.)

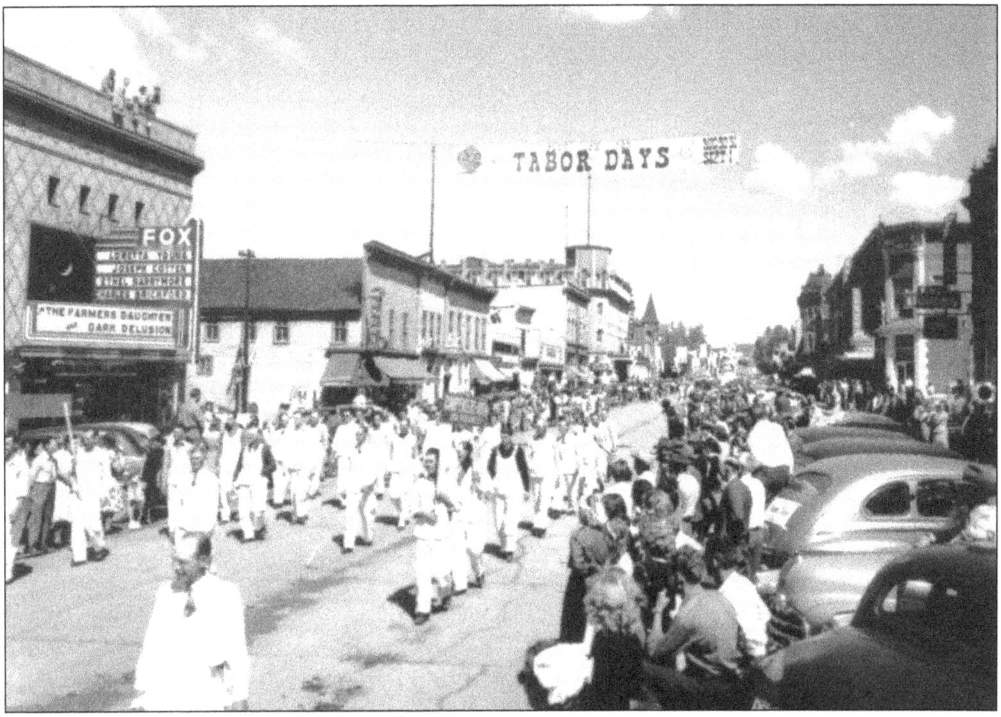

One of Leadville's longtime traditions was Tabor Days, a celebration of the influence of H.A.W. Tabor, the town's richest benefactor in the 1880s. Here, the 1943 Tabor Days parade marches down Harrison Avenue. (Courtesy of LCCC.)

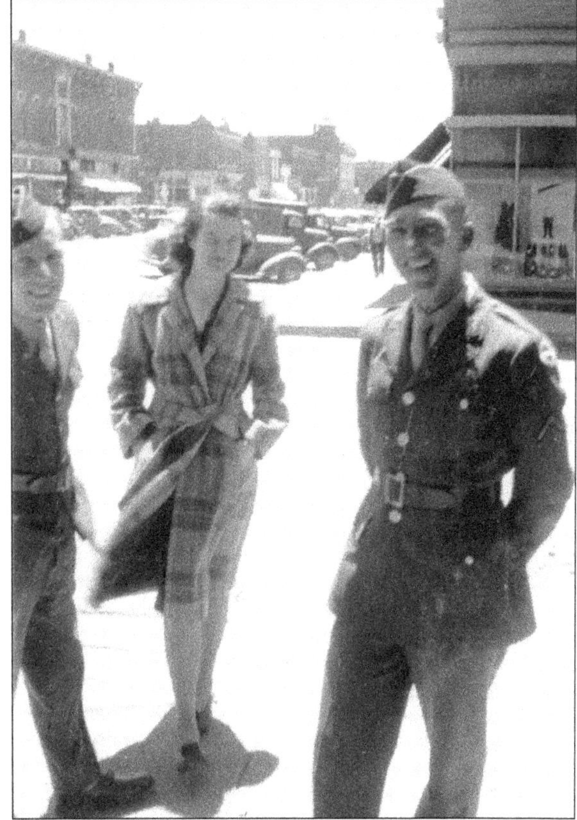

Two Camp Hale soldiers and a female friend smile for the camera in downtown Leadville. The saloon-rich town was frequently placed off-limits to soldiers due to crime and the rowdy behavior of some troops. (Courtesy of LCPL.)

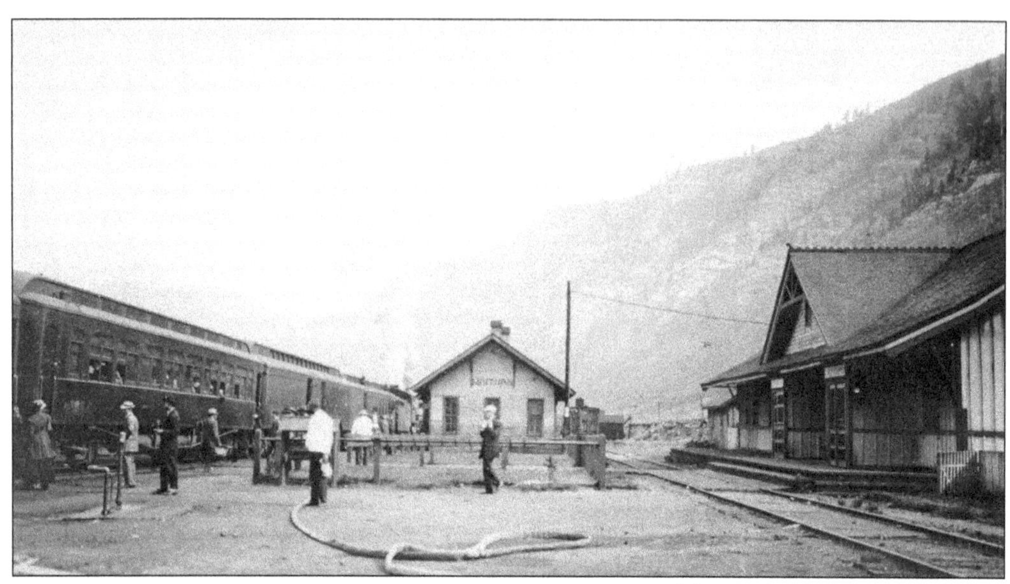

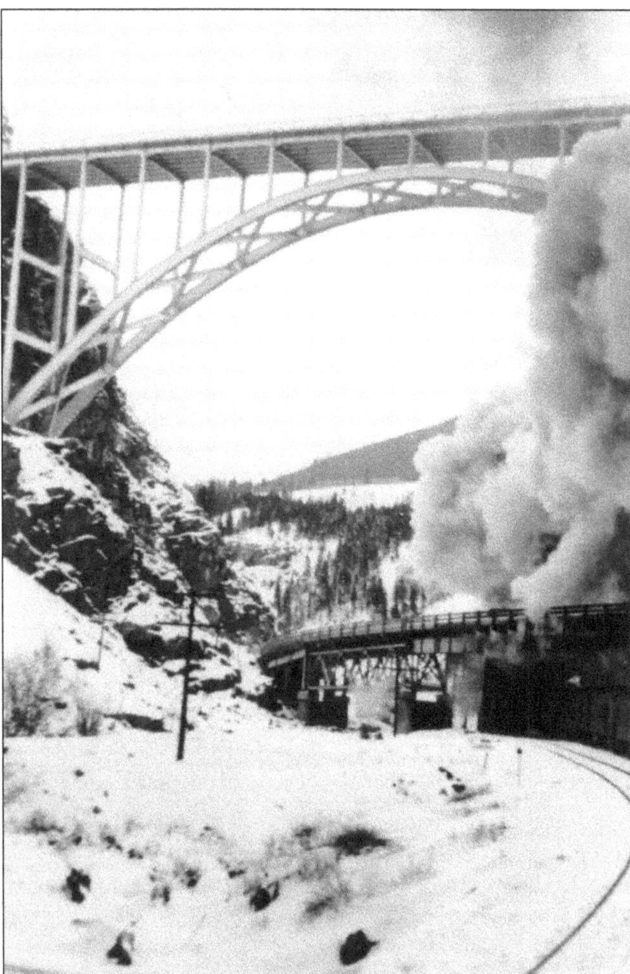

Thirteen miles north of Camp Hale is the railroad town of Minturn, incorporated in 1904. Although it was an essential crossroads for the mountain railroad system during Colorado's mining heyday, it had few amenities for soldiers wishing to spend some time off from training. (Courtesy of HC.)

As prosperous as Minturn was Red Cliff, six miles north of Camp Hale and tucked into a side canyon along Turkey Creek, a tributary of the Eagle River. It was settled in 1879 and was the Eagle County seat before the town of Eagle got that honor. Here, a train passes beneath the spectacular arched bridge, built in 1940 and still standing over Turkey Creek at Red Cliff. (Courtesy of Rouene Brown.)

Nine

Hollywood Comes to Hale

Wanting to attract more volunteers for the mountain troops, the US Army contracted with the Hollywood movie studio Warner Bros. to make a 20-minute recruiting film that would be shown in theaters across the country. In March 1943, Warner Bros. arrived at Camp Hale with truckloads of movie-making equipment to begin the filming of *Mountain Fighters*.

The film was directed by B. Reeves Eason, who directed a number of B-pictures in the 1930s. Probably his greatest claim to fame (or infamy) was being the second-unit director of the spectacular chariot race in the original 1925 *Ben-Hur*, starring Ramon Navarro and Francis X. Bushman, during which a stuntman was killed. It was said that a hundred horses had to be put down because of injuries. Eason was nearly blacklisted.

No such tragedies struck the set of *Mountain Fighters*, and the production—with a cast of a thousand extras provided by the division—wrapped after a few weeks on location at Camp Hale.

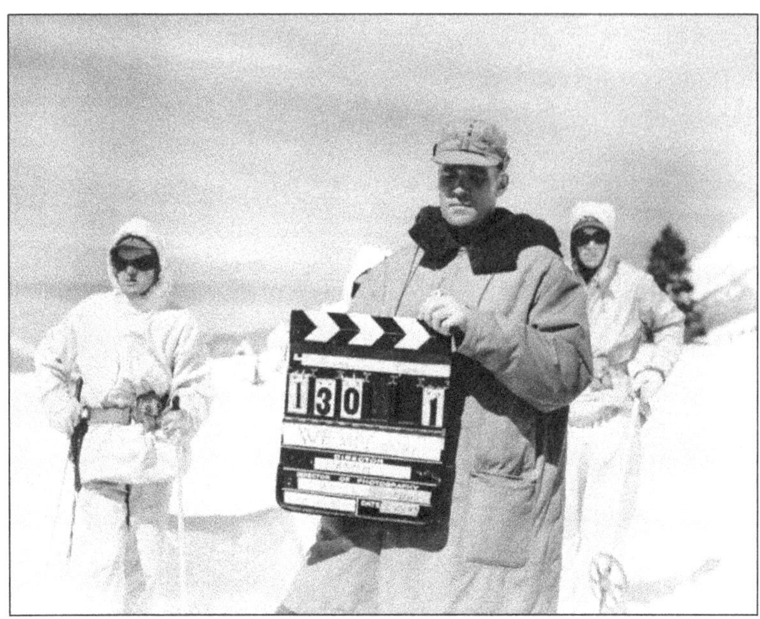

A Warner Bros. second assistant cameraman holds the clapperboard to mark the start of a scene in the snow above Camp Hale. (Courtesy of Rouene Brown.)

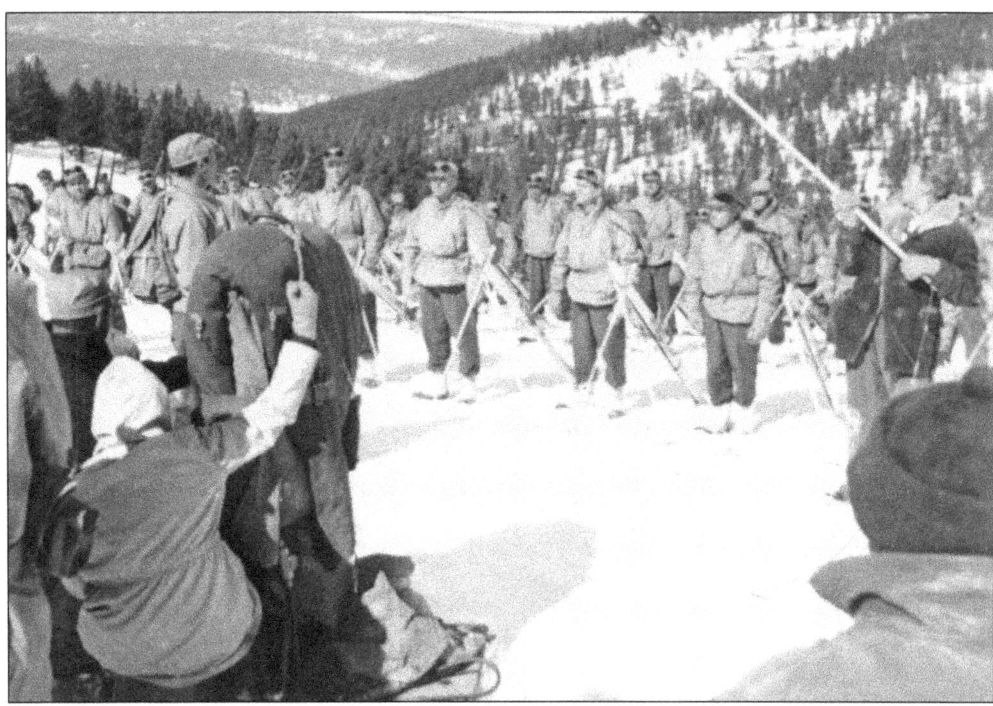

A cameraman (left foreground) operates a camera wrapped in a blanket to protect it from the cold, while a soundman (right) holds a boom microphone above an actor speaking his lines. (Courtesy of Rouene Brown.)

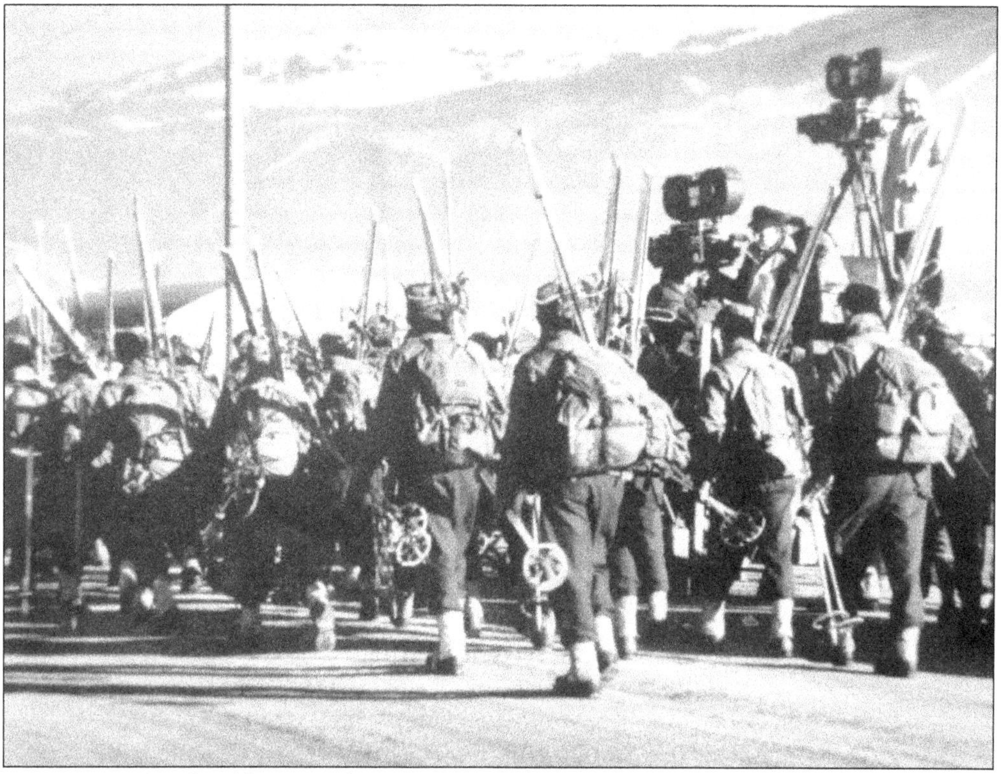

A company of 10th soldiers march past two Warner Bros. cameras. The filming provided a brief but pleasant diversion from the rigors of training and enabled the troopers to write home that they were now movie stars. (Courtesy of Rouene Brown.)

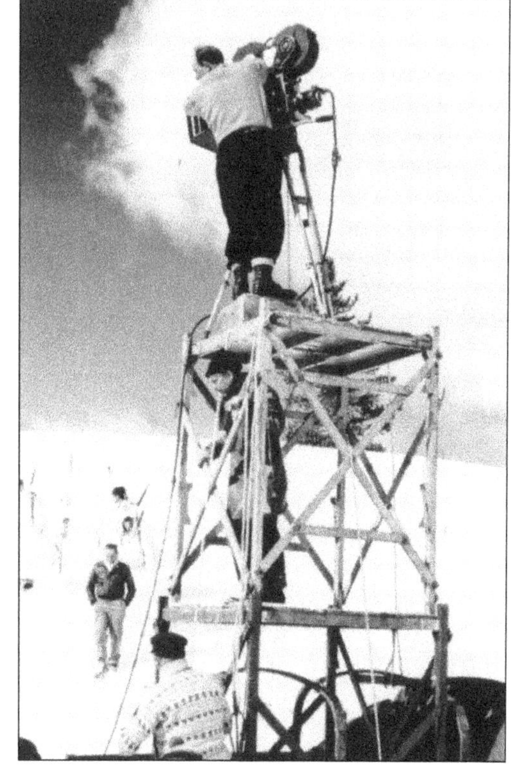

To get certain high-angle shots, the film crew constructed a platform for the cameraman. After Warner Bros. wrapped, a crew from Paramount Pictures arrived in November 1943 to shoot scenes at Camp Hale for its feature film *I Love a Soldier*, starring Paulette Goddard and Sonny Tufts. (Courtesy of Rouene Brown.)

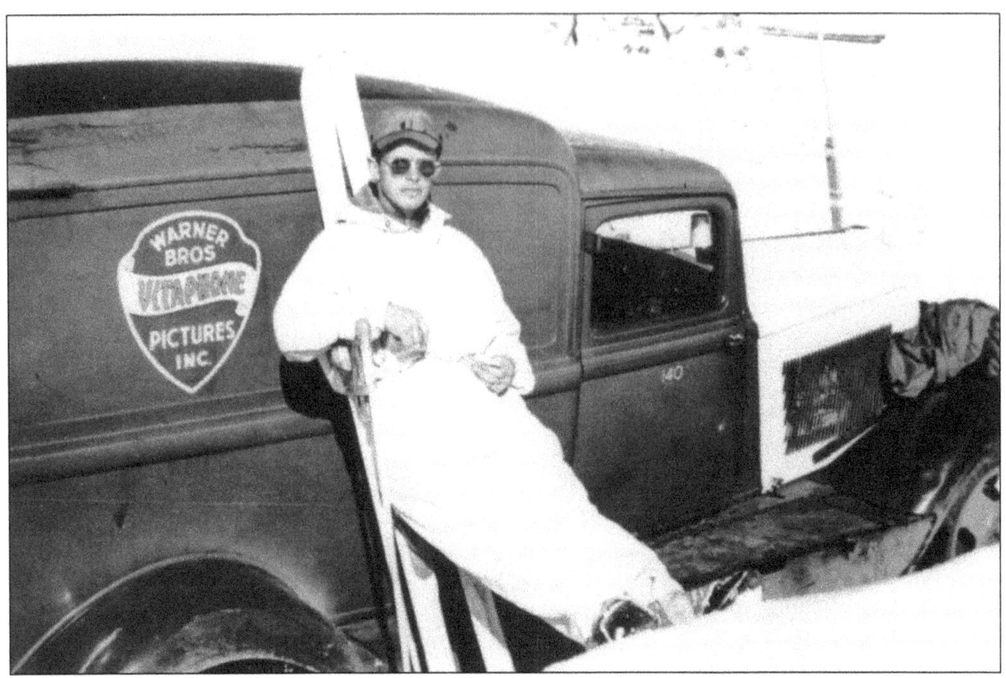

Between takes, a ski trooper relaxes against a truck bearing the logo "Warner Bros. Vitaphone Pictures Inc." Hundreds of 10th men became "extras" in the film. (Courtesy of Rouene Brown.)

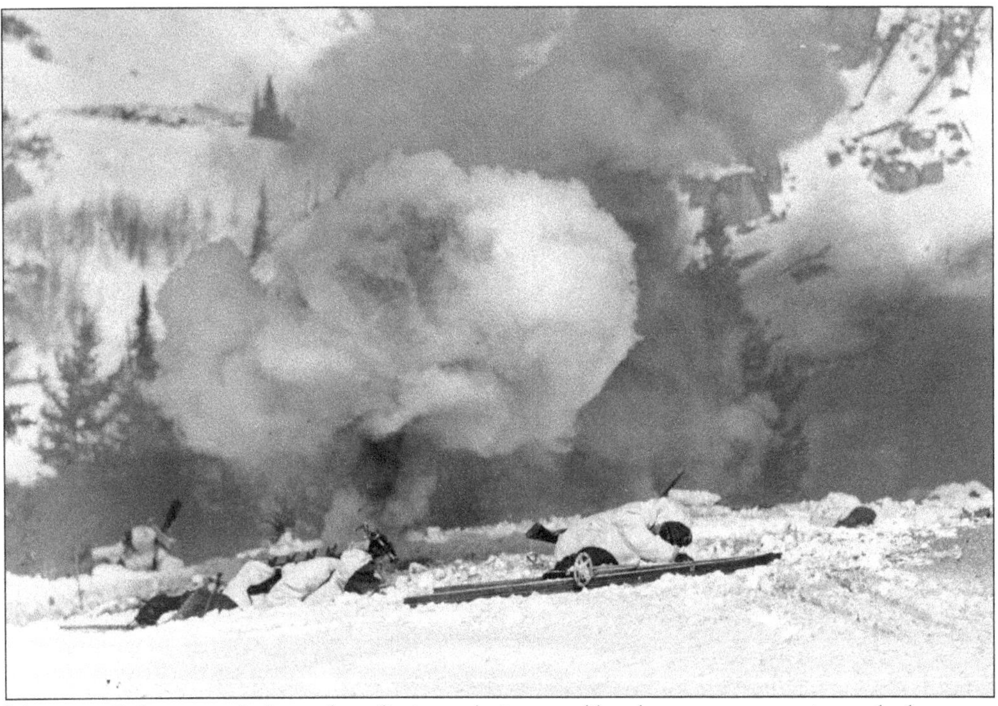

Mountain Fighters concludes with realistic explosions and battle scenes purporting to be between the 10th and a German unit. Even though the voiceover narrator says that the mountain troops "are engaging the enemy," it would be two more years before the 10th was sent into combat. (Courtesy of Rouene Brown.)

Ten

1944 AND BEYOND

The 10th Light Division presented a conundrum to the US Army. On one hand, the division was filled with some of the finest young men in any of the armed services. Because so many of them had attended or graduated from college (a relative rarity in those post-Depression days), their collective IQ was exceeded only by Army Air Force and US Navy pilots. Their months of training in the often-harsh environment of the high Colorado mountains had hardened their minds and bodies to an extent that few other American soldiers could match.

Yet there were serious negatives. The division was so specialized that it was unsuited to regular flatland combat. It had a lack of motor transport. The 75mm pack howitzers were fine for close-in mountain fighting but lacked the range and punch of the 105mm and 155mm artillery that the other infantry divisions could call upon. And then there was the issue of the mules and horses. They were, of course, essential for trekking through terrain that lacked roads, but they presented a logistical nightmare—requiring special feed, handling, and veterinary services.

The Army thought there were only two choices: either convert the 10th into a regular infantry division through re-training, or disband the division entirely and send the individuals as replacements to other divisions that had suffered heavy losses. So the Army decided to give the 10th the chance to prove its fighting mettle by scheduling it to take part in what was called the D-Series—a series of tests to determine its combat readiness. Starting on March 26, 1944, and lasting for three weeks, the men of the 10th departed Camp Hale and headed into the surrounding mountains to engage in maneuvers and field problems that would test their mettle.

While Army umpires watched, the men set up camps in the wilderness and endured a fierce spring blizzard and temperatures that dropped to negative 40 degrees Fahrenheit. Described as the toughest training any division ever experienced, D-Series caused 30 percent of the participants to be hospitalized for frostbite, snow-blindness, exhaustion, broken bones, and other cold-related injuries. Afterward, one soldier grumbled, "I think the Army was trying to kill us all."

Unfortunately, there was also a tragedy. A live mortar round was fired and landed in a company command post, killing one mountain trooper and wounding several others. When at last D-Series ended, the weary-but-proud troopers came down from the mountains, expecting to receive orders committing them to a combat theater.

But while the division had performed well in terms of fitness and esprit de corps, the Army was still not certain what should be done with the 10th.

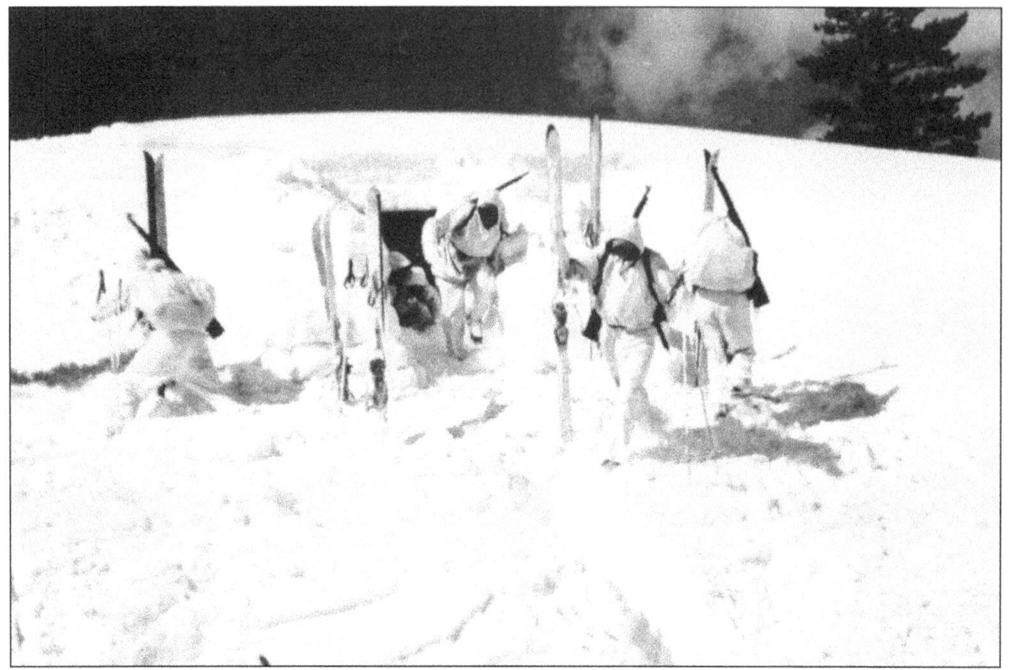

During D-Series, a group of ski troopers emerge from a snow shelter and prepare to set off on skis. The men of the 10th felt that they were ready for anything that the war could throw at them, but the Army had other thoughts. (Courtesy of Rouene Brown.)

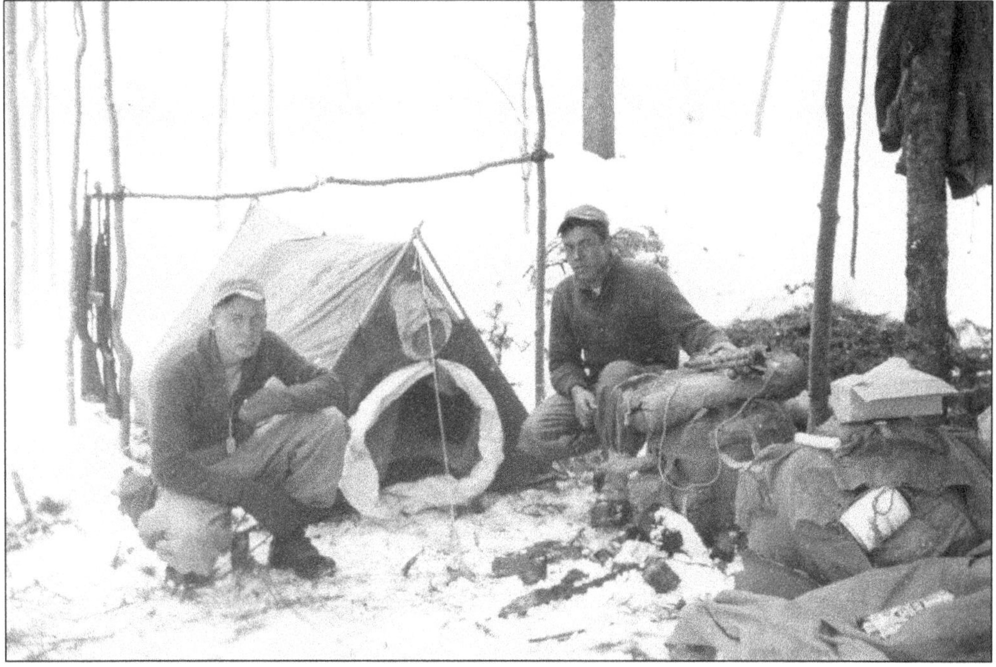

Two mountain troopers are shown outside their reversible mountain tent (green on one side, white on the other) while taking part in the D-Series maneuvers at "Camp Hell," as many of the men called it. The field problems went on night and day for three weeks and pushed every man's endurance to the limit. (Courtesy of DPL.)

Even the mules had to participate. Here, a mule is about to dip its hooves into an icy creek during D-Series. (Courtesy of DPL.)

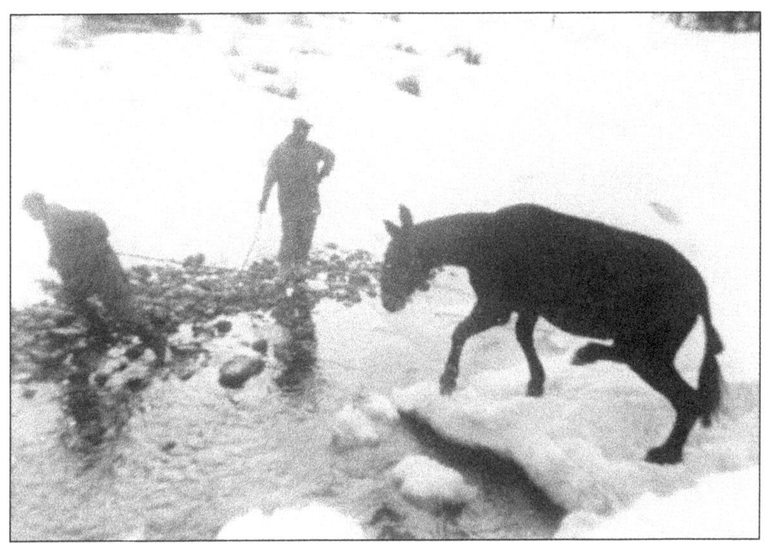

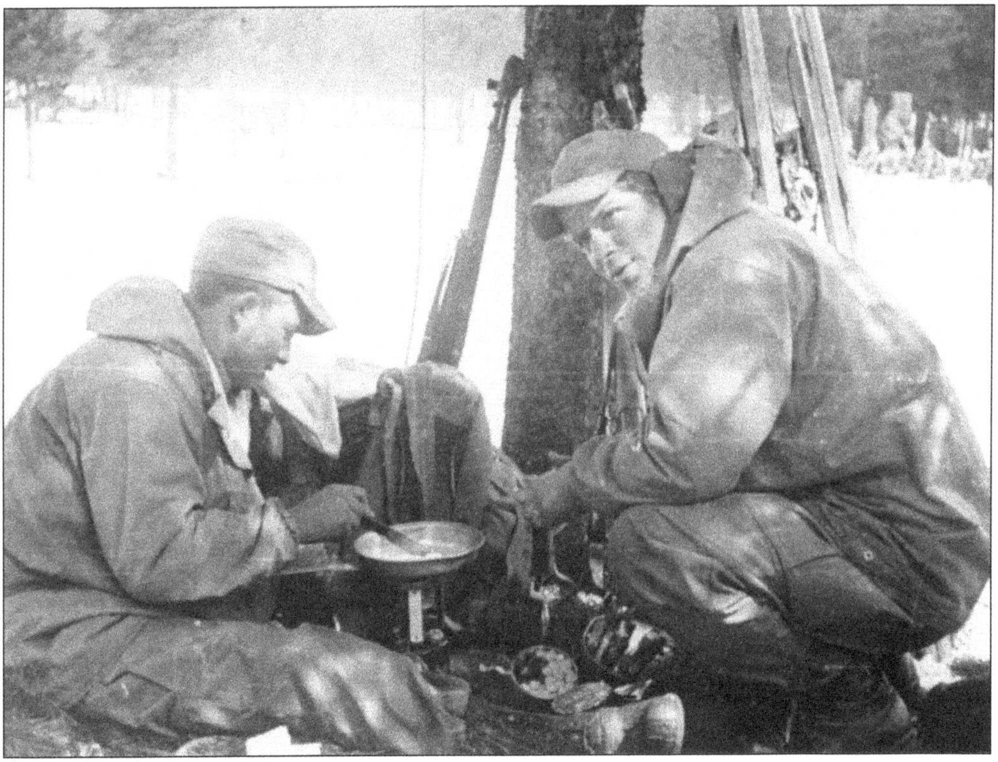

Two troopers heat up their rations over a small, portable stove. Gen. George C. Marshall directed that the 10th should leave Camp Hale and receive additional training so it could "fight as a mountain division in mountains." (Courtesy of DPL.)

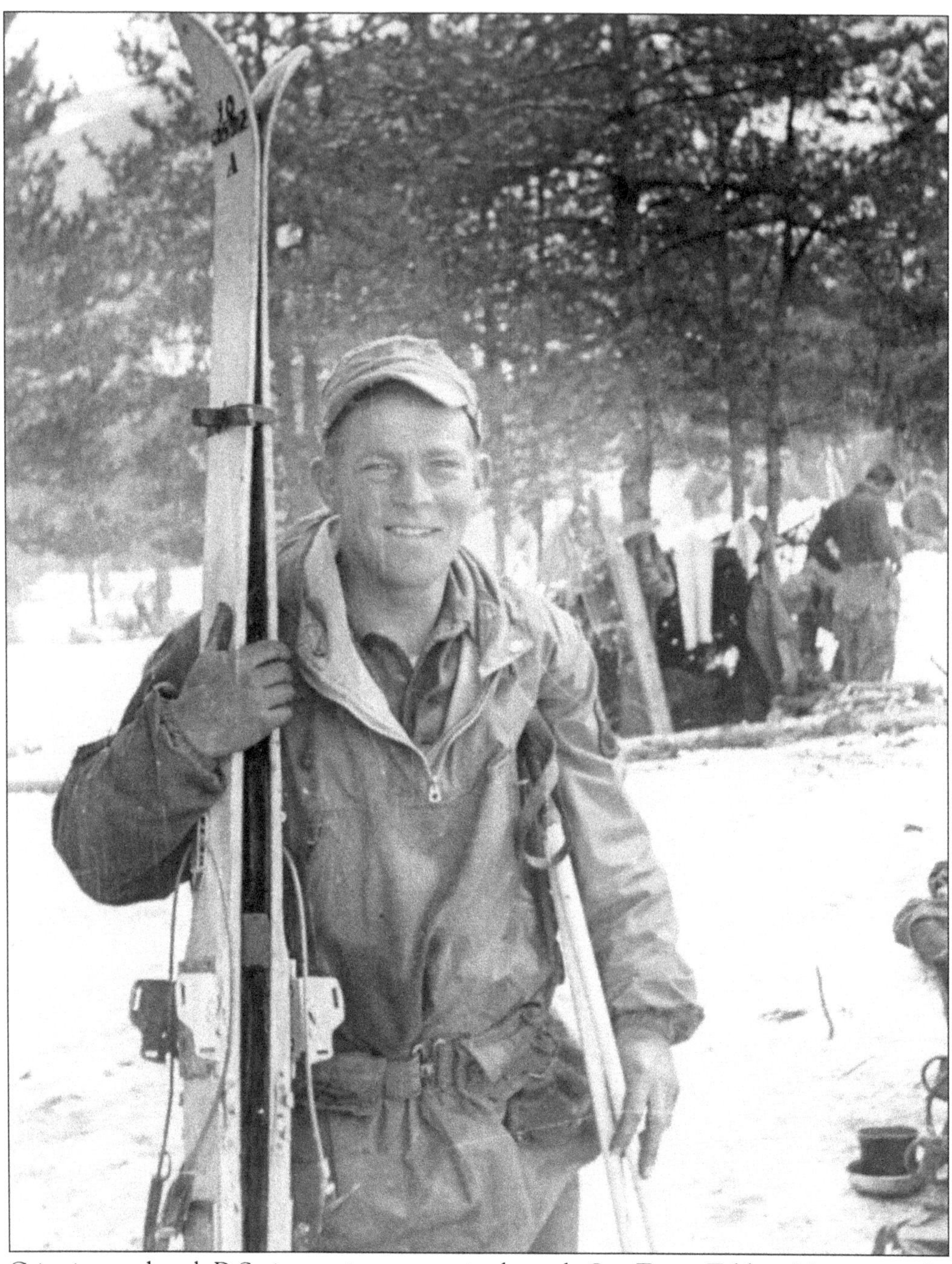

Grinning as though D-Series was just a romp in the park, Sgt. Torger Tokle, a Norwegian, the holder of the world record in the ski jump and one of the most famous men in the division, is photographed during D-Series. He would be killed in Italy in March 1945. (Courtesy of DPL.)

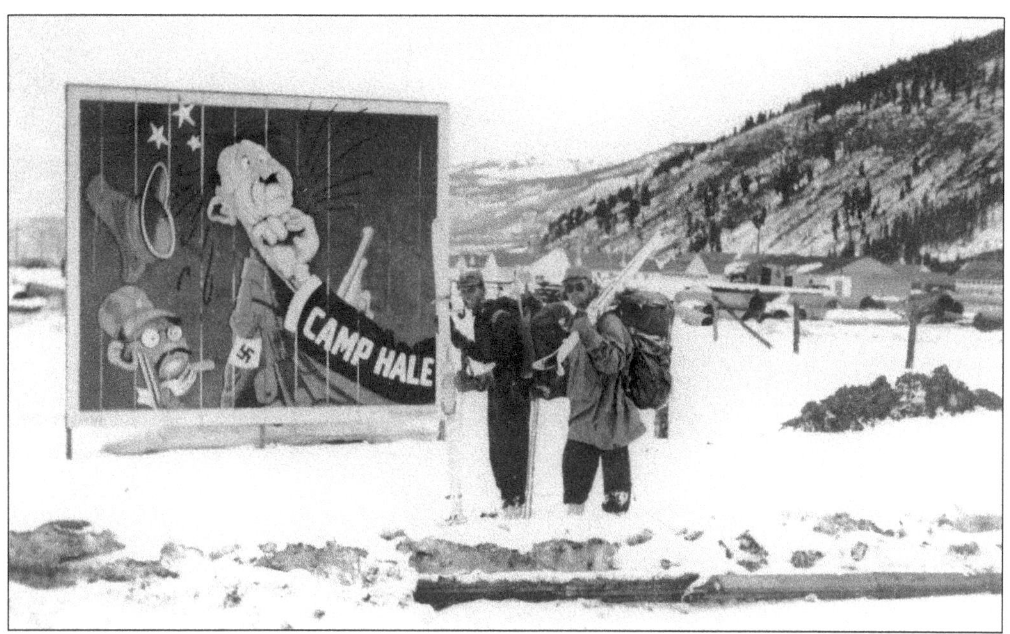

Two 10th men pose in front of a billboard that shows what the Camp Hale boys planned to do with the enemy once they got into the war, which did not happen until early 1945. (Courtesy of DPL.)

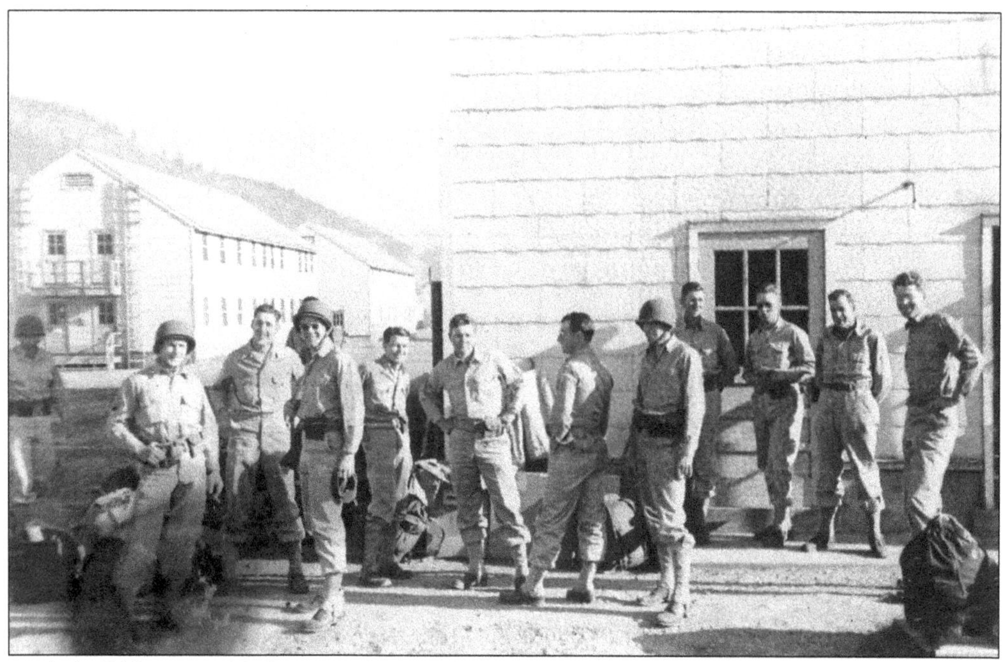

With duffel bags, steel helmets, and cotton khaki summer uniforms, these mountain troopers are ready to leave Camp Hale. Their next stop was additional infantry training at Camp Swift, Texas, where they would be made ready for combat in Italy, receive a new commanding general (George P. Hays), and a new designation: the 10th Mountain Division. (Courtesy of DPL.)

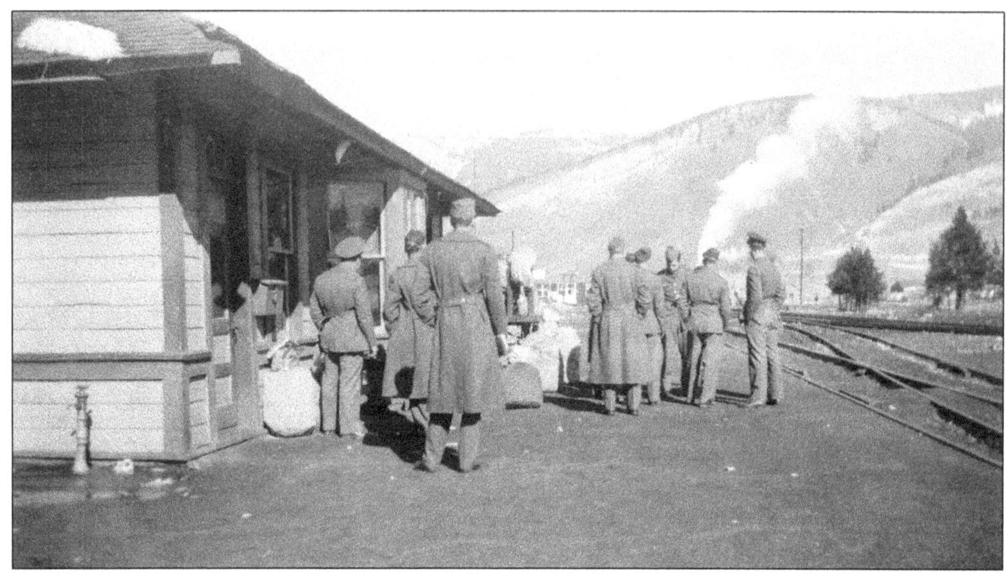

Although both these photographs were taken in winter, they represent the departure of the 10th Light Division from Camp Hale and the Pando depot in the summer of 1944. After six months of additional training at Camp Swift, the men of the 10th finally saw combat—in Italy's northern Apennine Mountains and Po River Valley. There, they lost 1,000 men killed and 4,000 wounded. But they never lost a battle or gave up a foot of ground—a testament to their courage and ability to persevere under extreme circumstances. (Both, courtesy of DPL.)

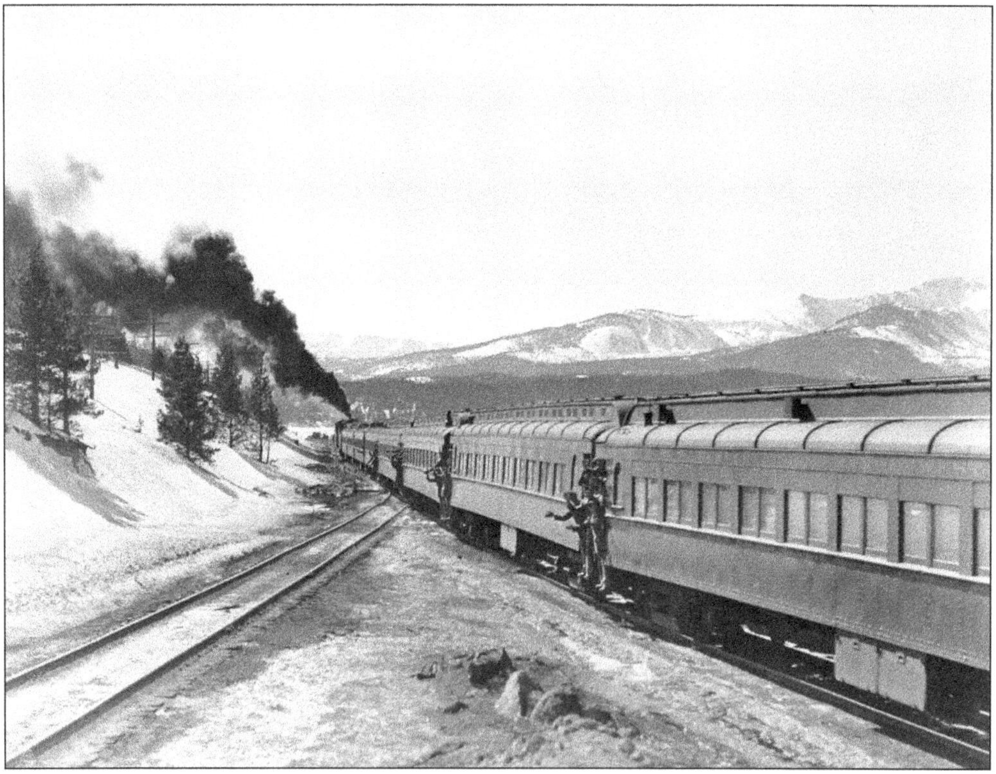

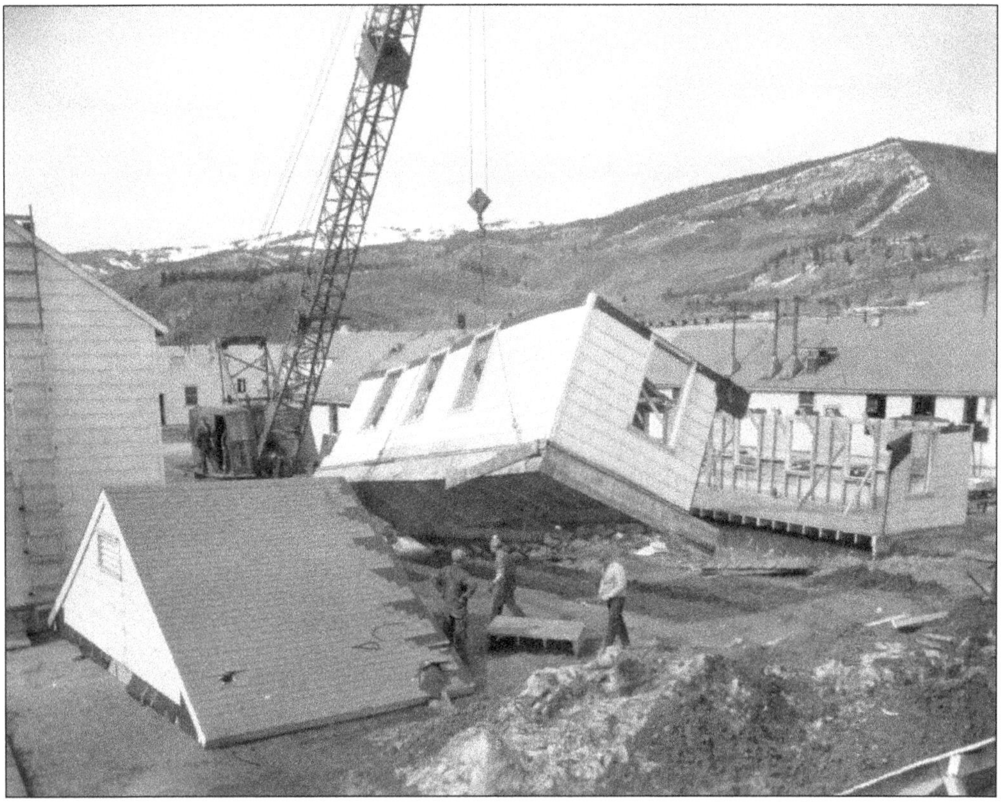

After the 10th departed Hale, a group of 3,500 German prisoners of war, held in over 40 POW camps in Colorado (there were some 700 POW camps across the United States holding 425,000 enemy captives), began the process of dismantling the camp. They were paid 80¢ a day for their labor. (Courtesy of DPL.)

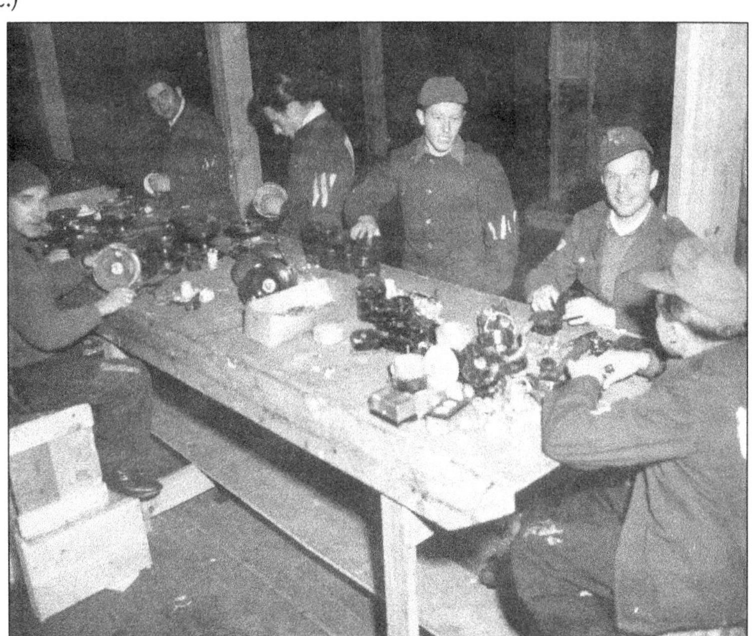

A group of smiling German POWs disassemble electrical components for re-use. Many POWs wanted to remain in the United States after the war was over rather than return to their war-ravaged countries, but were required to return home. (Courtesy of DPL.)

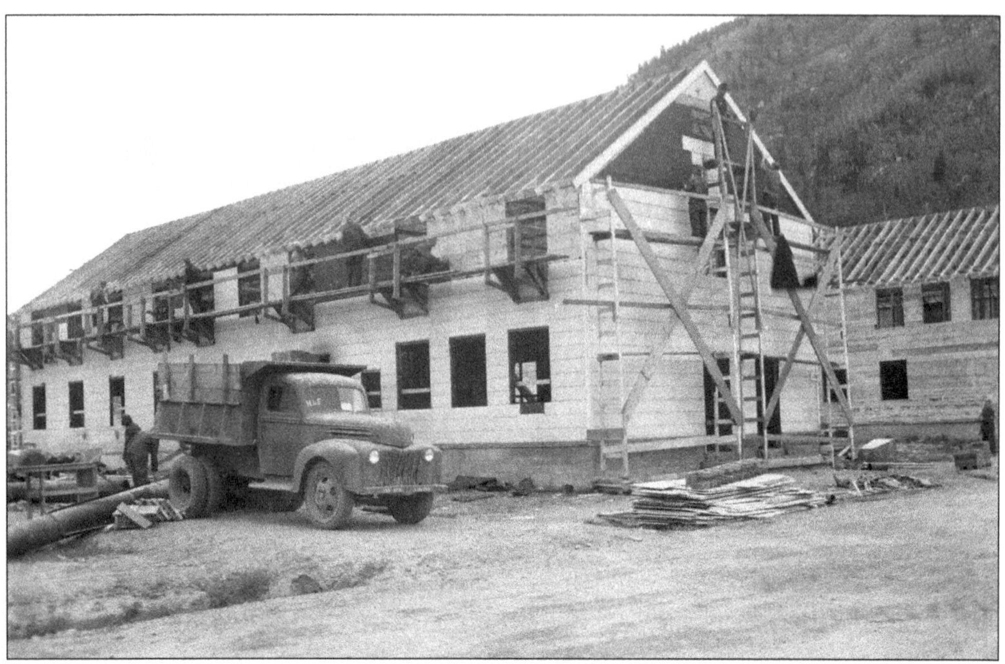

The German POWs were careful in their efforts to preserve the lumber, windows, floorboards, wiring, and asbestos-cement shingles so that the materials could be reused at Camp Carson and elsewhere. Local farmers and ranchers were allowed to purchase surplus building materials. (Courtesy of DPL.)

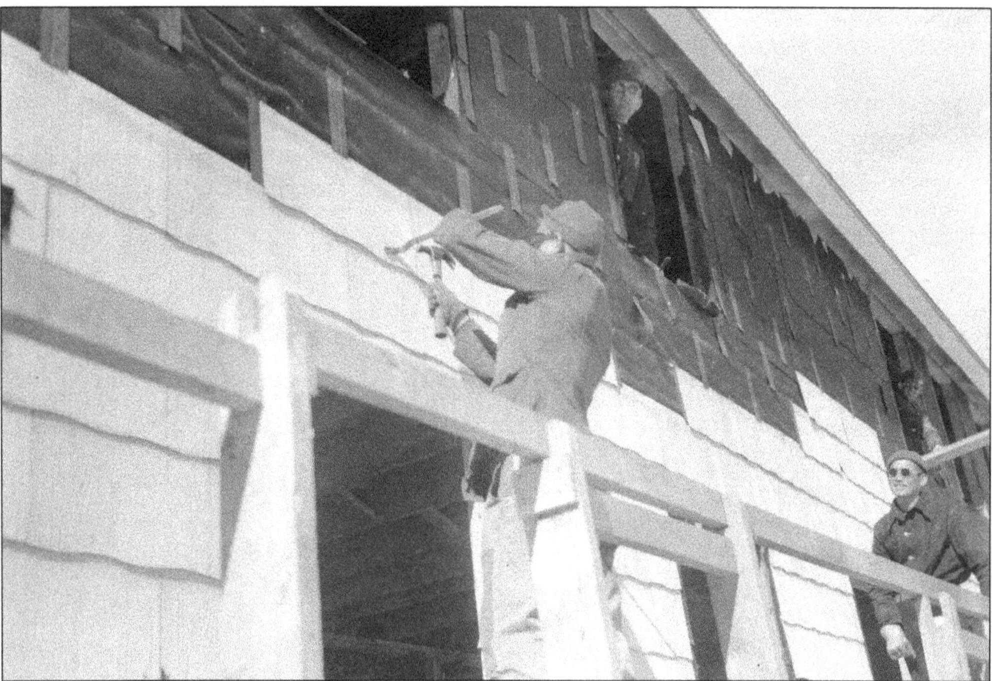

Several million feet of lumber and vast quantities of pipe, conduit, plumbing, electrical fixtures, doors, windows, and other materials that could be recycled were salvaged. Here, a German POW carefully removes siding from a building; even the nails were saved for future use. (Courtesy of DPL.)

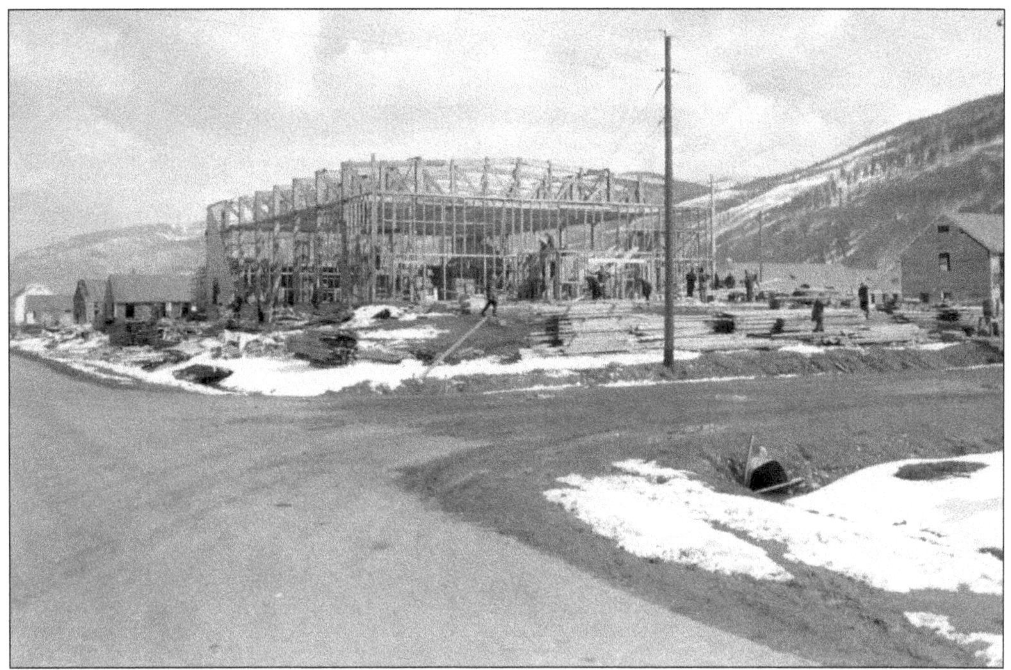

In April 1945, snow was still on the ground when Theater No. 2 was taken apart piece by piece. Soon, the camp that 10,000 workers spent seven months building at a cost of $30 million (nearly $500 million today) just three years earlier had ceased to exist. (Courtesy of DPL.)

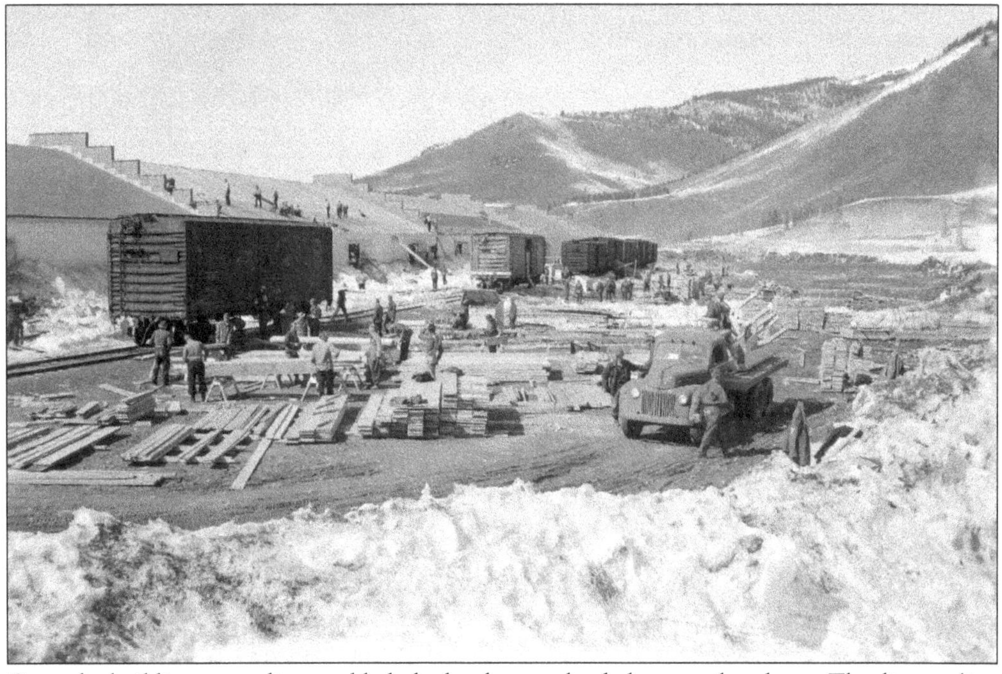

Once the buildings were disassembled, the lumber was loaded onto railroad cars. The dismantling of the camp continued through the summer of 1945. One of the huge warehouses is visible at left rear. Only the hospital was spared, being in use until the war's end to care for patients suffering from malaria contracted in the tropics. (Courtesy of DPL.)

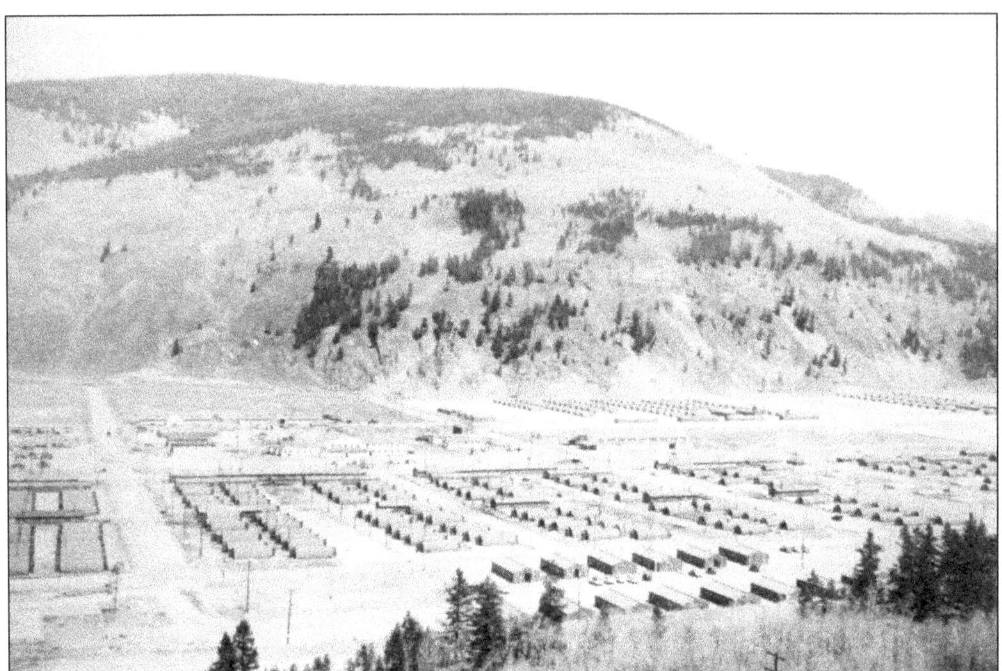

In the 1950s, the Army decided that the Camp Hale site would be good for cold-weather and high-altitude training, and so spent millions to install scores of Quonset huts where the wooden barracks once stood. The CIA also used the site in 1958 to secretly train 259 Tibetan guerillas who were parachuted into their homeland in an unsuccessful attempt to oust the Communist Chinese occupiers. (Courtesy of DPL.)

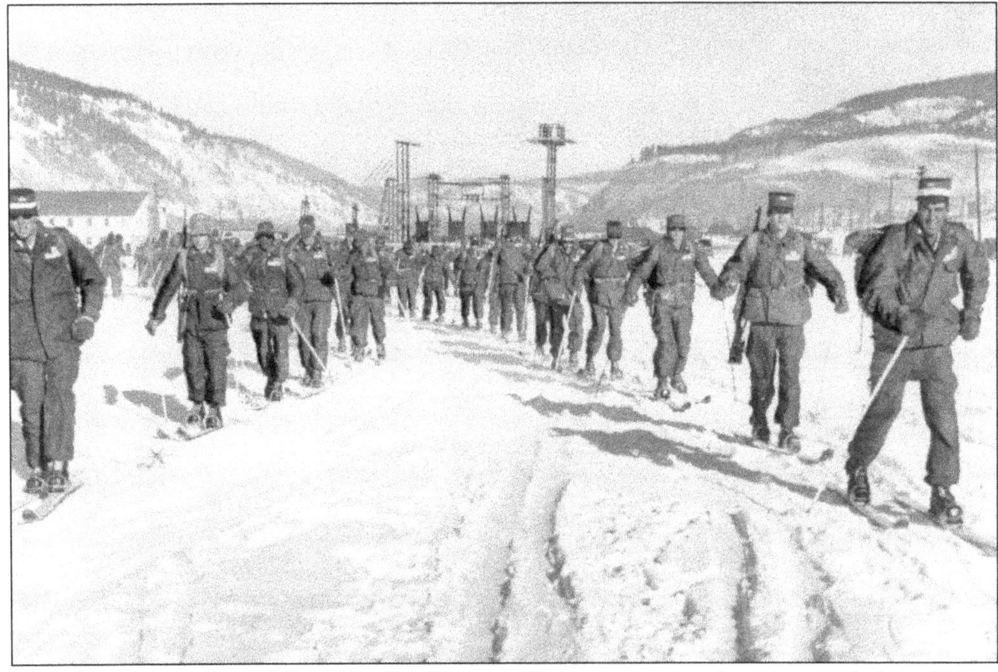

The Army's Mountain and Cold Weather Training Command operated at Camp Hale from 1952 to 1958. Here, members of an Army unit try out their ski legs on Camp Hale snow. (Courtesy of DPL.)

The rifle ammunition used at the rifle range was kept in these concrete bunkers, above which targets were hoisted. The berms on the rifle range, the outlines of streets, and the concrete foundations and a few broken bricks remain in the warehouse area at the northern end of the valley. Sadly, not much of Pando or the original camp exists today. (Courtesy of David J. Little.)

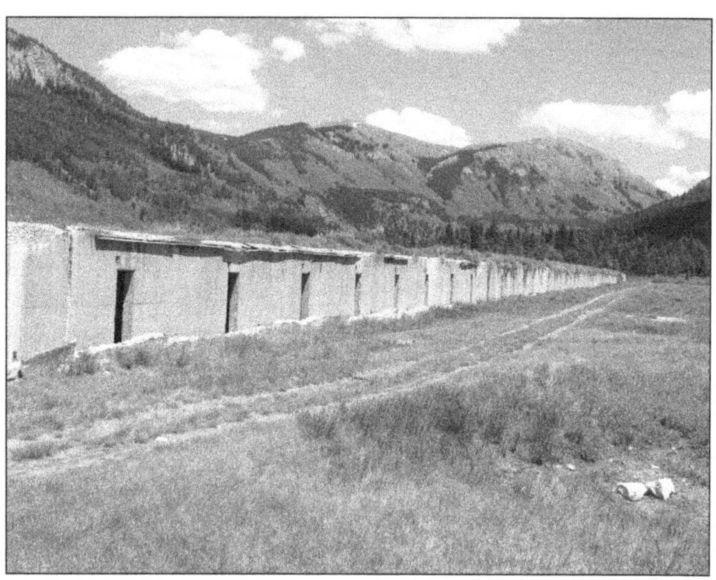

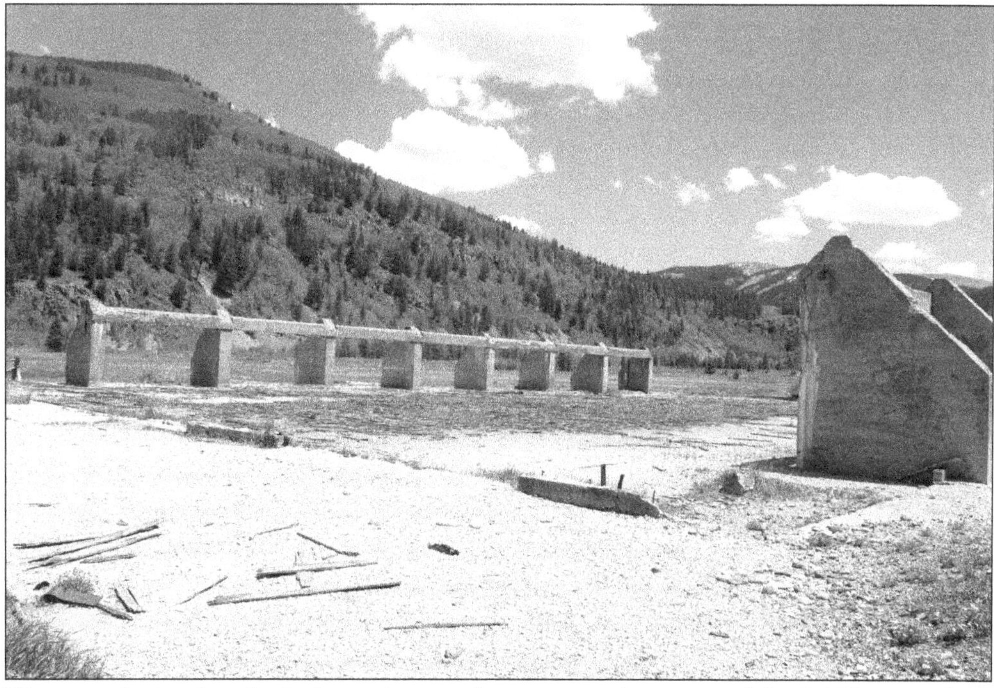

The most distinctive physical remains are the concrete abutments of the field house, which once supported the curved roof over the 18,000-square-foot structure. Portions of the camp are periodically declared off limits to the public by the US Forest Service, which manages the site, due to asbestos contamination and other environmental hazards—not to mention the occasional discovery of live munitions. Environmentalists have for many years wanted to return the site, or at least portions of it, to its natural, pre-war state. (Courtesy of David J. Little.)

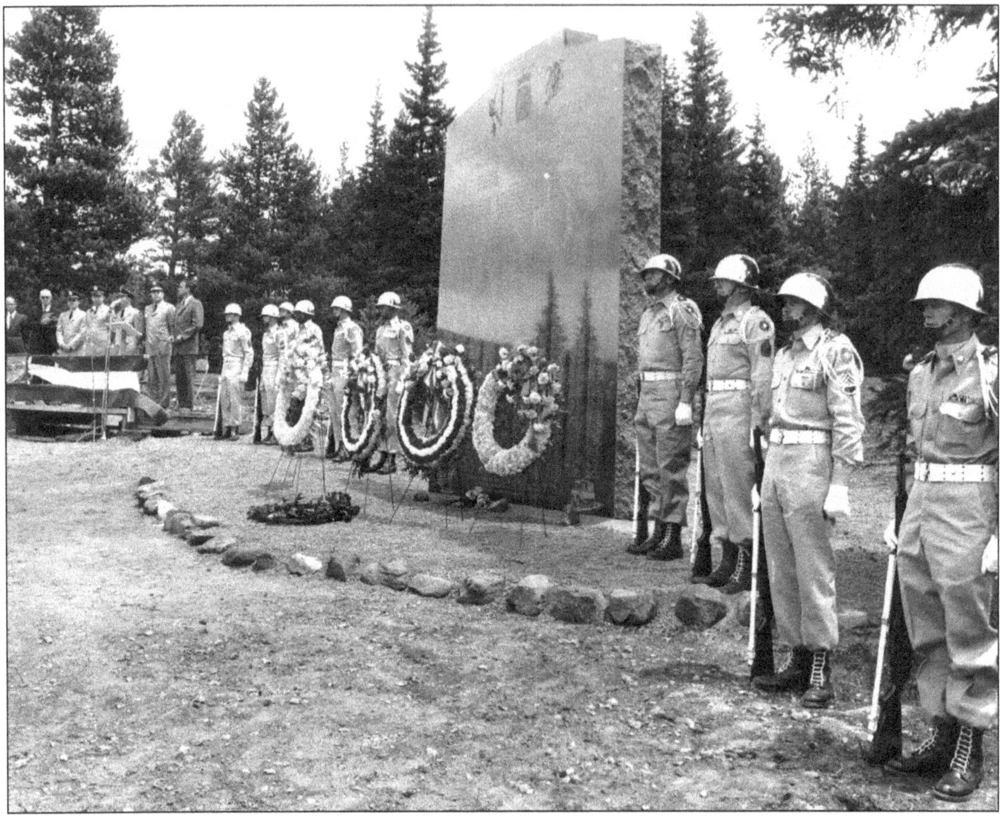

In 1959, the 10th Mountain Division Foundation dedicated a memorial to all of the division's combat deaths in a ceremony along US Highway 24 atop Tennessee Pass at the entrance to Ski Cooper, the former advanced ski-training area. A ceremony is still held there every year on Memorial Day. (Courtesy of CSSM.)

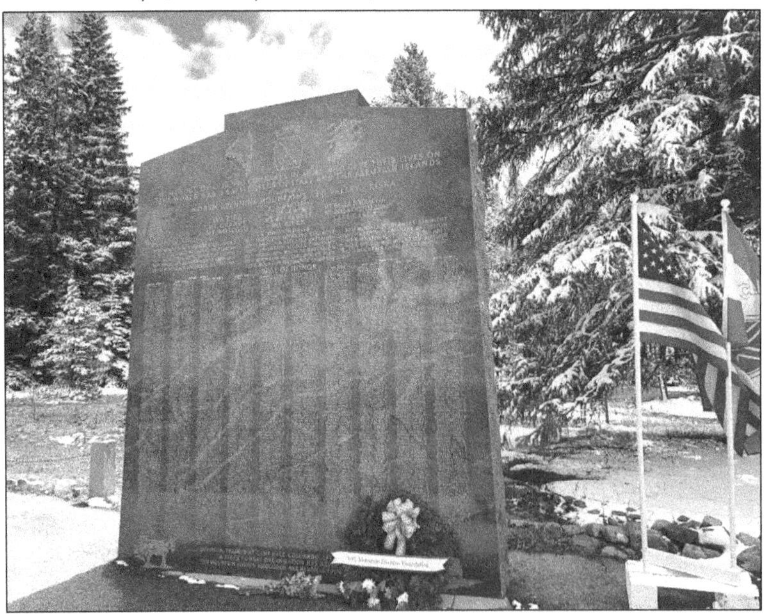

Originally, it was believed that the 10th lost 992 men in combat, but further research reveals the true number was 1,000. The memorial now has the names of all 1,000 of the fallen engraved onto it. (Courtesy of Flint Whitlock.)

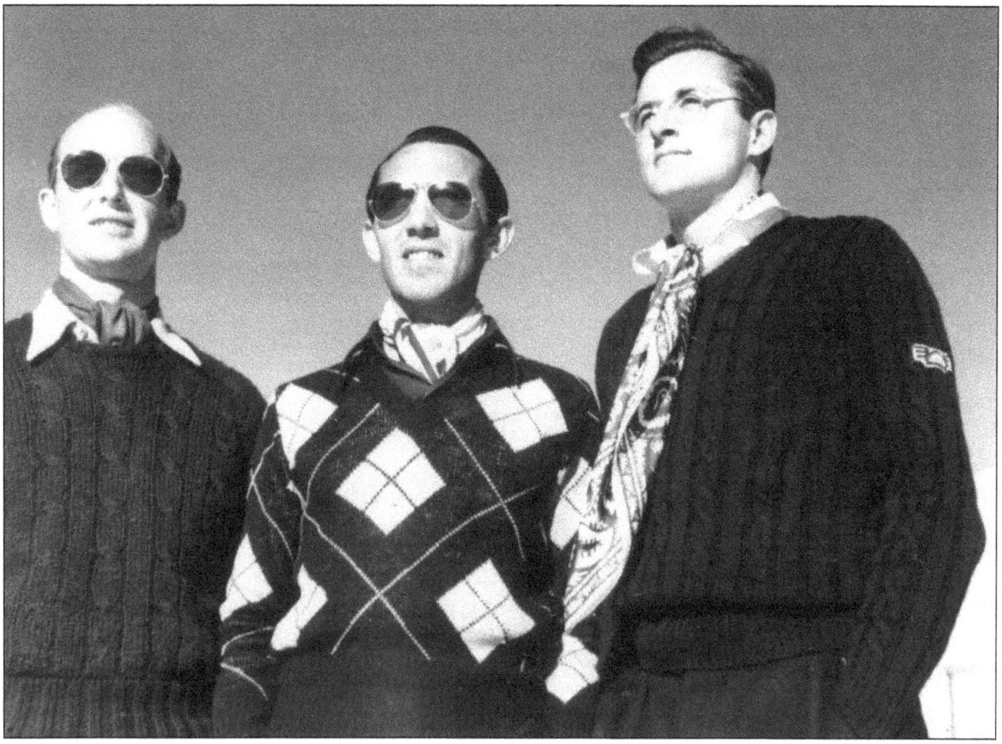

After the war, many of the veterans returned to the United States to become involved in the fledgling ski industry. Shown here are three 10th veterans (from left to right), Percy Rideout, Friedl Pfeifer, and John Litchfield, who were instrumental in turning the near–ghost town of Aspen into one of the world's premier ski resorts. The main financial benefactor was Walter Paepcke, founder of the Container Corporation of America. (Courtesy of AHS.)

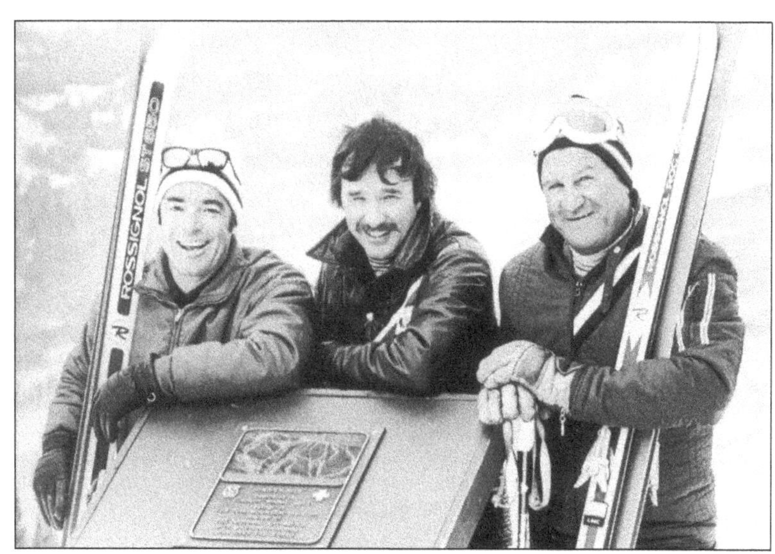

The glamorous Vail ski resort was founded by several 10th Mountain veterans in the early 1960s. Here, three of them (from left to right, Pete Seibert, Bob Parker, and William "Sarge" Brown) gather for a photograph in the 1980s. (Courtesy of CSSM.)

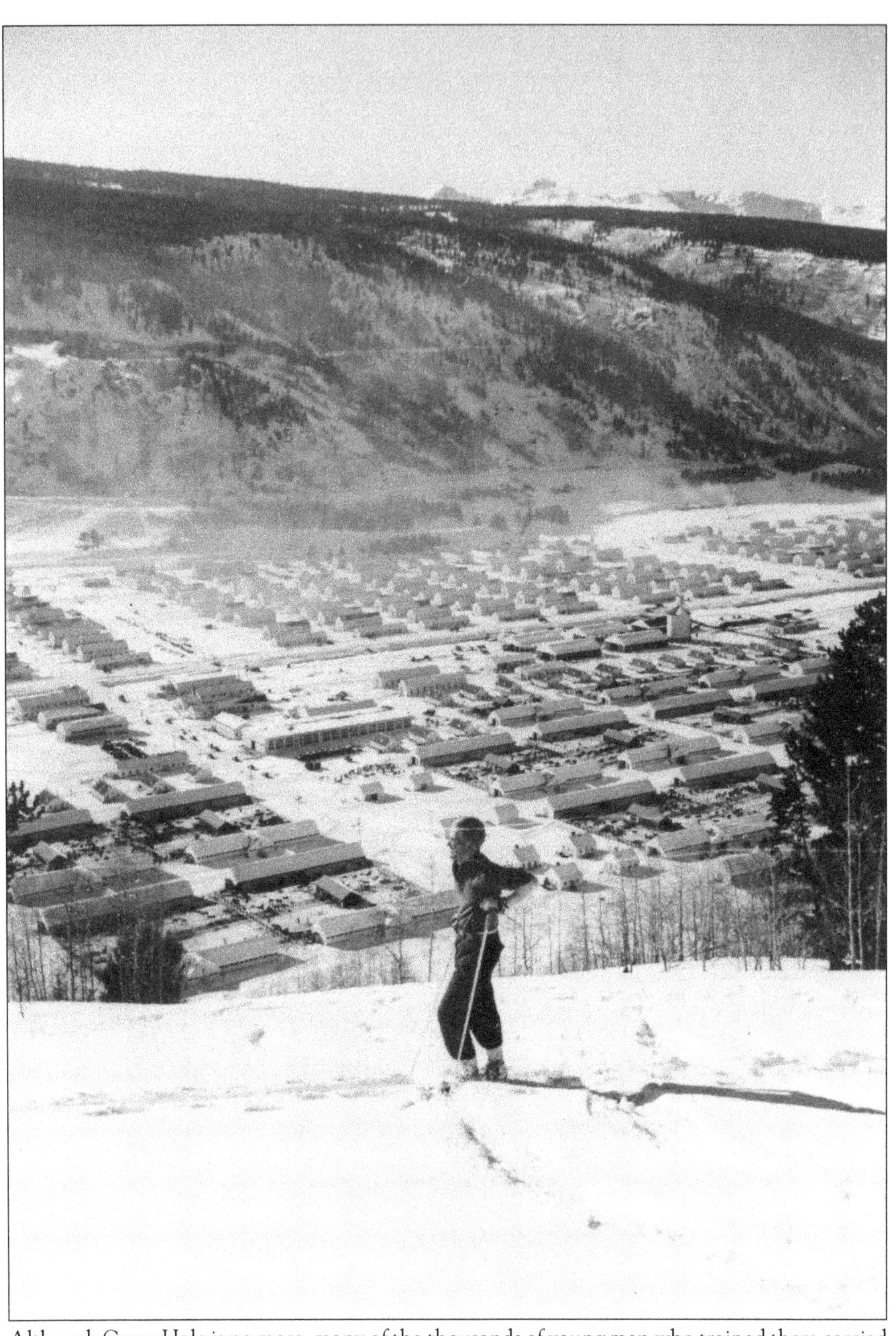

Although Camp Hale is no more, many of the thousands of young men who trained there carried memories of the place—both good and bad—for the rest of their lives. In October 2022, Pres. Joe Biden designated the Camp Hale site a national monument. (Courtesy of DPL.)

Bibliography

Chabalko, Justin J. *Forging the 10th Mountain Division for War, 1940–45: How Innovation Created a Highly Adaptive Formation*. Fort Leavenworth, KS: US Army Command and General Staff College Press, 2020.

Daneman, Marty. *Do Well or Die: Memoirs of a WWII Mountain Trooper*. Brule, WI: Cable Publishing, 2012.

Dusenbery, Harris. *The North Apennines and Beyond with the 10th Mountain Division*. Portland, OR: Binford & Mort, 1998.

Feuer, A.B. *Packs On! Memoirs of the 10th Mountain Division in WWII*. Mechanicsburg, PA: Stackpole Books, 2004.

Imbrie, John, and Hugh W. Evans, eds. *Good Time and Bad Times: A History of the 85th Mountain Infantry Regiment, 10th Mountain Division, July 1943 to November 1945*. Quechee, VT: Vermont Heritage Press, 1995.

Isserman, Maurice. *The Winter Army: The World War II Odyssey of the 10th Mountain Division, America's Elite Alpine Warriors*. New York, NY: Houghton Mifflin Harcourt, 2019.

Pote, Winston. *Mountain Troops: 10th Mountain Division, Camp Hale, Colorado*. Camden, ME: Down East Books, 1982.

Whitlock, Flint, and Bob Bishop. *Soldiers on Skis: A Pictorial Memoir of the 10th Mountain Division*. Brule, WI: Cable Publishing, 1992.

Witte, David R. *World War II at Camp Hale: Blazing a New Trail in the Rockies*. Charleston, SC: The History Press, 2015.

Various issues of *Camp Hale Ski-Zette*, *Blizzard*, *The Denver Post*, and *Rocky Mountain News*.

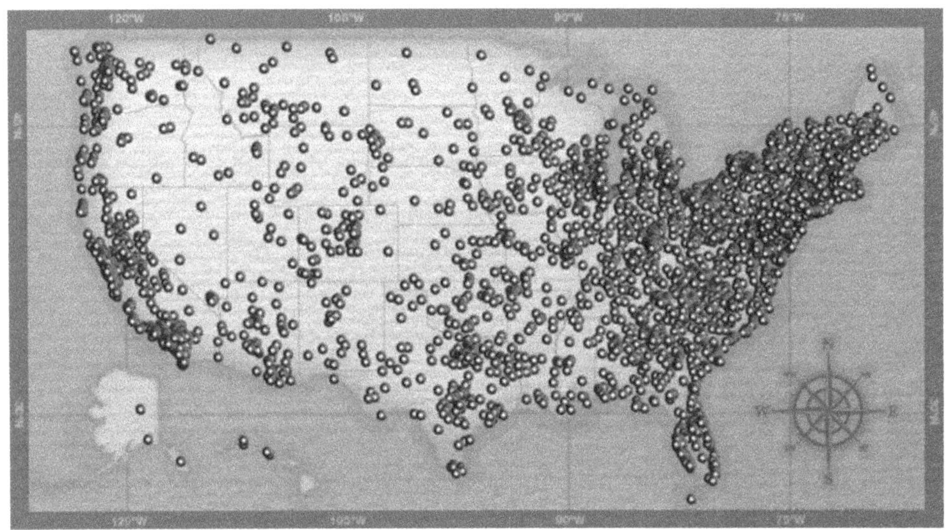

www.ingramcontent.com/pod-product-compliance
Lightning Source LLC
LaVergne TN
LVHW060623110826
845147LV00015B/926